Rethink
Social Media

Paul O'Mahony

Rethink Social Media by Paul O'Mahony
www.rethinksocialmedia.com
Order this book from Amazon.co.uk or on audio on iTunes or Audible

Design by Nick Hillson & Luke Bunting
Research by Paul O'Mahony
© Copyright 2018 Paul O'Mahony

Note for Librarians: A cataloguing record for this book is available from Library and Archives Canada at www.collectionscanada.gc.ca/a-z-index/index-e.html

Printed in Peterborough, Cambridgeshire, UK ISBN: 978-1909846-73-9

Published by Progressive Publishing
Progressive House
Units 8, 9, 10 & 11
Cygnet Park, Forder Way, Hampton Peterborough, PE7 8GX

Facebook: www.facebook.com/paulomahonyspeaker
Twitter: twitter.com/paulomahony
Instagram: instagram.com/paulomahony_
www.leftclickrightclick.com
www.paulomahony.com

Contents

Time Spent on the Toilet!

= 5 Mins

+ = 15 Mins

+ + = 55 Mins

+ + + = $$$

Acknowledgements

I wish to start by expressing my deepest appreciation and gratitude for everyone who I have met along my journey to date, whether supporting me directly or indirectly in getting "Rethink Social Media" out to the world! Since I started on my online journey back in 2009 as a complete novice to both social media and marketing, there have been so many people who have influenced me along the way, far too many to mention, literally tens of thousands! From the very first event I attended run by Gary Mcgeown, Donna Kennedy and Pat Slattery in Dublin 2009, I have been cast into a world full of amazing people who have assisted me in multiple ways, as colleagues, mentors, mentees, students and coaches but primarily as friends. I have learned incredible amounts from you all, so much so in fact, that it's hard to know exactly what I learned from whom any longer! I would also like to acknowledge everybody who assisted me in recently becoming a Guinness World Record holder for the longest ever continuous public speech!

All that being said, there are a number of people who I must highlight for special recognition for the significant contributions they have made, whether they are aware of it or not. I would like to give a very special thank you to all of the following; Mark Anastasi, Mili Ponce, Richard and Veronica Tan, John Demartini, John Assaraf, Tony Robbins, Jairek Robbins, Rob Moore, Sharon Moore, Mark Homer, Katherine Barratt, Jo Casey, Joanne Sweeney Burke, Chris Farrell, Mac Attram, Andrew Reynolds, Darren Winters, Shawn and Patricia Casey, Brian Koz, David Pocock, Jac Vidoret, Alexandra Vidoret Ponce, Frankie and Norma Sheahan, Andy Harrington, Simon Coulson, Paul Preston, all of the "Syndicate" mastermind group, Greg Secker, Piet Vannoppen, Maarten Verheyen, Jamie White, Telmo De La Cruz, Nick James*2, Pat Flynn, Randi Zuckerberg, Richard Branson, Robert and Kim Kiyosaki, Brian Tracy, T Harv Eker, Jay Abraham, Thom Luther, Nick Hillson, Pat Divilly, Clarissa Judd, Richard Nicholas, Harry Kumar, Damien Hope Tonkin, Samantha Kelly, Felicity Lyons, Helena Wootton, Tai Lopez, Russel Brunson, Ryan Deiss, Matt Lloyd, Jason Osborn, Mark Victor Hansen, Katie Morgan Bell, Matt Bacak, Harry Singha, Daniel Wagner, James Watson, Shaqir Hussyin, Daven Michaels, Tiji Thomas, Judymay Murphy, Mike Dooley, Dan Bradbury, Shaa Wasmund, Matt Thomas, Eric Thomas, Jean-Pierre De Villiers, Verne Harnish, Saj P, Alan

Moore, Rachel Gao, Anthony Hartigan, Kerwin Rae, Luke Bunting, Lyndon Wood, Chris Rowell, Thomas Power, Chris Black, Matthew Kimberley, Pat Mesiti, Steve Essa, Richard and Fe Watson, Oksana Tashakova, Keelan Cunningham, Jeni and Simon Fagence, Ralph Anania, Caroline Shaw, Kim McMonagle, Ian Lawlor, Michel Gimena, Tom Breeze, Grant Cardone, Brittany Lynch, Alan Forrest Smith, Dr Mike Woo-Ming, Molly Pittman, Keith Krance, Ralph Burns, David Sheahan, Larry Loik, Andrew Lock, Ben Lowrey, Sean and Pia Roach, Awfa Mustafa, Jack Bonson, Emma Hodgson, Daniel Swann, Anthony McCarthy, Ben Peresson, Lasse Rouhiainen, Jack Dorsey, Gary Vaynerchuk, Tim Ferris, Jack Canfield, Keith Cunningham, Dan Kennedy, Joe Polish, Victoria Whitehead, Matthew Armstrong, Brendan Burchard, J.T. DeBolt, Susan Zanghi, Tasha Cooney, Frank Kern, Brett McFall, Jason Buckner, Tom Hua, Marshall Sylver, John Lee Dumas, Darragh Colgan, Brian Haggerty, Andrew Baxter, Ted Thomas, Chet Holmes, Robert Rolih, Tom Beal, Raymond Aaron, Roy and Lyn Carter, Paul Casey, John Heelan, Pete Brady, Martin Healy, Dean Molloy, Jason Gaignard, John Lee, Sean O'Reilly, Anthony O'Connor, Twisted Metal, Mike Stelzner, John Chow, Colin O'Rourke, Ivor Browne, M'reen Hunt, Gal Stiglitz, Rehan Hussan, Darren and Rhonda Salkeld, the abandoned annual ski trip crew, the Tijuana six, both book writing bootcamp teams (too many to list everyone!) and Cian Conroy.

I would also like to thank Kazi and all of my teams that have worked with me closely along the journey and especially to the current merry gang of Donna, Vishal, Gina, Jake, Cam, Sooz, Alex, Tracey, Ralph, Gregor, Sean W, Nigel, Brooke, Robert, Andrew, Lou, Sean T, Ray and super Mariusz! I also wish to thank the beautiful hotels in which I wrote my book and all of their staff; Ashford Castle, H10 Lanzarote and Center Parcs Woburn and my shirt sponsors 7 camicie.

Finally, I would like to express my gratitude and love to Sarah and little Jess and all of my family, Dad, Mam, Sinead, Tom, Aoife, Donncha, John, Val, Bernie, Tony, Marion and Ian. Without Sarah's support, none of this would be possible, (so you can thank or blame her!), having put up with the endless travel, early mornings and late nights to finally get this over the line! I love you! I really hope you feel this was worth it all ☺! Let's hope that the sequel doesn't take nearly as long!

SECTION 1: INTRODUCTION

*"We cannot solve our problems with the same thinking
we used when we created them."*
- Albert Einstein

Imagine logging into Facebook in the morning to find out how much money it made you last night. Imagine going back into Facebook throughout the day to see how much more money it has been making for you. How much better would that make your social media "experience"? I'm guessing it would be very different! Believe it or not, there are hundreds of thousands of people who experience this on a daily basis, using the same social networks as everyone else but using them to make them money rather than purely for their entertainment value. This doesn't happen overnight; it is a systematic process that anyone can learn to do with the right guidance, a wifi connection and access to a certain smart device.

When you woke up this morning, was it natural or did some form of technology get involved and remind you that it was time to get up and into gear? I can probably guess the answer ☺. In modern society, most people are awoken by a "smartphone". Whether they are iPhones or Androids or something more classical or more modern, these devices typically not only wake us up and instantly inform us of all the latest news, like which celebrities passed away while we slept, but we generally carry them with us all day every day – they are usually the very last thing we say goodnight to! Of course, it would be rude not to finish our day by ensuring our phone is plugged in so it's fully charged first thing in the morning! Could there be a more horrendous start to your day than seeing that your phone has only 8% battery?!

If only we were as concerned for our partners' well-being and how charged they are in the morning! In fact, according to psychologists, "phone separation anxiety" now exists as a real issue when people get separated from their phone for any extended period of time. Many people I know would rather lose their wallet or purse than their phone!

When I was younger, people walked around with their heads held in the air looking ahead for potential obstacles to avoid. Now, when you look around you in any busy environment, the majority of people walk in a hunched over position glued to the device in their hand! It is like an addictive drug; a lifeline connecting them to their friends, family and celebrities they care about. This means that we are living in an era of unprecedented access to people, and with this comes unparalleled opportunity for businesses and entrepreneurs alike. We have never had such availability to people, literally at the touch of a button. Companies know this and they fight it out on a daily basis for your attention. People's attention is definitely the new currency of business, with the most successful businesses securing the most of your attention.

As phone and internet users, we are at the whims of sophisticated marketing campaigns designed to draw us in and keep us engaged for as long as possible, ultimately aiming for us to spend our time and money on their products and services. Yet most people don't realise that rather than being the target of such attention and being the person spending money, with a little knowledge and application of the new-found skills you will learn in this book, you could quite easily switch sides and be making money rather than spending it. This is how this book, RETHINK Social Media can help you greatly.

I want to take you from being in the 99%+ of people who use social media as it was intended – as a means of keeping you updated on your friends, families, celebrities, brands, etc. and spending your valuable time and money – to knowing how to be one of the exclusive few who learn how to use the same social networks to make you a serious fortune.

A simple illustration of the difference between a regular social media user and a social media profiteer can be outlined by answering the following commonly asked question: "Why should I care that Kim just posted on Twitter that she had her third cup of coffee today in Starbucks?" This is a question (or similar variations of it at least) very commonly asked of me by entrepreneurs and business owners in relation to why they don't feel there is a justification in using social media in their businesses, for example. Maybe this is you, or at least a certain part of you from time to time? It certainly started off as my opinion many years ago.

My answer to this question is as follows. "If you have NO plans to use social media for marketing purposes, then you absolutely have NO reason to care that Kim just had another coffee, unless you find that interesting in itself. If, however, you have a little business, for example, that sells specific types of coffee and promotes how regular coffee drinkers can make money while drinking it, you have just potentially found yourself the perfect person to help you grow your business. And do you know what, there are a lot more people just like Kim out there!"

If you are currently in business, or even thinking about it, you will very quickly need to learn how to market your business using the latest social networks in order to survive and thrive. However, to market successfully you need two things above all: you need to care, and you need integrity! As Zig Ziglar famously put it:

> *"Honesty and integrity are by far the most important assets of an entrepreneur."*

Marketing, in a sense, is caring about what people are saying and doing, and adapting your business offerings to meet those wants and desires. We are going to use social media to listen to those "wants" rather than to just barrage people with our opinions because we care enough to find out first what peoples' desires are.

When it comes to whether you should care about social media or not, it helps to start by looking at the numbers, which are just staggering. Today's users of social networks reach almost half of every single person on the planet. If you are in business, you MUST be there. There is no such thing as "my clients don't use social media" - unless they have passed on to the next world, and even then, who knows!

Social media is where people share their thoughts and deeds; it's the perfect place to find those who are soon to be interested in what you do. People are quite simply addicted to it, and the devices where it can be accessed and wherever there are addicts there is a LOT of money being made. If you are in business, or just considering creating one, you must stop wasting time, understand your audience and start making money. It is time to jump on board the greatest opportunity that has ever been, let alone of a lifetime, with virtually unlimited access to people all over the globe who openly share their deepest needs and desires and problems with complete strangers. In short, it's time to RETHINK social media.

In order to make this easy to digest for you, I have created summaries of each segment and chapter as you progress, in which I point out what the traditional business thinking currently is compared to the new RETHINK framework you will soon be adapting! Let's begin the RETHINK...

Chapter 1: What is Social Media?

*"If I had an hour to solve a problem I'd spend 55 minutes
thinking about the problem and 5 minutes thinking about solutions."*
- Albert Einstein

The year was 2008. It was a frosty morning, and I was driving a rented Ford SUV on my way to work in Waltham, near Boston in Massachusetts. I had the radio on, and I was slowly waking up enough to process what was being said. Let's be clear, first of all, I am not a morning person, in any time zone!

As I eventually "tuned in" to the barrage of US radio advertisements between the odd song, which I found a tad irritating, one particular advertisement grabbed my attention. It was an ad for Honda. Nothing about it was out of the ordinary until the very end, when the announcer asked the listeners to "Make your way to Facebook.com/Honda to find out more," or words to a similar effect. What jumped out at me was the reference to Facebook and not the more typical home website Honda.com.

I was not a marketer, and I did not work in marketing. I was a scientist who had accidentally ventured into engineering. I had, however, recently completed an M.B.A. (Master B.S. Artist ☺), which had given me some level of awareness when it came to such areas. I was intrigued that a social network I considered to be mainly used by teens and twenty-somethings was now becoming a focus of companies as big as Honda.

Then… CRASH!

Yes, like most men, my forte was not doing more than one thing at once; thinking while driving was proving difficult, and I drove into the back of the car in front of me at a traffic stop. Nothing serious, but little did I know at the time that it was the jolt that I needed! A few years later, I would find myself fortunate enough to be teaching tens of thousands of people every year all around the world about how to stop wasting time on social media and start making some real money.

This is not your run-of-the-mill book on social media, nor is it intended to be. While it has been years in the making, my challenge has always been "How does one write a book about social media that is not out of date by the time the book has been printed?" There is no shortage of "how to" books when it comes to social media, but I wanted this to be very different. I wanted this to stand the test of time, so that when someone picks it up ten, maybe even twenty years from now, the timeless concepts discussed will be just as relevant then as they are today, with a few tweaks here and there, which will be addressed through video updates.

The objective of this book is to help budding entrepreneurs, established entrepreneurs or business owners RETHINK many of the ideas and concepts that they have about social media. Most of what entrepreneurs and businesses do on social media quite simply does not work, and by that, I mean it does not translate into a measurable increase in profits.

This book explains why this is the case, and exactly what to do to fix it and start to make significantly increased profits as a result. In most cases, businesses struggling with social media are not clear what exactly the problem is – they just know it isn't working, or that it's costing them time and money (and certainly not making them any money). As Einstein's quote at the start of the chapter eloquently explains, first we need to truly understand the nature of the problem. I intend not just to diagnose the problems, but also to give you practical solutions to turn your business around, or indeed set one up from scratch, using these fundamentals. Most businesses are quite often focusing on the wrong problems.

So what is social media?

Social media as it is understood today means very different things to different groups of people. To teenagers, it is a place to share their pouting selfies; for young adults, a world to connect with school and college friends and look for jobs; for the middle-aged, it is for keeping track of children; and as one enters the later stages of life, it is often for more intermittent use, for looking at family photographs and videos. This book is not written for a specific age group but rather aimed at those who know they are ready to utilise social media and its phenomenal power to supercharge a new or existing idea or business. As a business owner, understanding the demographic of your ideal customer, and how they engage on social media, will be just as important to you when you need to figure out how to communicate with them in their "language".

Now let us look at the words themselves: "social media".

Media is from the Latin word "medius" or middle and is the plural for medium. A medium is a way or means of expressing your ideas or of communicating with people (Collins Dictionary). It is also defined as "an intervening agency, means, or instrument".

Put simply, social media is a means to socialise. Any type of medium that allows more than one person to engage with another is a legitimate form of social media. For as long as there have been people, there has been social media, and a deep and innate need and desire for human connection that I have christened our "Social Needia" ☺.

When considering how to write a book that would be still relevant years from now, yet amazingly impactful as you read it today, it was important for me to demonstrate that "social media" itself has stood the test of time. The perfect demonstration came to me at home one morning. As I collected my post from the letter box with the usual mix of anticipation and trepidation, it dawned on me that social media, of course, was nothing new. The postal service that we all know (and love) and have been using not only throughout our lifetimes but for the past 2500 years, is indeed just as legitimate a form of "social media" as any of the trendier social networks we are more familiar with today.

History and evolution:

When I ask audiences to put a timeframe to when they believe social media began, the average response is about 2005. In most cases, the reason why people consider social media to be so new and modern is that it's easy to confuse social media with social networks like Twitter and Facebook. Social media has been around since a lot earlier than 2005! Ever since the moment we were born, we desired contact from another human – it is in our DNA. Studies have shown that when newborns are not cuddled and held and supported in the first few days of life, they inevitably suffer in later life. We crave attention from our parents. Whether doing "good" or "naughty" deeds as a child, our behaviour is most often to get the attention of other people – usually our parents.

Being social satisfies a deep need within us that we have always had, and most likely always will; we are social animals. The basis of our society is around the core unit of the family, with the core of the family being the social relationships between us as we grow. This book talks about universal truths, the psychology that has been rooted in our DNA for millions of years and our need for connection – this won't be changing any time soon! This is what I refer to as our "Social Needia".

Fifty to sixty years ago, in the official "good old days" and of course long before that too, meeting in person was primarily the most common means of communication. Technology has always been looking to overcome the communication barriers between people caused by the lack of proximity to each other. The postal service, which traces back to Persia in 550 BC, was the first method outside of smoke signals used to deliver messages to people who were not in each other's company. Over time, we have moved into using communication systems that can connect people not only on opposite sides of a country, but across the earth and even between planets.

Our desire to be social and to communicate has driven technological advances. When people look back and comment on when, back in the day, they would speak face to face and truly cared about each other, they are implying that newer methods of being social are inferior. And it could easily be argued that they are correct. No other means of communication beats meeting someone in person. There are, however, other factors that need to be considered.

A hundred years ago, most likely the only people you knew were the people you grew up with in your family, extended family and local area. You would have known fewer people but known them very well. In the world we live in today, we have hundreds, if not thousands, of acquaintances, starting from when we were young at various schools, and then colleges, and multiple jobs, and various sports teams and hobbies, etc. It is no longer possible to meet all of these people in person and maintain some semblance of time to yourself in today's hectic lifestyle! Technology has allowed for and adapted to this change in our "social" being, making it possible to maintain relationships – albeit "lite" relationships – through a variety of social networks, text messages, instant messaging, live video and virtual reality, to name but a few.

As we look at social media a little deeper, we can see that progress in communication fields is now at a rate never seen before, and it is truly phenomenal. We have evolved from one-to-one personal meetings to the postage system, followed by a few thousand years' "break" to the telegraph, phone, internet, email, a variety of online social networks and instant messaging services, bringing us to today, when there never has been more of a choice in how to communicate.

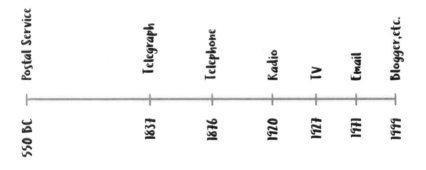

Fig 1.1: The evolution of social media

The media through which communication takes place have changed over the years. For a start, the speed at which the connection takes place has increased exponentially. What once took the time it would take for a horse to travel between towns to deliver a letter has now literally transformed to the speed of light. Your message can travel from one side of the world to the other in much less than a millisecond. While this has its advantages, it brings with it any number of challenges.

The ease with which we can contact people has changed dramatically too. Only 20 years ago, it was not possible to contact somebody without knowing either their physical address or phone number. Now, do a quick search on Google and 20 seconds later you can be making direct contact with anyone from a friend to one of the most influential people in the world.

Social media can also be about building a community. This is something we have perfected over thousands of years in Ireland and the UK, with the local pub being central to communities as a place where people share their life experiences with each other – with the assistance of certain liquid lubricants to help with the "social" aspects and make the stories more interesting. So, the next time you find yourself in a bar and you need to explain your actions to your better half, you can say that you were working on your social media ☺.

The fundamentals of what social media truly is have never changed. It is about the connection between people. Many have major objections about the new wave of "social media", which often revolve around the lack of face to face ("FaceTime" ☺) interactions and comments like "people just don't speak to each other any more". In many cases, what is missing here is the understanding that human beings' innate need for connection has not gone away; the means of doing so has just changed form.

The change in the means of communication media from physical form into energy or light is a reflection of how the means of exchanging money has adapted too. The word "capital", which today we use for describing a sum of money, originates from the Latin word "caput" – quite literally the head of livestock or cattle. Obviously, carrying around pieces of animals to exchange had its challenges, and over time coins, then notes, then plastic began to replace each other. Now we use electronic forms of money transfer, making it nothing more than energy or light. We rarely get to "see or touch" money any more, as it moves through the ether from our employer to our creditors and banks and through the blockchain.

That brings us back to today and the journey at hand, whether you are reading this through physical means, electronically or indeed listening to me on an audio file!

There are five sections to this book, each building on the previous ones. This allows you to start from scratch, assuming you have no experience in this field, and build the concepts as we progress. It is set up in this way in order for you to start using social media in its current forms to leverage it for any individual or business owner who is looking to make major changes to their current financial situation.

Firstly, in stage one, I wanted to give you a brief overview of the history and evolution of social media, but only briefly as this in itself doesn't help you with the creation of your business.

Secondly, I will present you with an explanation of the overall concept of this book and the urgency behind stopping wasting time on social media. 99%+ of people on social networks, from my experience, are there out of boredom and spend hours on end looking at what is happening in other people's lives. I wish to show you how to look at these social media users and find the particular individuals who you can help with your current business or the new business you are considering starting. I will point out some of the most commonly made mistakes so that you can immediately identify them and eliminate them. I will also share with you that right now you are living in incredible times where, literally starting today, you have the opportunity to build a highly profitable business online from your phone or tablet! I will also explain why, unlike the incredibly low success rates of traditional business models, your chances of success with an online business using the RETHINK model are 99%+ ☺.

Thirdly, I am going to focus on the overall success strategy behind this book. I will introduce you to the RETHINK social media framework and show you why it is a must for anybody starting out on this journey and existing business owners. I will explain in great detail the importance of fixing problems that people are willing to pay for and analysing who the right people are for your business. We will discuss how easy it is to build your credibility, how to find the right people across different social networks, how we can help them for free as well as offering them products to purchase, and where to find products when you don't have your own. Shortly after that, we will start to understand the importance of building trust with our followers and how to measure the success of our business so that we can set up an asset that pays us over and over again and that only grows more successful with time.

I will then show you the exact tactics for cashing in on your new-found knowledge, using tried and tested online marketing strategies regardless of your experience. In the last two sections, I will conclude by highlighting some of the main watch-outs for the future and how you can be prepared for this, before wrapping up by sharing how I can assist you further if you would like more help from me.

Let's start from the beginning: why should we even think about using social media? What is the end result that we want?

I'm sure you have heard from some social media expert or another that social media is all about getting "branding for your business". Every time I hear people speak about getting branding with social media, it reminds me of a story I was once told by my uncle Joe. Back in my late teens, I was looking for work experience and was discussing options with my uncle. He asked me if I wanted to make decent money or to get work experience. I was confused! I wanted both, I guess! Joe said to me:

*"Experience is what you get when you are not getting
what you really want!"*

I believe the same applies to "branding" and social media.

**Branding is what you get from social media when you are not
getting what you REALLY want!**

I am yet to meet a small business owner who would rather "get branding" than make serious income from their social media strategies. For bigger organisations, of course, branding in itself is a worthy goal – this is often done through the sponsorship of sporting stadia and the like, and larger organisations have tested the return on such major outlays in investment. Branding and generating income don't have to be mutually exclusive, however. Branding is often used as an excuse when the experts are not experienced enough to show you how to use social media to impact the bottom line positively, with a real-life return on investment for all to see.

When I started out on my online journey and focused specifically on Twitter, no amount of branding with Twitter was going to put food on the table or pay my bills. Through necessity, I worked out how truly anybody can use social media, not just to get branded, but to make millions of dollars in just a few short years – like I did. Business, first and foremost, is about solving problems for people in exchange for a financial benefit. When you think about it, if business is about people and social media is a means to connect people, then it would logically make sense that, if managed correctly, social media SHOULD be a power house in building your bottom line significantly – and it can be, and will be, when you follow the steps outlined in this book. That's the bottom line: we should use social media to make us more money, plain and simple! Let's find out how…

Summary:

Social media is nothing new! It has been with us for thousands of years in various forms, but the advent of new social networks in the early 2000s has brought it into the limelight like never before in history. It is a huge part of normal daily life now, as are smartphones. Currently 99%+ of people who use social networks have no intention, or no idea that it's possible to make some serious money using the exact same networks on the exact same devices. This is the essence of this book: to show you, regardless of your experience, that rather than being the target of marketing messages 24 hours a day, 7 days a week, and spending your precious time and money, you could be making money all that time by learning how to leverage the biggest phenomenon and opportunity of our generation. It's time to RETHINK social media!

Traditional Thinking:

Social media is a relatively new phenomenon and a place to go to follow what my friends and family are doing. It can be used for business and is good for building relationships with customers and getting branding, but it is extremely time-consuming and it is difficult to measure its exact benefit to the bottom line.

RETHINK:

Social media is not a modern phenomenon. When using it for your business, it does not have to take up a lot of time and can be structured in an easy to manage way. It should be an integral part of your business, but it is not in itself the entire solution. Social media is not just about branding. Its benefits can be measured with accuracy down to the last dollar.

You can now start to forget about social media being used exclusively for personal reasons; in fact, it's just got a LOT more personal! Let us instead learn how to use the precious time you may already spend on social media to start making a serious income.

SECTION 2: CONCEPT

Chapter 2: Why Do Businesses Fail?

*"Entrepreneurs are the only people who will work
80 hours a week to avoid working 40 hours a week."*
- Lori Greiner

Did you realise that as an entrepreneur, you have a 90% chance of failure in your business? That's what the facts say about TRADITIONAL business using a traditional business model. Let's be clear for a moment. I am not telling you that the solution to business owners' current or impending financial issues will be simply opening a Facebook page, there is clearly more to it than that!

Let us look at the facts for a moment about the likelihood of success of any business before I explain how you can completely turn things around. According to Neil Patel in his article in Forbes magazine, nine out of ten business start-ups will fail. That is the unfortunate truth.

Generally speaking, I feel this is a little optimistic; I have read elsewhere that this number is in fact much closer to 97%. With those odds stacked so highly against a new business owner, why would you even begin? We would much prefer a 99%+ chance of success rather than failure, right?

But why is there such a high rate of failure? There are many reasons, as we will soon discover. Let us start with what the key goals are for most new business owners when they begin: 1. To free up more time, and 2. To make lots more money.

As business owners soon find out, the more "successful" they become,

Ref: (https://www.forbes.com/sites/neilpatel/2015/01/16/90-of-startups-will-fail-heres-what-you-need-to-know-about-the-10/#1b0be72d6679).

quite often the more money it costs and the less free time they have! Most entrepreneurs unknowingly set themselves up for failure right from the start. This might surprise you, but I truly believe it. Many people open a business with the mindset of an employee and zero experience of what it takes to run a successful business. Traditional business is hard! Being an employee and a business owner are completely different roles; one is specific and specialist, while the other is about being a great generalist.

Let's look at how this can happen. A significant proportion of business owners started their journey as a result of being upset with their boss. They realised that they were better in every way than their boss but getting nowhere near the same rewards. It sickened them taking orders from someone who wasn't as good as them at what they did. People join companies but leave bosses, as the old saying goes! Then one day they'd had enough and they decided that they were going to go do their thing, but this time by themselves with no interference from their boss. Let's say on the Friday that they were a personal assistant, and the following Wednesday they were the proud owner of a thousand new business cards stating, as fact, that they were the CEO of their new business. It's an exciting prospect and certainly gets the heart pumping!

What a buzz! This is going to be great. I'm going to do this... It's really happening! It's time to enjoy the life of a business owner, time to enjoy abundant cash and lots of free time... oh boy, are you in for a surprise ☺.

Now let's put you in the position of this newly-made CEO. Imagine you're sitting on your bed with your laptop and you think, "Hmmmm, perhaps I need to move the 'office' out of the bedroom and into the kitchen." You then quickly realise that having business meetings in the kitchen may not exactly be ideal either. You decide to look for premises to rent. Now this, too, brings a degree of a buzz, until you realise that you need to pay roughly three months in advance for even the smallest grotty office. And you may need to kit it out yourself, and then pay for a landline and wifi, etc. and banners and logos for the company, which are yet to be created.

You take a look at local offices and rent a space that requires a three-month deposit in advance and comes with the additional costs of heating, lighting, parking and local business taxes. You must also get yourself set up formally as a business and hire an accountant. Let us hope the office is furnished, or you may just have to rent or buy your office desk and chair as well as a new printer and possibly an upgrade of your work laptop, which hopefully you have now returned to your old boss.

Assuming this is all in place, you are sitting in your office and wondering if the phone is going to ring. "How do I get the word out that I am in business?" Well, you need to get started on marketing and sales. This most likely means you now need to find a web designer, and a budget to run local ads in the paper or on the radio. You've also heard that getting set up on social media is a must. When the phone finally rings, you realise you are not comfortable with making sales and really have no idea how to price what it is that you do. Who is going to deliver the product or service? You are already too busy learning how to market, keeping tabs on your web designer, and setting up and managing your social media to have time to also deliver the service. It looks like you need to pay the bank a visit and request a loan, because the next step is hiring someone! You may be asked to put up the very home that you live in with your family as security, and now you are really not so sure if this is your best ever brainwave.

If you haven't given up at this stage, you start to realise that the one skill you were paid for as an employee is almost completely irrelevant when it comes to a business. Until now, you never needed to worry about things like marketing and sales, not to mention your next step, hiring and managing people! Perhaps you involve a recruitment agency; you eventually find the right person who can do what it is you planned on doing to begin with, or take over your marketing and sales from you. And let's not forget, now you need to involve a lawyer to draft a contract of employment and make sure everything is above board. At the end of the month, payroll needs to be organised and now you have obligations as an employer to pay various taxes and insurances for your employees. On pay day, you suddenly realise that your employees get paid first and if there is anything left over, you just might get paid!

I could go on. What about customer service, managing the diaries, meeting clients and potential clients, attending networking events, creating logos, brochures, filing tax returns, inventory management, invoicing, metrics, scaling up, market research, even simple things like purchasing some clothing so that your appearance looks somewhat professional ☺? We haven't even touched the tip of the iceberg here – there are endless jobs that need to be done, consultants to be hired, contracts to be written and agreed, and various insurances to be purchased, to name but a few.

What about your family? They have hardly seen you since you left your job. What happened to all the extra money and free time you had expected? This scenario is all too common among new business owners. You have exactly the opposite of what you set out as your two main goals: you have less money and less time to spend doing the things you love with the people you love. Is it any wonder that most businesses fail when the owner realises that it was easier to be guaranteed payment, not just the scraps left over? Ok, you have to put up with a boss you don't like, but you can sleep at night with the security that money is coming in when it's meant to – and you don't have to sleep with your boss every single night. At least you can go back to having your weekends off!

Here is a breakdown from *Fortune* magazine of the top reasons business owners felt their business had failed.

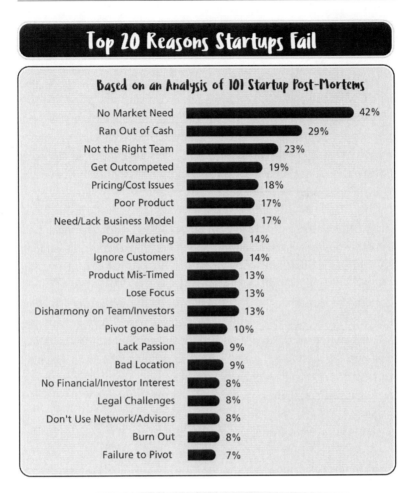

Top 20 Reasons Startups Fail

Based on an Analysis of 101 Startup Post-Mortems

No Market Need	42%
Ran Out of Cash	29%
Not the Right Team	23%
Get Outcompeted	19%
Pricing/Cost Issues	18%
Poor Product	17%
Need/Lack Business Model	17%
Poor Marketing	14%
Ignore Customers	14%
Product Mis-Timed	13%
Lose Focus	13%
Disharmony on Team/Investors	13%
Pivot gone bad	10%
Lack Passion	9%
Bad Location	9%
No Financial/Investor Interest	8%
Legal Challenges	8%
Don't Use Network/Advisors	8%
Burn Out	8%
Failure to Pivot	7%

Fig 2.1: Top 20 reasons start-ups fail

The overwhelming winner with 42% is "No market need" for the product. This makes me smile as it is such a common misunderstanding for business owners. Please highlight this next sentence until you almost create a hole in the page!

Ref: http://fortune.com/2014/09/25/why-startups-fail-according-to-their-founders/

People do not buy what you think they need; they buy what they want!

To keep things really simple here, your job as a business owner is to give people what they want, and make a profit. Traditional business thinking from the leading business schools would dictate that the key to a great business is to come up with a great idea that involves finding something that people really need. I truly believe that this idea, well intentioned as it may be, is fundamentally flawed and ends up setting up most budding business owners for failure right from the outset!

There are two aspects to it, and both are misguided. Firstly, having a great idea for a business has nothing to do with being successful. The business that wins is the business that knows how to market that idea successfully. Just look at Facebook – it wasn't their idea, but they knew how to market it better. The second flaw is to find something that people "need". If your business is based around something that people "need", but not what they "want", you are bound to fail. As a minimum, you should make sure that what people "need" and "want" are the same thing. Otherwise, like most business owners do, they project their values onto the consumers, telling them that this is something they should buy, which they have no intention of doing. At the end of the day, people will purchase in line with their values and not yours – we will study this in more depth later in this book.

But it's definitely not all gloom and doom here. This is how business used to be! The world of business has changed dramatically, as have the chances of your success. Every one of the issues above can be overcome with the framework of RETHINK social media. This is a big claim, I know, but you can judge for yourself shortly. With the advent of the internet and social media, things have become a whole lot easier. The process of finding the right people and offering them the solutions they "want" to purchase is something that can be delivered in its entirety online, without ever leaving the comfort of your own home and without the need of any bank loans or major risks.

Summary:

When you start out with a new business, run in a traditional way, there is an overwhelming chance that your business will fail. 90% of the time, in fact. Most business owners believe that the reason for their failure was that there was "no market need" for their product. It is all too common for a business to come up with a great idea that people "need", only to find out all too late that it wasn't something that people actually "want". Even if you have an amazing product or service, that doesn't guarantee success either. Running a typical business is extremely hard work, often resulting in business owners working twice as hard for half the reward and being last to be paid in the business. That all changes through the clever leverage of the tools that are available to us now, such as online social networks and smartphones. The world has changed right in front of our eyes – and so have the odds of your success: they are dramatically stacked in your favour right now!

Traditional Thinking:

The key to business success is to have a great idea to create something that people really need. Once you overcome the initial humps of creating that business and learn the ropes, more money and lots of free time are just on the horizon!

RETHINK:

Learning to leverage tools such as the internet and social media can completely transform how you run a business from day to day and massively increase your chances of being successful. We must adapt to providing people with what they truly want, not what we think they need, and learn how to market ourselves better than our competition.

Chapter 3: An Unprecedented Opportunity

"Great opportunities may come once in a lifetime,
but small opportunities surround us every day."
- Rick Warren

A once in a millennium opportunity…

Never, since the beginning of our civilisation as we know it, has there been such an advancement in technology in such a short space of time as has occurred in this generation. The mantra of certain phone networks of "connecting people, not places" has become a reality. Children of today cannot imagine, let alone remember, a time when it wasn't possible to get in touch with somebody literally in an instant. Only a few short years ago we relied on having to know somebody's exact location at a very specific time and, in addition, know the phone number for that location; we even had to hope that nobody else wanted to contact anybody at that location at the same time, or we'd be out of luck! Teens of today are mystified by the idea that we just picked a location and a time and actually showed up in order for us to meet ☺. Imagine, no last-minute texts changing location, or explaining that you are running late.

With the advent of smartphones, iPads and other tablets, wireless internet, PCs, laptops, virtual reality and whatever the latest gadgets are, we continue to be brought closer together and made more accessible. Technology advancements have changed the communication landscape forever. I know you are generally aware of this, but so few people are aware of what this could and should mean to them financially; it could completely transform your personal or business financial destiny in incredible ways!

As mentioned in the introduction, we live in a time when people literally carry around their phones with them 24 hours a day, 7 days a week. Most often, they are the source of the first and last activity in our daily lives. We are addicted to the devices, relying on them not only for general news and updates, but also connections with our loved ones and peers, and in many cases, to assist with our emotional well-being. Activity on phones can result in the release of endorphins and dopamine, – two chemical substances that drive addictive behaviours.

We are living in unprecedented times. If we choose to, we can access over half of the people on this planet, 24 hours a day, 7 days a week. Consider that for just a moment. That's 3,500,000,000 people! With this power at your fingertips, surely it makes sense to get involved in harnessing such opportunity rather than meekly watching the biggest opportunity of a lifetime pass you by. Imagine being able to tap in and listen to the conversations and musings of complete strangers who are willing to share with the world, or anyone who cares to listen, what their major problems are at any given moment. Why people share their problems with complete strangers is not really that important; what is important is accepting this, moving forward and learning how to take advantage of it.

If we consider that the purpose of business is to solve people's problems and get a financial reward for this undertaking, wouldn't it make sense to see if we could somehow connect the two; listening to people's problems using the latest hot social network and then offering those people instant solutions to their problems for a profit? Learning the skills to do this will not only make your phone worth its weight in gold, but a lot more than that!

While we're certainly living in times when technological advancements of the day never cease to amaze, it could also be viewed that we are living at a time in history when there has never been more uncertainty, political upheaval, economic shocks, and genuine fear and panic among people about not only their safety but their financial futures. Whenever you're reading this, you will probably remember that when the results of Brexit and the election of Donald Trump were announced, a glance at any social media network would show you the overwhelming sentiment of fear, anger and uncertainty among the general population. Adding North Korea into the equation certainly didn't ease the tension much either.

While this fear is understandable among the general population, as none of us particularly like change, spending time on social media venting about issues that are completely out of our individual control is probably not the best use of our time. I don't intend to choose a side on either of the political decisions mentioned – it actually doesn't really matter, because regardless of which side of the fence you are on, complaining on social media about it changes nothing. In fact, it reinforces what I explained earlier about how the 99%+ use social media on a regular basis. This is where you need to distance yourself and learn how to turn the passion of others into profit for you.

I would like to shift the mindset of worrying about the external environment that we have no real control over, to focusing on what we can control as an individual or as a business. We can completely determine the level of success of our own personal micro economies when we focus only on the areas within the locus of our control. How can you secure your business' viability and/or your personal financial future when your environment seems more uncertain than ever? Is it even possible?

I would suggest that it absolutely is, using a combination of using the RETHINK social media model, RETHINKing the traditional business model, leveraging the power of the internet and using the proven models that are sitting there ready for us to discover. This is exactly what you'll learn in this book.

With an online business, you immediately remove a lot of the costs and risks you have with an offline business; let's look at all of them here.

- No premises to rent
- No additional heating, lighting, wifi or phone for an office
- No big deposits for an office

- No recruitment agency
- No sales team
- No marketing team
- No web designers
- No graphic designers
- No sophisticated websites
- No products of your own
- No customer service
- No merchant accounts
- No complex payment processing systems
- No meeting room hire
- No operators
- No paying insurances for staff
- No salaries
- No need to leave your home ☺
- No loans
- No big risks

This list, while extensive, is not complete. With an internet business leveraging social media, you take away almost every single risk associated with running a "regular" business, and you can do it all without ever leaving home. Sounds great, right? Well, that is exactly why I got started, and it's very doable, even for the complete beginner. Now, before we move on, let's address what I would consider the elephant in the room at this point. "But Paul, if it was that easy, wouldn't everybody be doing it?"

> "If it was easy, everyone would be doing it."
> - Anonymous daredevil ☺

This quote is really powerful to me, as it is the thought process that stops most people from ever focusing on doing tasks that can completely change their finances. My first business coach really disliked it. When I had just made my first money on Twitter while I had literally been sleeping, I asked him the next day, "If it's this easy, why isn't everybody else doing it?" He looked at me and said something along the lines of: "That one question, Paul, is what stops most people from taking any type of positive action." He continued, "If you are going to ask this question, at least change the wording to "If it's this easy, why am I not doing it?"

When you ask this question, at least you can answer it. You have absolutely no control over what other people do. So, ask yourself the question, "Why am I not doing this?" and then you can get to the root of the issue. It could be fear, lack of knowledge, uncertainty or, quite commonly, it could be that you are very concerned about what other people might think. I recently had the pleasure of sharing the stage with the author of Chicken Soup For The Soul, Jack Canfield, and I loved what he had to say on this:

"What others think about you is none of your business."

What a freeing affirmation that we could all do very well to keep in mind from time to time. Let us look for a moment at what "everyone" is doing, starting with some facts. What do we consider "normal" behaviour for "everyone"? I could not write my first book without referring to one of my all-time favourite quotes:

"Normal is getting dressed in clothes that you buy for work, driving through traffic in a car that you are still paying for, in order to get to a job that you need so you can pay for the clothes, car and the house that you leave empty all day in order to afford to live in it."
- Ellen Goodman

Most people are too busy keeping their head above water, unfortunately, to have the time to learn new strategies, let alone implement them. In a society in which we are encouraged in our 20s to put ourselves under the maximum possible stress with our home mortgage for the next 30 years to be considered "successful", perhaps we need a new role model – perhaps "everyone else" should not be the gauge of what is right or wrong in terms of what we choose to pursue.

In my own case, ever since my late 20s, I have liked to study what the most financially successful people do and model them instead. Do you know how many millionaires (in US dollars) there are on the planet? We can define millionaires as those with "investable assets of US$1 million or more, excluding primary residence, collectibles, consumables and consumer durables."

According to *Fortune* magazine, there are about 17 million millionaires. This might appear like a lot of people at first, but as a percentage of the people on the planet it's approximately 0.23% of society. Put another way, only 1 in 500 people have hit the heights of traditional financial wealth. I don't know about you, but I would not consider 1 in 500 people "normal" or "everyone". Clearly these people do things differently, financially at least, and if we are going to model anyone's behaviour, I would suggest that this is where we start. In fact, if you are doing anything that is different to the norm, you should congratulate yourself, because you might have a much better chance of success ☺!

Having established that we must look at things differently to get new results, and model those who are already successful in the areas in which we wish to thrive, let me share with you some examples of businesses you will already be aware of that are using the model I'll be suggesting we plug into very soon. I have been promoting this model for many years, but never has the evidence been so roundly supported by the amazing success of some of the world's biggest companies. What do Uber, Facebook, Airbnb, booking.com, Amazon, eBay and Alibaba have in common? They all have annual revenues of billions of dollars. They all have something else in common too: they all serve as the "matchmaker".

Uber, the world's largest taxi company, doesn't own any cars; instead, it matches the drivers of cars with passengers looking for lifts. Facebook, the world's most popular media owner, does not create its own content; it allows people to connect with each other and share their own content together.

Ref: www.businessinsider.com/world-wealth-report-countries-with-the-most-millionaires-2016-6

Alibaba, the world's largest retailer, doesn't own its inventory; it allows businesses with lots of inventory find businesses that are looking to distribute products globally. Airbnb and booking.com are two of the world's biggest accommodation providers, yet they don't own a single hotel, apartment or B&B; instead, they match people looking for accommodation with the providers of accommodation. Amazon, the world's largest book store, does not write its own books; it matches authors all over the world with avid readers keen to consume and read their books. eBay, one of the largest stores in the world, does not make the products it sells; instead, it matches excellent product providers with people looking to purchase those products.

Fig 3.1 The changing face of business

Are you starting to see the picture?

None of these companies take on many of the big risks associated with traditional businesses. They don't make the all-too-common mistake of creating a product or service first and then forcing it out to the market. These companies let the market demand dictate what solutions they provide. Looking back at the number one reason why most business owners felt that their business failed, the clear winner with 42% was there was "no market need" for what they created.

It is very common for business owners to create something that they feel the market "needs". From my experience, however, people very rarely purchase what they "need", they tend to purchase what they "want". I'm sure you'll agree with this from your own experience; you might need to upgrade the fence around your house, but you want to use that money for a foreign holiday instead ☺. Let's take a look at a graphic to explain what I am suggesting we can do together as a RETHINK of traditional business and of the traditional use of social media.

Fig 3.2: The matchmaking model

How can we apply the same "Uber-esque" model to our real-life examples? The concept is actually very straightforward. While people all over the world are freaking out about financial uncertainty in their futures, for a number of years I, and many others, have been sharing a simple concept that anyone can follow, which can bring you control of the financial world of both you and your business. We often hear that "there is nothing more certain than change", or words to that effect. I certainly agree with this comment in most instances. If, however, we wish to find financial certainty at times when there is nothing but uncertainty and continuous change, what if we could find certain areas where we have absolute certainty and where there is little or no change? Surely this could help us out significantly. Is this even possible? I definitely believe so!

Have you ever met a person without a problem? Seriously, have you ever met anybody, be they financially rich or poor, who doesn't talk about problems they have? I certainly haven't! In fact, I would be willing to wager that there's not a person on this planet who does not come with a whole host of problems, which you'll discover if you speak to them for long enough. There is certainty in this: no matter what happens in the economy moving forward, people will continue to have problems, whether they are about having too little or too much money, and I for one cannot foresee this changing for many, many years to come.

Lots of people just LOVE to complain about their problems! We even compete with our problems, to see who has the worst one. Case in point: at a recent event, I heard somebody complaining over coffee about how long it took them to make it to the event because of the traffic, when a complete stranger butted in to share how it took them twice as long, and yet another person explained how it had taken them almost another hour on top of that ☺. We can't help ourselves, it's in our very nature. Just take a look at your favourite social network and look at how many complaints there are. Problems drive desires and wants, and peoples' "wants" drive the economy!

Something else that we like to do on a consistent basis, as a general rule, is spend money. Most people know exactly how they are going to get rid of their money before it ever even arrives in their bank accounts, in my experience ☺.

Put these two human attributes together for a moment: people will always have problems and they like to spend their money, in many instances, on solving those problems. Look at figure 3.2 again, with the three people – this "typical" person is represented in the diagram as the individual on the left-hand side holding the green jigsaw puzzle.

The person on the right with the blue jigsaw puzzle represents another particular type of person – your typical entrepreneur, someone who loves to solve problems. Generally speaking, entrepreneurs and business owners are really good at creating solutions to problems, but where they fall down is in learning how to market themselves properly and how to perform the sales function of their business well. In fact, many entrepreneurs really dislike marketing and sales – it is not their forte. Add to the mix that there is a 90% chance of failure, and suddenly your opportunity may become clear to you.

While businesses are busy with operational issues (blue jigsaw person) and people are busy complaining and looking for solutions to their problems (green jigsaw person), wouldn't it make sense for you to position yourself in the middle as a "matchmaker"? This is the perfect place to be! Regardless of what happens in the economy, as people's problems change, so will the solutions produced by busy entrepreneurs and business owners. Business owners will continue to struggle to find customers, and customers will continue to look for solutions, regardless of changes in the economy. Why join the struggle? Why do something that has a 90% chance of failure? It's time to RETHINK the "normal", time to RETHINK how we use social media and do business and stack the odds right back in our favour.

What does "positioning yourself in the middle" actually mean in real terms? Am I suggesting that you do not need any business, or if you have a business, just to abandon it?

The matchmaker will have a business, but a very different kind to the norm. The concept is as follows: the matchmaker uses social media to find people who are complaining about very specific problems. (They learn the tools for how to do this and contact these people, etc., which we will elaborate on later in this book.) Once they have found the right people, they can now introduce these people to the products and services they want in order to solve the problems they have.

This does not mean that you have to create the products or services. Neither does it mean that you must be the expert in this field. Instead, you introduce the people with the problems to the very best solutions that are available for their specific problems, and you get paid an introducer fee or commission for having found the customers for the businesses. You do not need to deliver the products or services at all; in fact, your "work" ends once you have introduced the person and the solution. You get paid if that person purchases the solution following your introduction. If this seems confusing, please don't worry, I'll explain it in terms I guarantee you will fully understand.

Uber meets Walmart…

One of the major hang-ups that people who are fresh to the idea of building an online business commonly have is how little focus needs to be placed on the product or service that will be sold. In the traditional form of business, the product or service is right at the core of the business model; however, in the matchmaking model, it is only one piece of the puzzle.

When a business creates its product or service and it is proven to work, the next rational step is to get it out there in front of as many relevant people as possible and look to win those people over so they will test the new product or service. One of the issues with this is that, most likely, there is a lack of knowledge of the brand and possibly a distinct lack of trust when it comes to the product, especially when it's new to the market, unless perhaps it is from a historically trusted brand.

How do supermarket chains overcome this hesitancy, this lack of trust relating to newer products? Major supermarket chains have this aspect of business absolutely nailed! This is where they truly stand out from other businesses.

Think about the model of the Walmart, Tesco or any major supermarket brand you commonly use. They build enormous warehouses very close to where lots of people live, fill the warehouses with empty shelving and put cash registers at one end. They then proceed to allow literally tens of thousands of separate companies to fight it out among themselves to determine what products get stocked on the shelves in their stores. They allow the individual companies to do all of the branding, advertising, marketing, etc., so that by the time the consumer walks into the store, they already know exactly what product from which brand they want to purchase as **they already know, like and trust** the brand. Major supermarket chains do not try to convince the consumers of the need to buy their own branded products, they just set up a scenario in which the consumer can conveniently come to just one location and find the brands they want. Tesco and Walmart have no emotional attachment to any particular product; they make a commission on every single product that sells! The products that sell the best get priority in terms of product placement on the shelving. The supermarket chains do not need to get involved in things like product complaints, as these are filtered back directly to the manufacturer.

This concept is called affiliate marketing – where one business sells another business' products or services and takes a commission from every sale without ever having to create the product itself. It is often explained in complicated ways, and as a result, it can confuse people a lot. Most major organisations allow regular people like you and me to become partners of theirs completely free, allowing us to sell their products and make a commission on any sales we make.

Let's take two typical examples, eBay and Amazon, two of the world's largest online sellers. You can go to their websites and apply to become a partner (affiliate) of theirs completely free of charge. They ask for your email address, home address and other contact details, and your payment details so they can pay you your commissions. In return, they give you personalised links to their websites that you can use to promote products on their websites and get paid a commission on any sales that take place.

This is one of those things that when you become aware of it, you really wonder why more people aren't aware of it or doing it regularly, as it truly is a game changer. It means that any regular person, regardless of experience, can get started today promoting the products and services of other businesses in an instant. This is how I made my first sales online the very first night I attempted it – I immediately felt like I had cracked the code ☺. You can get paid commission from other business' products of anywhere from 5% all the way to 100% on your sales. Yes, even up to 100% in some cases, as businesses may be happy to give you all of the initial sale so they can then promote more products to the customer at a later stage through something known as a sales funnel (this will be explained later in this book).

For now, all you need to understand is that our concept is very simple: we are going to look for people on social media who have certain problems, let them know about the very best products in the world that can help solve the issues for them, and get paid for every single sale, even though we won't be creating any products or services ourselves. We've just started to RETHINK social media and RETHINK business!

There may be a number of questions that you already have about this model, especially considering how simple it seems. Why would anyone buy from me? Can I really do this? How much experience do I need? Do I need to have a business already in place? Where do I find companies that allow me to sell their products? Will businesses let me sell their products even if I have no experience? Why do businesses give so much money away to someone like me as a commission? Will there not be too much competition? Where do I start?

These are just some of the many questions that I too had when starting out, and I will answer them for you. However, one of the more important questions for right now is one not mentioned above. What I have neglected to mention is that Tesco and Walmart are already brands that people know and trust, and you most likely don't have this credibility, so how can it work for you? Now if this is a question you were considering, I'd like to congratulate you, as this was something I did not even think about for quite a long time after I started my first online business. This is where social media can really be your friend – when used correctly.

We live in an age when it could be argued that the perceived levels of credibility of a person or business can be proportionate to the level of following that person or business has on social media. Just thinking about it logically, if you met two entrepreneurs with identical experience and know-how and you were going to do business with one of them, all else being equal, if one had a much more significant social media following than the other, there is a strong chance you'd choose that person. It gives a level of social proof and added confidence to one's buying decision.

Traditionally, building up the credibility of any brand was a very costly and very time-consuming process, which often required years of expensive branding exercises or relying on word of mouth recommendations to build up over significant periods of time. With the advent of social networks like Facebook, Twitter, Instagram, YouTube and the like, there has been a major shift to make this process easier than ever before. One of your major objectives in this book is to learn the uncomplicated strategies that can allow you to start to build you own credibility through the clever use of your time and money on social media. It does not need to be difficult. In fact, this is exactly how I started. At one point in time, I had no Twitter accounts, no followers and no social media credibility – exactly how most people start. Following some very simple strategies that I will share, that changed dramatically, and this is how you too will overcome credibility as a potential obstacle, and instead make it one of your major strengths.

In the next chapter I want to turn this concept into a seven step RETHINK model that you will be able to get started with very shortly, regardless of your experience.

Summary:

The world that most of us grew up in is not the world we live in now. Yet even with all the advancements in technology, people seem to have more problems, anxieties and things to complain about than ever before. While people continue to have problems, entrepreneurs and businesses continue to go out of business due to lack of customers, among other reasons. In recent times, however, a number of companies have emerged that have bucked the trend of failure and generate billions of dollars per year in revenue. Rather than focusing on creating products and services themselves, they take on the role of the matchmaker. Alibaba, Booking. com, Airbnb and Amazon are just a few examples. At the same time, billions of people have joined the online conversation in social networks. While most of us either watch or engage in conversations about our perceived problems on social media, a tiny minority, of which you are about to become, are following these conversations to identify how the people with these problems can be helped. Once we know who these people are and can start to collect their details, we can then focus on finding the most innovative and best-selling products that can solve their problems. We get paid just for introducing the solution to the person looking for it; there is no limit to peoples' problems or the products that can solve them. Many of the products that will make you wealthy do not even exist right now!

Traditional Thinking:

In order to run a business, there are a number of very costly things that must be in place to begin with, such as decent premises, website, list of product offerings, brochures and staff. Your core product is central to your success, and you must do everything in your power to grow this brand so that people start to trust you. If the business can afford it, you can hire marketing and sales teams to take on these tasks and hope that it all works out.

RETHINK:

Products are not the core of businesses any longer, peoples' problems are. The success of a business can be determined by how well it solves the person's problem as opposed to the product it created to solve the problem. Social networks have completely changed our level of access to people, which has made it relatively simple to identify them based on the problems they have. We are living in a time when you can look for people on social media who have certain problems, let them know about only the latest and best products that can help solve the issues for them, and get paid for every single sale. Best of all, we don't even have to create any of the products or services ourselves.

SECTION 3: STRATEGY

Chapter 4: It's Very Different to What You Might Think

"The secret of business is to know something
that nobody else knows."
- Aristotle Onassis

Traditional business is difficult. No matter what anybody tells you, there is a huge amount of graft involved, especially at the beginning. But so is having a job – it certainly comes with its difficulties too, and no matter how well your job goes, you still have to go back again on Monday! But this doesn't mean that business needs to be difficult all of the time. With the right systems in place, once the initial work is put in, anything is possible. Using leverage and being clever in how you function can remove a serious amount of heartache that is just plainly unnecessary. As the quote from Aristotle Onassis above indicates, when you know something that's not commonly known in business, you certainly have a huge advantage.

We have just looked at the "matchmaking" concept and how this can be something worth seriously considering for most people. I would now like to elaborate on this, add more meat to the bones and explain the overall RETHINK strategy. The strategy that I wish to share consists of seven steps. This system is an opportunity to leverage what is not commonly known, especially as it relates to the use of social media in business. To explain this model correctly, let's just look at a fairly traditional model of a business for a moment.

Let's take a local hamburger fast food outlet as an example. When an entrepreneur decides to open one, the first thing they do is look for an area that may be best suited. They look for places where large hungry crowds of people are likely to hang out. Ideal locations might be near large shopping centres or near entertainment venues, for example. This is key to any successful traditional business: having a hungry crowd of people on tap who are likely to want to buy what you have to offer. Having ready-made customers, if you like, is key to making relatively easy money. The burger company could have the smartest looking shop with the latest recipes and they could have the best tasting burgers, but if there's no hungry crowd of people (ready-made customers) passing outside all day long, they will very soon go out of business.

Fig 4.1: Standard retail business model

The RETHINK Social Media Model is very different to the retailer's model, and with many advantages other than those mentioned above. Firstly, it is set up online, so you don't even need to leave the house to get started. Secondly, with paid ads on social media, you can figure out if a business model can work within a few hours rather than years, and as a result, your business can be scaled up or scaled back by pressing a few keys on your keyboard.

Now look at the RETHINK social media way of doing business. To begin with, we start by ensuring that the basic criteria are in place to set up the matchmaking concept.

1. Finding a business area where there are already millions of people with a specific problem (hungry crowd).

2. Ensuring that there are at least hundreds of great products already created to solve the problems in this area that we can sell ourselves.

With these two basic criteria met, this allows you to become the matchmaker. Once you have selected your niche area, you then look for a hungry crowd of people using social networks, like Facebook and Twitter. The system I'll teach you essentially shows you how to then capture their details and then introduce them to a product or service so you can then bank the cash.

In essence, here are 7 key steps:

1. **R**ight niche – choose a niche area that is already proven to work, rather than reinventing the wheel

2. **E**valuate who your ideal people are – understand the interests, mindset and perspectives of the people who have these problems and assess where they hang out online

3. **T**arget the right traffic – target these people online with different traffic strategies, such as advertising, testing different networks as you go

4. **H**elp them for free – offer a free and incentivised solution to the problem in exchange for their contact details

5. **I**mmediate upsell – learn how to offer a product or service immediately after contact details have been exchanged

6. **N**urture your list – build a long-term, profitable relationship with the people you are assisting through email and other means

7. **K**now your numbers – understand the key indicators that will drive increased profit from your online business, allowing you to adjust as you progress

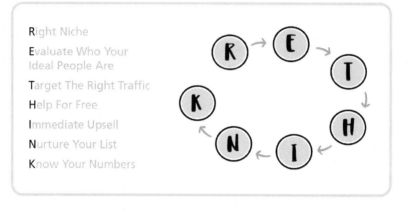

Right Niche

Evaluate Who Your
Ideal People Are

Target The Right Traffic

Help For Free

Immediate Upsell

Nurture Your List

Know Your Numbers

Fig 4.2: Stage 1 – RETHINK Basic Model

Some of the steps are similar to that of a traditional business, but obviously with some major differences too.

For a start, if you wanted to start a physical shop today in your local high street, you'd certainly need some very deep pockets. We have already been through the common startup issues, and these days most shops are open seven days a week, so if you wanted to compete you'd really have to do the same. Honestly, these days I wonder why people bother to start a traditional business knowing that they'd need to find tens or possibly hundreds of thousands of dollars before they even made their first sale. Why go into huge debt to open your shop in the town, for instance, when you can start a business online with none of these costs at all?

With a simple one-page free website you can be in business today for almost no cost. But what products are you going to sell in order to make a profit? We touched on this already briefly, and it depends on your current situation. You may have your own traditional business that you want to take online. Perhaps you have an ecommerce business and you may be in the process of leveraging the amazing power that Amazon or eBay have in the online retail space. You will be finding new people on social media for your business every single day and sending them to your shop front.

When I first looked at making money online, I briefly investigated having my own website that sold my own products or services. However, the thing that put me off was the thought that I'd need to develop (somehow) my own website and I'd have to develop (again, somehow) products of my own to sell on that website. It would be possible to license someone else's product to sell on my site, assuming I could figure out how, but that was costly through traditional channels. Immediately I was stuck: I had no idea how to develop a product and I certainly had no idea how to license someone else's… until my coach showed me how.

What I did not understand at the very beginning was that there are loads of product owners in business who have products and are willing to pay as much as 100% of the profits basically for sending customers to their website. Hang on, but why would anyone pay up to 100%? Simple: because you know (or will know, after I've shared it with you) something they don't. To sell a product, the product owner needs to get "targeted" people to their website. That's to say, people who are likely to want to buy their products because they have an interest in the subject matter. Without people coming to the website, or "targeted traffic", they make no sales. It's therefore worth the business paying you handsomely for bringing people or traffic to their site so they can get the visitors to look at various offers. They also know that they can make more sales to these people later on. This is why sometimes they may pay you 100% commission to encourage you to become their affiliate.

After all, to get people to their website, to sell their stuff, they would normally have to pay out a lot in advertising, perhaps offline with ads in newspapers, on TV or on billboards, or they'd have to use online ads on other websites or pay expensive agencies to run Google Ad campaigns. Don't worry, you won't have to run expensive TV, radio or Google ads either, thankfully. Times have moved on, yet most businesses have not. Later in this book, I will explain this concept in a lot more detail so you fully understand, so for now please just go with this. The RETHINK Social Media Model is much easier, and requires very little money to get you up and running.

"Ahh, sounds good, but I have no idea how to get 'traffic' or how to send it to someone else's website…" Neither did I, but that's the secret behind the success I discovered, and it's so simple to do. After all, almost half the population of the planet are using social media, and it's growing every second of every day; there are almost 2.5 billion people on Facebook alone, and they are all easily accessible, all easily grouped into various interest groups. Through this system, you'll be able to quickly find out which groups of people want to buy which particular product or service.

First things first, social media is not even relevant to you until you first know what business you wish to be in. What problem would you like to fix? What type of people do you wish to serve? Do you even care?

Step 1: Right niche

It is hugely important that we immediately tie this down from the outset, or we don't have a business to begin with. Let's make sure we get this part right, as a good start is half the battle. Too many people fail at the very first step by either choosing a niche that they feel has great potential but is not yet proven, or take on multiple niches at once so that they leave no money behind. Whatever niche you choose does not have to be a lifetime commitment! For now, you just need to select one niche to be able to learn the RETHINK system and start generating an income, first and foremost. At a later date, you can come back and use this system for other niches if you wish. The key thing to begin with is to choose a niche that is already proven so you can focus on the system, not on a particular product. This is why I recommend to business owners to generally avoid using their own business as a guinea pig for social media, as too often the focus becomes the business and products you know, rather than the marketing system we are looking to learn and leverage.

So which niche should you choose? What is the perfect niche for you? Firstly, there is no such thing as the "perfect" niche, but there certainly is the "right" niche for you. Choose one that's a proven hit and stick with it until you at least match your current salary. Once you do that, you will realise that there is unlimited potential here! While it took a lifetime to get to your current salary first time around, it is more than possible to match it in just a few months with this RETHINK system... and then you can repeat it as often as you like, and that's when it gets really exciting! You're no longer exchanging your time for money, you are free! However, the key words that I mention are "one niche only".

"F.O.C.U.S. – Follow One Course Until Successful"

As I write this, something that a good and wise friend of mine, Richard Tan, once quoted to me comes to mind, about getting started with your business.

"I do not believe in taking the right decision,
I take a decision and make it right."
- Muhammad Ali Jinnah

This is as true for niche selection as it is for many areas in life. Once you have chosen your niche, that's it, job done, it's time to set sail and solely focus on making money with that one niche first. I will make sure that you only select from options where there are millions of dollars spent on a weekly basis, so you are setting off into a niche with a river of money!

There is another view that you should focus on your passion or your hobby and set your business up around this. "Do what you love, and the money will follow!" is how the saying goes. My take on this is that it very much depends on what you love! Ultimately if others don't "want" what you love, you're not going to be receiving their money. Remember, the most important person in your business is the person you are serving, as they have the money. So it's what they are passionate about that's the key!

As nice and hopeful as this idea sounds, I think this advice, although well intended, is one of the main reasons why ordinary people like you and I can fail when trying to make money from home. Think about it; if your hobby is making cakes, or writing poetry or playing the piano at the weekends, chances are you will not be making decent money any time soon using those niches. At least, you won't be pulling in the life-changing sums that you may hope to in other areas. It may be difficult to hear but I strongly believe this.

To quote my friend Piet Vannoppen, "My hobbies cost me money, a lot of it, which my business needs to fund!"

My advice on this, for what it's worth, is to choose the right niche based on what people want and are willing to pay for so that you can earn a significant income and spend your newly found money and free time on your hobbies! One place to go in order to find out if there is money to be made in a niche or not is www.dummies.com. This is the home of the "… For Dummies" series of books. While this is a good starting point, in the last 20 years, "Dummies" books have been written about absolutely everything as far as I can see, so I don't truly believe that all of these niches are potential goldmines, but it's still good for getting ideas.

I will get you started on one of the "sure thing" niches – you can choose from the top three areas. Once your niche is selected, you can then begin with the next steps in earnest, starting with where to find and evaluate who your ideal people are.

2. Evaluate who your ideal people are

Once you know the right niche for your business, its only then that you can realistically start to think about who exactly it is you are looking to target. There will be many different types of people who will fit the profile, but there will be some who are easier targets than others. Your goal is to target people based on who will be the easiest candidate for you to start with as your lowest hanging fruit.

Later in this book, we will look at how to determine what your ideal target looks like, and then once you know who they are, you can start to think about the places that they are most likely to hang out. The general rule is to find the people who have the most urgent pain but also have the funds to pay for the solution.

3. Target the right traffic

Once you know what your ideal target market looks like and where they tend to be most of the time, I will grant you permission to get started on social media ☺. Most people jump into Facebook ads, for example, not really knowing who exactly they are looking for, or just having a general target. The results will most likely will be very disappointing. It is only after you have done the work on the various avatars for your business that the real fun starts with finding them online. If Facebook and Twitter are used correctly, once you know your avatar, it can be like shooting fish in a barrel and when set up, you can get paid every single day, no matter the business. So why would you receive daily payments, you may ask?

Especially if you:

- Don't supply or have anything to do with the merchandise being bought on that website,

- You don't have anything to do with the website (i.e. you don't own it or haven't created it),

- You've had minimal costs, and

- You never deal with any of the people buying their merchandise on that website.

Well the answer is simple: basically, someone else has all the merchandise on their website, but what they don't have is a targeted group of people to sell to, which is what step 3 is all about. Your ability to get traffic is what distinguishes you from the product owner. That, quite simply, is not their specialty, which is understandable, as they are busy creating products! However, thanks to the system, you could have access to huge numbers of virtually any interest group, be they individuals interested in health and beauty, online marketing, snowboarding, beekeeping – in fact, in any area.

Look at a very simple model of owning an online store that focuses on weight loss: a quick search on Twitter for a specific problem statement like "I want to lose weight" shows you hundreds of people complaining about their weight loss. These people are willing to share that problem with 350 million other people, so there is a good chance they might be ready to do something about it! Or if you have a pet business online, wouldn't you love to know where all the dog lovers are? It is as simple as logging into Twitter and searching for terms like "I love my dog" and you will instantly have access to people who have used variations of these terms within the last few days.

This is a massive shift from any other form of internet business. Previously, if you had a website selling a product, or even if you were offering other people's products (as an affiliate), you would have to advertise to get traffic to that site. You'd have to really learn about search engine optimisation, too, to get yourself ranked up high in the search engine listings for particular keywords. Even the simplest internet business was fairly involved and time-consuming. In this seven-step system that I use, it is the complete opposite. We will review this extensively in the coming chapters.

4. Help them for free

The key hinge that swings the door is step number four! You really need to master this step. The reason for helping people for free is to build a database. What does this mean? Simply put, you offer people a free gift that can help them with their problem but in order for them to get it, they need to provide you with their email address. Simple, right? This is the main reason you're on social media in the first place, so you can find the right people to have in your database. You must build a database or list of people's contact details for this system to work. Your database is your business! The more targeted people on the list, the more people you can help, and the more money you can make.

In fact, your income is a direct outcome of the number of people you help and the relationship you build with them moving forward. Current estimates show that most businesses or successful entrepreneurs, should make on average at least $1 per person on their database per month. This is the formula that puts you in control! If you want to make an extra $10,000 a month, your goal is to build a database of 10,000 people in that niche. This simple formula can put you in control of your financial future!

When helping people for free, you must ensure that this takes place before you ever look to make a sale. One of the ideas that I will repeat throughout this book is not to sell directly on social media where at all possible. Keeping in mind that people are on social media to be entertained, it's far from ideal if they are being barraged by sales messages, as it will upset them. Our goal is to start off our relationship on the right note by offering a free gift. If they are not interested, that's not a problem, but if they are, then we can collect their contact details and the process really begins in earnest. Fortunately, this process has become very straightforward to set up with the software that is available, and we'll walk through this process very shortly.

5. Immediate upsell

As soon as you have contact details secured, this is your best possible opportunity to close a sale, after a complete stranger has expressed a keen interest in what you do. The challenge most people face is not having something to sell, or not knowing how to set up a process where they could sell products to people immediately after that initial contact. We will be discussing what your choices are around selling products and what to do if you wish to create your own or simply sell other peoples' products. We will also look at the concept of how to maximise the likelihood of immediately making a profit from your first communications a little later, using a combination of psychology and clever software. We will then discuss the idea of creating a "value ladder" of products and services with ever-increasing profits, and see how these can be set up online as sales funnels to automate the sales process. This is how we move from a few thousand dollars a month to potentially hundreds of thousands of dollars a month.

6. **N**urture your list

As I've already explained, your list is your business. How well you manage your list will determine how much money you have to manage. This is not as simple as the odd email every now and again promoting a product, either. Later on in this book, we will walk through the 10 "Rs" of relationship building with your list, so that your people will truly know that you care for them and have their best intentions in mind, while you maximise the profitable return for your business. We will find out how you take a complete stranger and take them on a journey with you that can eventually result in them being raving fans of your business and becoming lifelong clients.

7. **K**now your numbers

This might be considered the boring bit to most, but once your business is up and running, it will be the key determinant of your success in the short, medium and long term. The good news is that it removes all need for guess work and gut feel. When you know what numbers to watch out for as your key indicators, and what to do based on those results, you will become an unstoppable force! We will spend plenty of time together simplifying your numbers to the basics you must know and then also introducing you to the additional metrics that will really allow you to laser-target your pain and profit points.

So, these are the seven stages in the exact order I follow and implement them. Starting with nothing but my previous employer's laptop, a wifi connection, a lot of determination and a coach, my journey to my first million began in earnest.

Let us now look specifically at what the tactics are to bring these seven areas into real terms for you; get ready to kick off your very own business, starting now.

Summary:

The standard retail model for setting up a business involves taking out a loan, hiring staff and looking for premises in the middle of an area that has a high footfall. This has many inherent risks, including, of course, the level of stress a financial loan imparts on the new owner. Money can only be made while the shop is open. By applying the RETHINK model, this completely changes, and your odds of financial success improve dramatically. You are open 24/7 without any of the financial burdens or risks.

Traditional Thinking:

Follow your passion and the money will naturally follow. Everyone is your target market. Get your business in front of as many people as possible from the outset. Sell at every opportunity. Once initial purchase is complete, time to find a new customer. Continue to get brand new customers in the door without a follow-up plan in place. Let's just focus on keeping the debt collectors from the door.

RETHINK:

Right niche: focus on people's urgent problems and solve them and you will have all the money you desire. Evaluate who your ideal people are: prioritise them in terms of who to target first. Target the right traffic: once you know who you are looking for, now you can start to advertise and match the right message with the right people. Help them for free: begin the relationship by offering something for free to build a database; your database is your business! Immediate upsell: the moment you have their details, follow through to determine their level of interest. Nurture your list:

how well you manage your list will determine how much money you have to manage. Know your numbers: what gets measured gets improved; know where the real issues and successes are occurring and adapt accordingly.

Chapter 5: You Must Learn For The Right To Earn

"If you think education is expensive, try ignorance."
- Derek Bok

I would like to spend a little time introducing myself before sharing with you my in-depth insights to the system I followed, and continue to use daily, across my businesses. Thankfully, this system has resulted in my life being completely transformed over the past several years, taking me from having a full-time job to being mostly free to do as I wish with my time and money.

I am a complete paradox when it comes to social media. I'm an introverted biochemist by profession who is not even a big fan of social media! This may come as a surprise to you. Yes, I am definitely not the biggest fan of how people can spend hours on end living their lives by monitoring others' lives. Without doubt, it has its downsides, which certainly receive their fair share of publicity. Yet social media completely changed almost everything in my life over a very short period of time. The way I think about now is like how I feel about electricity: I don't have to create it or love it in order to turn on a light!

By sharing parts of my story, I hope you'll feel at least a little inspired to learn from what I have done and to implement it for yourself or your business, regardless of your experience.

When I got started with my online business a number of years ago, I had absolutely zero experience in anything to do with running a business, let alone an internet business using social media! Here comes the start of the good news: you don't need any previous experience with an internet business or social media, and you certainly don't need to have used sites like Facebook or Twitter before being able to leverage them in a highly profitable way.

As I write this, I have just disembarked from my 101st flight in the past 8 months. In the past few months alone, I have been fortunate enough to have been in UAE, India, South Africa, USA, Hong Kong, the Canaries, Singapore, Fiji and all over Europe to name just a few! If you had met me just a few years ago, you would not have believed this was possible! I LOVE to travel, and I LOVE experiencing other cultures, and being able to change others' lives while doing it is a HUGE bonus! The fact that in a regular job, for most people at least, you can only have four to six weeks off in a year to do what you love was definitely one of the main triggers to get me off my backside and seek a new life I would be in control of for once. Think about that for just one minute - if we spend 80% or more of our lives doing things we don't enjoy, it doesn't seem quite right!

Fig 5.1: 11-year-old Paul!

I don't have a rags-to-riches type story to tell you where you're going to be rooting for the "little guy" or the "underdog". I've never been homeless.

I've never been a drug addict until I bought an old book and found the ancient secrets to wealth (you know what I mean!). In short, I've never been down and out; I was just like most ordinary people – just getting by but never really considering doing anything much about it. I had a full-time job for over 9 years, which was nothing unusual. Actually, I really liked my job. However, like most people, I suspect, I just knew deep down that there had to be more to life than getting up every morning, going to work, coming home tired at the end of the day and getting up the next day to do it all over again. Isn't that the existence for most adults pretty much until they retire and then ultimately die? Well I was just one of millions of other Mr & Mrs Average. To be honest, I didn't really think much about my life, as I figured that it's just how things are. Growing up, my parents, who were both teachers, instilled in me what they knew to be true at the time, which was that you needed to work hard and get a good safe "permanent" job and retire on a steady pension.

That was fundamental to having a steady life. I guess that's the sort of life plan we are all taught to follow. You try and get good grades in your exams and get yourself a good job and rise up through the promotion ladder for the next 45 years. You then retire with a nice little pension, of maybe half what you are used to earning at work (if you are lucky), and if you've not died of a heart attack beforehand, you live out your final years on modest means. Now I am not even addressing the fact that many people will now outlive their savings, so what then?

I often wonder why I never thought that there may be more than a slight flaw with this life plan. Why had it taken me 9 years to do anything about it? But we all generally buy into this life plan and just get sucked along, even if we promise at the start it will never happen to us. I was no different. I remember as a child listening to my parents get up at 7am every single weekday morning and thinking *I will not do this for my whole life, this is misery because I really am not a morning person and never have been!* I didn't want to have to get up and work for someone else my whole life. However, whether it was me forgetting my childish ideals or just being sucked into the standards of society, I set my whole life up to follow the original plan of working for my life. Well it is very easy to do this, isn't it? As children we are like sponges and our parents are our role models. We tend to end up doing what they did as a default mechanism – and I did, I too became a teacher. I mean, we almost all believe that at some stage or another we must get a job or the only alternative is to become a bum, right? That's what we were all taught from when we were knee-high. There just weren't any other options, or that's what I was led to believe anyway.

I had a very happy middle-class upbringing along with my two sisters and one brother in a suburb of Limerick in Ireland, known as Raheen. It was a great time ☺! We lived in a 4-bed semi-detached house with my Grandmother, so it was a tight squeeze for the seven of us. Both my parents, as I said, were teachers at the same school (where they taught English and history). I was pretty good at school, not the best but not the worst, just a pretty normal student who, like most kids, had no real inclination to do anything other than go to college and get a job.

Making money on my own was something I'd never considered. I had no entrepreneurial streak from my family, and I didn't know anyone who did anything other than have a job, or work as a farmer, so it just never crossed my mind once. After school, I went on to further education. I don't know if you've been to college or not, but one thing was crystal clear about college for me: I didn't learn much of value that I used in the real world. I learnt nothing about making money, or how to manage money, or the importance of having the right mindset for the attainment of wealth. I learnt nothing about how to market or sell anything. Indeed, having spoken to many people about this over the years, it's clear that in general, the education we receive from the age of around 4 years old to when we are let loose in the work place does little more than teach us how to join the rat race and never leave. But at the time, I wouldn't have noticed, because during my years in higher education my main focus was on having a good time.

The first real job I had was a part-time job in Supermac's, which is basically an Irish version of McDonalds, flipping burgers, gutting chicken and dealing with customers (in no particular order of preference). Not a great job, I have to admit, but I learnt a lot more there about the importance of hard work, teamwork and meeting deadlines than I could ever have learnt in college. It was also the first time I noticed how easy it can be to make money from a business providing something to a "hungry" market - something which later became the crux of our social media and online business systems. It also provided me with all the motivation I needed to make sure I finished college with a qualification so that I could apply for a "professional" office job. Cleaning toilets at Supermac's at 3.30am was enough to wake me up to that fact.

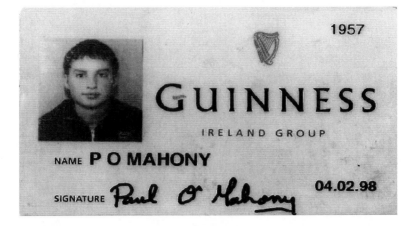

Fig 5.2: The dream job for a student

Actually, the highlight of that time in my life can be summarised in one word... GUINNESS! As part of the course I was studying, luckily for me I had a 9-month work placement at the home of Guinness, in St James's Gate in Dublin. Now there's a dream job for an Irish student! My highest values at the time are starting to be unveiled ☺. That takes us up to 1999, when I decided to stay in college for another year before finally realising it was time to take up full time employment. I started working in July 2000 at a medical device company in Galway, starting on €18,000 a year. Living the dream, right? I stayed there for 9 years, until April 17th 2009.

As I said, I didn't hate work; I actually enjoyed it most of the time, and I met some great friends there. The only thing was, I knew I'd never make the money to do the things I really wanted to do in life, and at the top of that list was travel. I definitely got the travel bug from travelling to the US with my job, and it never left me. Of course, when I started earning a wage, before knowing the finances of it, I presumed it meant I could afford to travel all over the world – and regularly! The problem was, to pay for holidays abroad I always found myself using a credit card, and before I knew it, I was firmly imprisoned. All I was really doing was working just to pay the bills and to meet the credit card's minimum payments each month. Not only that, but my "wealth advisors", who consisted of my work colleagues in the canteen, advised that I should buy some property in 2006 in Ireland. I bought two houses with the bank's money and the rest, as you can guess, doesn't need much explaining. Feel free to google "Celtic Tiger Ireland" ☺. I was completely caught up in life's rat race, with two houses worth less than 50% of what I'd paid for them only a couple of years earlier! They say education is expensive, well then try ignorance! I am living proof ☺.

Still, this was the way most people seemed to live their lives – in massive debt – so I just plodded along and went with the flow. And I doubt if anything would ever have changed for me if it wasn't for something that came right out of the blue. I was asked to tell 40% of my department at work that they were being made redundant, which was something I found very difficult to do. I'd worked with some of these people for almost 9 years, and they had become my friends. They couldn't believe they were out of a job, in much the same way I couldn't believe I had to tell them. They all had permanent jobs, which turned out not to be so "permanent". This really got me thinking about the so called J.O.B. (just over broke) that

I had, and it reminded me how reliant my entire financial affairs were on keeping it. For the first time in my life, I started to look at how I could possibly take control of my financial affairs and start to make additional income outside of my job.

I needed a financial safety net so no-one could ever fire me and cause me to lose my livelihood. As I said, it's something I'd never thought about before, because when I was growing up, I was told that a permanent job is the ideal scenario for the perfect life. And I honestly, though I guess naively, thought that's exactly what I had. But believe me, when you're sat across the desk looking into the eyes of your friends at work, you soon begin to realise what a farcical notion that is in today's world. It also hits you that you are just as likely to end up in the same position as them, very soon, unless you choose to do something about it.

It is highly likely that at some point down the line, you are going to lose your job, regardless of how "permanent" you think it may be now. If we look at examples in the UK and the US alone, I'm sure the people who worked for the News of the World could never have imagined they'd lose their job; it was a newspaper that would be around for another 100 years. I'm sure the people who worked for Woolworths thought their futures were secure; after all, how could this famous British institution, which always seemed busy with customers, not be around? And these were both in pre-BREXIT times! We then had the fall of Lehman Brothers, the fourth largest investment bank in the US, collapsing after 158 years of business. If it can happen to established companies, believe me it can happen to any.

That was a turning point for me. I set about finding a new way of educating myself. The traditional methods had failed me when it came to financial independence at least. Now I understood what Grant Allen meant in his famous quotation:

"No schooling was allowed to interfere with my education."

It was time for my real education to begin. I started reading many self-help books, such as Rich Dad Poor Dad by Robert Kiyosaki, which I cannot recommend highly enough for someone starting out on this journey. Actually, I ended up reading most of his books, including Cashflow Quadrant, Retire Young, Retire Rich and Before You Quit Your Job, all fantastic reads. (Little did I realise then that only a few years later I would get to share the same stage with him, his wife Kim and his co-author Sharon Lechter!) That began to turn my thinking around. After reading these books, for the first time I really started to get the itch to potentially leave my job. I wasn't in a hurry, I set myself a 10-year goal of having made enough money (somehow) to leave my job by 2019 for good. Let me just add, before this time I had never been interested in reading, and for me to start reading these books was a big deal. However, once I started them I became consumed by them and realised that my time to take control of my financial affairs had arrived. I started to realise that you must learn for the right to earn! It is often said that your biggest voids dictate your highest values, and my lack of security around money was suddenly driving my focus to learn all that I could about it. And so began my 10-year countdown to financial freedom ☺.

However, once I made this decision, a strange thing happened. I started to get lazy again, as it all seemed so far away into the future. I suppose I felt I had plenty of time to work on this; there was certainly no rush. So, predictably, I began to procrastinate and returned to normal life. Here I was, I had information in these books on how to make money for myself, but I simply put them on a shelf and did nothing with them. I call these my "shelf-improvement" books ☺. Perhaps you have been guilty of this yourself in the past? No matter what information is in a book, it is of no benefit to you until you have consumed it and implemented it! You may have heard the quote before from T. Harv Eker, claiming that the three most dangerous words in the English language are "I Know That!". Knowing and doing are completely different things; one results in inaction and the other provides results. This is what I would like to make sure you do: take this system and put it to use to completely change your financial life for the better.

So how did I go from procrastinating to finally leaving my job and changing my financial situation forever? It was 2009 and I was still working full time, even though I'd read a mountain of books on creating financial freedom and made the decision to change my life. So how did I escape this? How did I end up with the RETHINK Social Media Model in my hands and making money from it? Well everything changed for me during spring 2009. I attended two seminars that completely changed the course of my life. The first was a seminar on how to create a successful online business. Here is a picture of me at that event!

Fig 5.3: My first ever online marketing event Dublin February 2009

It was an interesting event for me, as I had never been to anything like that before. Most of the speakers were from the US and Australia, and you could tell that many of them had not spoken in Ireland before. Their requests for us to "high five" each other and to massage our neighbours' shoulders did not go down very well ☺. In Ireland, we are one of the most, if not the most sceptical beings on the planet, especially after the Celtic Tiger. We tend to avoid touching each other, if at all possible, until after dark. We don't drink because we like it, we do it out of necessity to keep our population alive!

I ended up investing almost €10,000 at that event after being told on numerous occasions, "If you want new financial results, you must change your daily actions". I decided to educate myself on new skills in online marketing in order to get vastly different results.

One month later, I flew to NYC (courtesy of my boss) and went to a Tony Robbins seminar about leadership skills – or so I thought. In case you haven't heard of him, Tony runs motivational events all over the world to assist people in getting up off their backsides and taking "massive action!" I highly recommend that you check out his documentary I am not your Guru on Netflix, and any of his books.

Fig 5.4: 2009 in front of Tony Robbins

The event was quite surreal, to say the least. Once again, there was a lot of backslapping and massages and high-fives, and I felt quite early on that this was not really targeted at an Irish audience, or especially someone as sceptical as me. When he kicked the event off by asking everyone to dance around like lunatics, I was stunned to see almost three thousand people partake without batting an eyelid! I was seriously considering backing out at this point, and I bumped into another Irish person who looked at me in disbelief. I said to him, "Before you say anything, I just want you to know that I didn't use my own money to pay for this!" He said, "I think I've seen something like this before… it's like one of those cults you see on the Discovery channel… I don't think I'm going to hang around! Who knows what he'll have us doing by the end of the night! Do you fancy going for a pint instead?" I admit, I was very tempted by the offer!

There were also a couple of Germans nearby, standing together with their arms folded, looking around with a confused look on their faces, saying something that sounded like "Vos is dis?" That was when Tony reminded us all that we were to walk on fire that night, and that if we did not do everything he said, we were going to burn! Well, all I had needed was a little motivation, and that was enough for me. I decided against having barbequed feet and began to commit fully. I started by moving away from anyone who resembled being Irish; anyone with red hair or freckles was in my "no go" zone! It was time to find my inner "Yank": no scepticism, no cynicism, no holding back, I just went for it 100%. A few hours in, I was so hooked on the idea of living the dream and making money from home and "fake it until you make it" and "living with passion" and "taking massive action" that I actually did the craziest thing I had ever done in my life on the first night of the event. No, it wasn't the walking on fire, that was the easy bit… I texted my boss to let him know that his "services would no longer be required"!

A word of warning here: I don't recommend you do this! It was definitely the wrong way of going about it. Just be careful when you go to motivational seminars that you hold off a couple of days before making such life-changing decisions, especially when, like me, there's no plan B. My boss surprisingly (to me at least) didn't even try and keep me. In fact, he seemed quite acceptant when letting me go. He did have some words for me as I walked out the door, which have stayed with me ever since: "We all think about leaving and making our fortune, but it's rare any of us have the balls to do it! So, if you do make that fortune, make sure you give me a ride in your helicopter in 5 years." Well when he said that at the time, I know he genuinely hoped this would happen. Today, however, just a few years later, I just want to say "thank you" to Daragh for that encouragement.

On Friday April 17th 2009 I walked out of my office for the final time and what did I walk into? Well, nothing actually. For the next few weeks, I must admit I skipped the making money part of becoming wealthy, the "working" side of it and "learning for the right to earn", and instead I simply started to live like I was a millionaire. I just sat in the sun (when it showed itself) reading books I'd wanted to read for years but never had the time to. I made up vision boards, a journal with my goals and pictures of the life I wanted. In short, I sat there pondering what my next step should be. After a few weeks of this inactivity, I finally decided, rightly or wrongly, that trading the stock market would be a great way for me to make money fast. This took me to the end of May, when I decided to implement my plan and to use all the money I had saved, to trade the stock markets.

Well to cut a long story short, the first thing I did was to pay for a self-proclaimed stock trading "guru" to choose the stocks and make the trades. The result? Within just two months I had blown every penny I had saved!! I had learnt a valuable lesson about trading, investing and who you should take your trading advice from! The theme was the same, I kept trying to avoid paying for education, but my ignorance always ended up costing me more! I was now much worse off than I ever was while in a job, as I still had all my debts, but this time with NO INCOME to pay them off.

It was time to hit the "PANIC" button! One July morning, I woke up in a bit of a panic and decided to ditch the stock market for now and instead put my effort into mastering the internet. I got all the material out from the events I had attended since February 2009 and began to take massive action rather than just to "study" the materials this time. The main thread that seemed to run through making money online was centred around the need to get involved in "niche marketing". This was basically finding yourself a niche that would make money, which sounded easy, right? Find yourself a hot niche market with thousands of hungry buyers waving credit cards but with no competition, and you're set for life!

Easier said than done. It had initially taken me a long time to really get going up until then, because choosing the "perfect" niche was proving very difficult for me, hence why I will not allow you to delay yours! I kept overthinking and hesitating and it ended up with me not taking any decisive action. That's when fate took a hand…

It happened when I received an email that really got my attention, about a lady in the UK who was making £3,000 per month using Twitter while maintaining her full-time job. Her name was Mili Ponce, and I will be eternally grateful for meeting her. She was coming to a workshop in London the following weekend, which I had already paid to attend. That was enough for me; I was going to make Twitter my niche! I didn't know if it was a good niche, or even if I was "allowed" to pick it as a niche, but I decided to explore and see what I could find out about Twitter.

So, I googled this social network, which I knew absolutely nothing about. I'd never used it, or even knew anyone personally who used it, and I didn't even see the point in it. Actually, I didn't understand much more after my Google search. I only knew two things: one, from what I'd learnt at the seminars I went to, was that the secret of making money online is firstly to build a list of email addresses of potential customers; two, I'd found out that this woman was making her money because she had found a way to get "followers" (essentially targeted potential customers) on Twitter for free. The more I read about her success and her system, the more I realised this was what I was going to do; her way of making money was so much easier than trying to set up a traditional business.

In addition to the benefit of it being pretty simple to do, the main attraction for me was that it cost almost nothing to set up, and just a few dollars a month to get up and running. There were almost zero risks, especially when compared with any of the other options. That was perfect for me, as I had hardly any money left and had lost nearly everything I originally had on stock market trading, which is all about taking calculated risks.

Years later, I did get back into investing and made sure that from then on, I would always firstly learn from the very best before taking risks around money. A major thank you is due to the very best stock market investing trainer, my friend Darren Winters, for restoring my faith in trading and investing and putting me back on the right track. For me, the key to changing everything was to get educated first. I lost money in property and on the stock market, and I could not get my online business to work until the penny eventually dropped – you must get educated first! As soon as I paid for coaching from people who had already made millions in their field, my results changed dramatically.

Now back to Twitter for a moment. Without really knowing what I was doing, I set up my first Twitter account and wrote myself a note: a personal target of getting 1,000 followers in just one week. Of course, I had no idea how I was going to do that and no idea if it was even possible! All I knew was that I needed to do something, and setting myself a specific target would at least encourage me to go do it. After all, I only had to take action for a week and I was sure that even I could manage that. I sat down and decided I would start testing Twitter by using it in five separate areas, which were fashion, business, personal development, writing and health, to see how quickly I could grow those accounts. How did it go? Did I get 1,000 followers in a week? No! I did even better – much better. In fact, in my first 7 days I'd managed to get 7,000 followers! It was a great thrill to see something work so quickly.

Apparently, I wasn't the only one impressed either. I attended the seminars that Mili was speaking at that weekend and happened to be sitting next to a guy called Michel Gimena, who was a software developer. He had developed a simple piece of software for Twitter users, so we ended up chatting quite a lot, especially when I mentioned during the coffee break that I had just got 7,000 followers on Twitter in a week. You should have seen the look on his face, I could tell he was impressed. Apparently getting 7,000 followers was unheard of in this timescale. I had no way of knowing that, of course. He simply could not believe that I had got 7,000 followers in just 7 days! Excitedly, he ran off and spoke to the seminar organiser. All I had at the time were Twitter followers, and I still didn't really know what to do with them.

Making money from the followers was the one part of the jigsaw that I needed – I personally didn't know how to start making money from them. However, everything was to change for me that afternoon. I showed the software guy what I'd been doing on Twitter to get my followers. He then asked me if I had a product to point my followers towards. I told him I didn't, as I was only just starting out. He looked at me rather oddly and said something along the lines of "Have you not been listening to anything that is going on here? This event is about how to find other business' products to sell!"

He was right, of course! The event had been teaching us how to find and sell other people's products. The organiser came to see me and suggested that I should look to make money from my Twitter followers, as it would be a great story for the other event attendees. I told him I was all ears. He too looked surprised that I didn't know what to do next; to him, the answer was very obvious, but it wasn't to me.

Thankfully, he took the time to explain it to me step by step. He told me to send out some Tweets that encouraged people to click on a link to some products that were for sale. I explained that I didn't have any products. Now he was puzzled! He asked me if I'd even been in the room up to that point, as having products of my own was not necessary. I explained to him that as good as "affiliate marketing" sounded, it wasn't really for me, and he asked me why. I told him that I would be uncomfortable selling products that I hadn't tested out myself first. He then said something to me that really changed my perspective forever. He told me I could spend the next five years buying other businesses' products and deciding if they worked or not and go broke quickly, or use a magic tool called Google and type in the name of the product followed by "reviews", to instantly find out how good the product is. He then added that ideally I should sell a product with a money back guarantee, so that there is no risk anywhere along the line!

He used the example of how we mostly make decisions about buying a book on Amazon by checking the reviews first, and he was exactly right! You can't read the book before deciding if you are going to buy it. Suddenly the penny dropped, and I realised I was completely blinded to the opportunity until the right people explained it to me in the right way at the right time. He then pointed out that if I wasn't sure which product to pick, I could start by promoting the software he could see I was already using on my laptop. It was a simple program I had bought that flashes up your personal goals on your PC screen discretely every few seconds. It was a kind of subliminal message intended to train your brain. It runs quietly in the background on your PC or laptop and you don't know it's there. It just pops up your goals that your brain registers but your eyes hardly see, which was very cool. You can check it out for yourself here http://resources.leftclickrightclick.com. It had been working very well for me (and has done ever since) as I was meeting my goals (although I hadn't set any financial ones yet).

I told the Twitter software guy about the subliminal tool I used, and we then checked their website to see if they had an affiliate program for it that paid a commission for any referrals – and sure enough, they did! What I did next was to send out some tweets throughout the night letting people know about this subliminal software. I must admit it wasn't something I thought would appeal to every one of my followers, but it was a test. I set it up, finished the rest of the day at the seminar and forgot all about it. I woke up the next day, after sleeping on the floor on my aunt's apartment outside London, and started getting ready to go to the second day of the seminar. When I switched on my laptop and checked my emails, to my absolute shock and surprise, I had two emails telling me I had made two sales! I logged into my PayPal account, and yes it was true, I had positive figures in my PayPal account for the first time! Who knew that you could use PayPal to collect money rather than just spending it, as I had done until that day? Yes, I had implemented and made money on my first day trying!

Best of all, the money had come in on autopilot while I had been asleep! It surely was a MIRACLE! Making money while I slept. My first thought was that I should sleep a lot more…☺☺. I was hooked! Yes, it was just two sales, I know, but when you actually see that something works, it gives you an incredible buzz. Especially when you get money for doing nothing much really – for sleeping, in my case. I wanted to do more, especially as more money began rolling in from my little test. I concluded that if I could make money without knowing what the heck I was doing, then if I focused on doing it some more I could make some real and serious money!

So on the second day of the seminar, I immediately sought out the organiser Mark Anastasi again – who also became my first coach and a good friend – and got talking with him and asked his advice. He suggested that I stick to just one niche, which was making money with Twitter. Following his guidance, that's what I did over the next few months. I simply decided on one niche and started focusing all of my efforts into harvesting Twitter followers who were interested in that niche, and more importantly, I started to collect their email addresses. Through email, I then began to introduce them to products I knew they would be interested in and from which I would earn a good percentage of the profits. Mark began to guide Mili and I on how to create an online business and then how to create our own products and services that would end up bringing in millions of dollars over the coming years.

A strange thing happened a few months into this new business. Requests started to come in from individuals and companies who wanted to be trained on what I was doing and to show them how money could indeed be made from social media. There was a lot of talk about the great branding that social media could bring, but it was a difficult task to find someone who could clearly show a path to consistently grow revenues from it. With the help of a very good friend of mine, Chris Farrell, we put together a basic one-page website and before I knew it, I was consulting with large companies, some of the most successful in the world, and at the same time teaching entrepreneurs and people who were just keen to get started in a step-by-step manner.

Now I am in a fortunate position to speak at some of the most amazing venues in the world and share event stages with some of the major experts in the fields of marketing, business and personal development, who were and still are heroes of mine, such as Tony Robbins, Jay Abraham, John Assaraf, John Demartini, Jack Canfield, Robin Sharma, Lisa Nichols and Sharon Lechter, to name but a few.

Fig 5.5: Speaking in front of 3,500 people at the Entrepreneurship Bootcamp UK 2017

One thing that I haven't yet expanded on is the impact that having a Twitter account with lots of followers had for me. When my Twitter account had over 70,000 followers, I started to get contacted by media channels basically asking me who I was and why I had more followers than U2 or Westlife or Bono, for that matter. Because of that, I ended up writing for the Sunday Independent newspaper for a couple of years, and from that came more credibility. At one point, I had the third largest following within Ireland, although most of my followers were people I had initially followed from all over the world.

In the crazy world that we live in today, a social media following provides instant credibility. I don't agree that it should, but it certainly helps a lot. That's the good news, because anyone can learn how to grow a following on social media – it is just a case of applying the rules and strategies that work. Once you build this into a habit, you will have a tribe of your own before you know it! The image below is one I am most proud of. The biggest and best event organiser in the world is Success Resources, and the owners Richard and Veronica Tan have been so good to me over the years, providing me with the opportunity to grace their stages with global stars time and time again.

They had belief in me long before I could see it, and when I was added to their banner below, it truly was an amazing day for me. I couldn't be more grateful. Most people in that image are household legends who spent decades learning their craft in order to get where they are now. Just look at what RETHINKing social media did for me, and what it can do for you too! See if you can spot me ☺.

Fig 5.6: Success Resources line-up of world renowned speakers – and me!

So, there you have it, the behind-the-scenes story. Surely if I can do this then so can you! It's time to discover the next tactic for how to bring your targeted clients along on the journey to your financial freedom.

Summary:

I started out with a background in science and worked in fast food chains, a famous brewery and then a medical device company. It was not my schooling or my work experience that set me free financially. My real education began in 2009 at an online marketing seminar when I realised that if I continued to do what I was doing, I would continue to get what I always had. I invested in completely new skills and education and focused on Twitter as my niche. I was guided by my coach to do exactly what I needed to do to RETHINK my life and financial future.

Traditional Thinking:

The key to a financially secure life is to go to school, do well in your exams and get a permanent job that will "set you up" for life.

RETHINK:

You must learn for the right to earn. Financial freedom begins with education, continues with coaching, builds momentum with consistent action and brings you to unimaginable heights with persistence and the right support.

SECTION 4: TACTICS
Chapter 6: Right Niche

"You can have everything in life you want, if you will
just help other people get what they want."
- Zig Ziglar

Would you like to become wealthy, let's say very wealthy? You would certainly not be alone with your answer to this. I would guess in most cases that the answer is "yes". Here is another basic question for you; is there enough money on the planet right now to make you wealthy, or does more money need to be printed? This may seem like a silly question – of course there is enough money on the planet right now to satisfy all your financial desires. But if this is the case, and the money that you want to have right now is not with you, then who has it? Have you ever considered that for a moment? Who has "your" money right now?

Perhaps on first thoughts, your answer is that the company that you work for has your money. If you are a business owner, your answer is possibly that your clients have the money you desire right now. Either answer indicates that your focus is quite limiting in terms of your earning potential – it is either on the idea of exchanging your time for money or from serving your current client base. Maybe you thought that your money is in an institution like a bank and if you could just get legal access to this, then all your financial worries would be solved once and for all. I hope that you are starting to realise, however, that this is not the reality, that the company you work for or the clients you serve are only two potential sources of the money you require.

In very simple terms, **other people have "your" money!**

Yes, all the people around you on a daily basis, and the many more that you have never met, are carrying around your future wealth in their pockets and bank accounts! Our goal is to figure out how to move it from their pockets to our pockets in a legal and ethical way as quickly as possible to meet your financial dreams. In order to do this, you need to position your offering so that people feel that the offering is worth more to them than holding on to the money that it costs. For me, it really highlights the essence of everything that is fundamental to the concept of RETHINKing social media. If you really understand this concept, it can give you a real clarity when it comes to who is the most important person in your financial relationships right now – it's the person with the money, not you! In other words, the person you need to serve in exchange for cash.

This chapter opens with Zig Ziglar's famous quote about helping others get what they want in order for you to get what you want. This was a slightly different way of stating the same thing. It is such a refreshing approach to business to realise that it is not about how much money you can "make", as this term suggests that you can manufacture money, which of course is illegal! You can't make money and stay out of prison for very long. Instead, it is how much you "earn" and hold onto that determines your wealth.

This is why having a great idea is not the best focus for your new business, unless of course its focus is on providing a solution to people that they **really want,** as soon as possible, and you know exactly what that is. Too often the focus of the great idea is "I know exactly what people need" or "everybody needs this". What we need to figure out is the following: how do we position the offering that we have in such a way that people will not only want it, but will also feel that they are better off having this product or service as opposed to keeping the equivalent amount of money in their pockets or bank accounts?

The thing is, the odds are stacked in your favour here and you may not realise it. People love to spend their money! Most people are not very comfortable in the possession of money. The term "burning a hole in my pocket" is often used in relation to the feeling many people have when they acquire money, such as after pay day. Before they even get paid each week or month, most people have already planned out in perfect detail exactly how they are going to get rid of their money. Whether that's by spending it on the mortgage, the children, clothes, groceries, car loan, credit card bills, etc., once it arrives, the money isn't going to be hanging around for very long.

Imagine for a moment that you're single and you've already planned out how you're going to get rid of your new partner before you even meet them; how long do you think they'll hang around? It seems farcical, doesn't it? This, however, is how most people think and plan around money. This is great news for you, because the odds are really stacked in your favour – people really love to spend their money, they just need a good reason to spend it. If it's not spent with you, it will inevitably be spent elsewhere. With this in mind, let's consider what is the essence of choosing a business area that gives you the best opportunity of maximising your profits with the least effort and smallest degree of risk.

Choosing the right business.

What does it take to have a great business? A great idea, a great team, a great product? Could it be any or all of these, or perhaps something completely different? Having attended many short business talks over the years, it often seems to be that the focus initially is on having a great idea; that having a great idea is the cornerstone of a highly profitable business. In my experience, I have not found this to be the case. A great idea in isolation is not the sole answer, as we saw in chapter 3.

Let's start by thinking about your own behaviours when it comes to making a purchase. When you ultimately decide to make a purchase, do you make the call based on how much you need the product or service, or how much you ultimately want the same item? When it comes to business ideas, in a lot of instances the decision is made based on how much somebody needs a product.

Let's say for example that you have a PhD in human psychology and that after years of dedicated research, you have just figured out a fool-proof way for people to completely change their mindset that will make them much more successful in life. You are absolutely certain that most people need this and are very excited about your business opportunity. You could possibly even run it by your friends, who no doubt will support the idea, confirming that indeed it is something people really need to help them get better results in all areas of their lives. Assuming that you have the finances and move ahead to launch the product, you might wonder why it was a complete flop. Surely everything was as you expected – the product that everybody needs was now ready for the world but nobody seemed to want it. What gives?

In general, people very rarely buy what they need, they tend to buy what they want. This is a huge determinant of the success of a business. If your focus is constantly on what people need as opposed to what people want, it is almost always inevitable that you are not going to be as successful as you expected. People will always tend to spend their cash in the areas that they value the most and often will tell you that they "can't afford" products or services that they definitely need. Have you ever found yourself deciding against attending a training course that you need, for example, but instead deciding to book a family holiday that you want? Taking this concept at a larger scale, if you continue to ignore the wants of people in favour of their needs, you really are making your likelihood of success much lower than it could be.

Remember the reasons why business owners felt their businesses failed? The big winner with 42% was "no market need". I would suggest that maybe there was a "need", but that a more accurate representation of the problem was that there was "no market WANT"! When selecting your niche, keeping this in mind is absolutely critical.

When starting out on your journey of maximising the time and money spent with social media, if you have chosen a niche that is not a good match to the market, regardless of how well you manage your message on social media, it is very unlikely that it will be successful. Social media is not the silver bullet that will fix all the gaping holes that may exist in your business; if anything, it will bring them more into focus. So if you intend to use social media for your current business, turn your focus on your business to begin with and plug the holes as quickly as you can.

For example, if your website is not performing as you would wish, you may need to RETHINK its purpose and what you want to get out of it. If you don't have a sales team in place who know how to convert your prospects into customers, then no amount of additional marketing is going to fix this. Most important of all, you should ensure that the product or service that you provide is top class. You really need to be able to stand behind whatever it is you provide before you put your energy and focus behind the marketing project.

These are very different skills to those of marketing, and as a result, it is not uncommon for a business owner who is looking to implement their new social media strategy to constantly focus on the areas they are more comfortable in – their business, the product, the service… anything but the marketing process. This is why I strongly suggest that if you're a business owner whose business isn't developed to the level it needs to be at before you announce it to the world, an excellent starting point is to choose a niche where the "want" is definitely and clearly defined by the customer base.

I suggest that we completely RETHINK how we look at our concept of business, and rather than starting with the focus of a particular product or service, that instead we first focus on the specific problem that people have. Ideally, we want to find a problem that people need immediate solutions for and are in enough pain from that they are willing to pay for a solution right away.

In my experience, there are a few different areas or niches that have stood the test of time in terms of being an area where people have problems and are willing to pay for solutions. Remember, for right now, we are not thinking about products or services at all, our focus is completely on the problem area. Wherever there is a problem for people, there is likely a strong reason for people to part with their money for a solution, and that is what we are after.

Ideally, you want to choose a problem area that has a major "how to" element to it. By this, I mean that we can explain to people in real terms through education how they can learn how to solve this problem for themselves. Selling educational products as opposed to physical products can have a massive impact on your profit margins. If you are selling physical products, even a physical book, for example, there are innate costs associated with each individual item, such as the printing costs, the paper costs, the cover costs and the shipment to a store or your home. These are to be factored into every single book. In addition, there are the product creation costs, such as the proofreading and editing costs, and creating the online listing for the book.

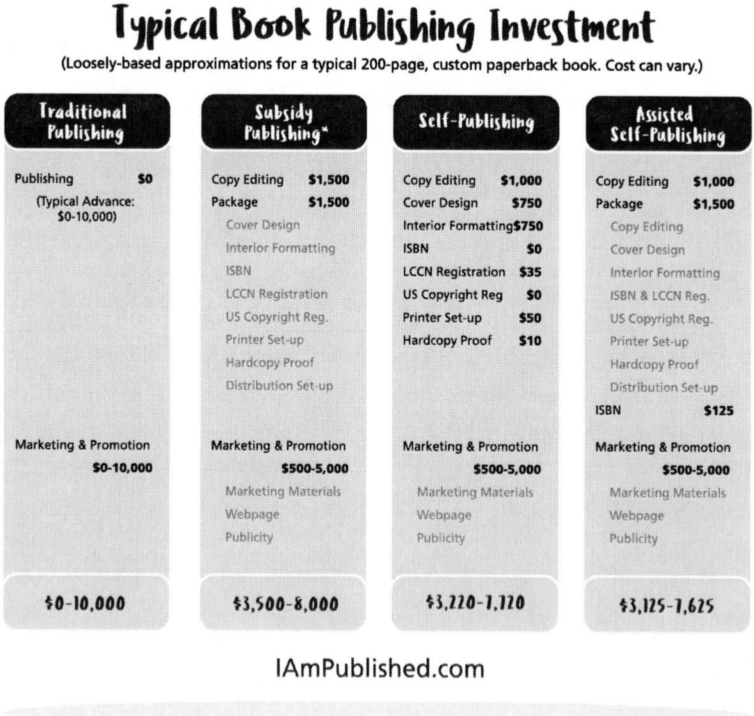

Typical Book Publishing Investment

(Loosely-based approximations for a typical 200-page, custom paperback book. Cost can vary.)

Traditional Publishing		Subsidy Publishing*		Self-Publishing		Assisted Self-Publishing	
Publishing	$0	Copy Editing	$1,500	Copy Editing	$1,000	Copy Editing	$1,000
(Typical Advance: $0-10,000)		Package	$1,500	Cover Design	$750	Package	$1,500
		Cover Design		Interior Formatting	$750	Copy Editing	
		Interior Formatting		ISBN	$0	Cover Design	
		ISBN		LCCN Registration	$35	Interior Formatting	
		LCCN Registration		US Copyright Reg	$0	ISBN & LCCN Reg.	
		US Copyright Reg.		Printer Set-up	$50	US Copyright Reg.	
		Printer Set-up		Hardcopy Proof	$10	Printer Set-up	
		Hardcopy Proof				Hardcopy Proof	
		Distribution Set-up				Distribution Set-up	
						ISBN	$125
Marketing & Promotion $0-10,000		Marketing & Promotion $500-5,000		Marketing & Promotion $500-5,000		Marketing & Promotion $500-5,000	
		Marketing Materials		Marketing Materials		Marketing Materials	
		Webpage		Webpage		Webpage	
		Publicity		Publicity		Publicity	
$0-10,000		**$3,500-8,000**		**$3,220-7,720**		**$3,125-7,625**	

IAmPublished.com

Fig 6.1 Typical book publishing investment

If, however, you are not selling a physical book but just a digital version, such as an e-book, then the costs of creating the physical book disappear, increasing your profit margins dramatically. While it may not always be possible to sell only digital products, it is certainly something that you can look out for, increasing the percentage of your offerings that are digital. This becomes even more important when you are selling other businesses' products, as there is a lot more margin to go around when the products are digital. With that in mind, let's look at particular areas that you can focus on to get started.

The three biggest areas that I have found that make excellent choices for a business focus are, in no particular order, **1. health & beauty, 2. wealth, and 3. happiness.**

These three areas (along with the weather) take up a lot of thinking time and conversation on a daily basis, I'm sure you'll agree. They provide a very solid cornerstone for you in thinking about who in particular you may wish to serve. Let's take a look at each of these three in turn, in terms of the possibilities of using one of them for your niche choice.

1. Health & beauty

You would need to be living under a rock for your entire life to be unaware of the amount of money spent each year on our obsession with having the perfect body, looking a certain way, the latest diet, the latest pills or the latest exercise routine. There are many specific areas that one can focus on within this rather large niche, such as cosmetics, weight loss, getting fitter, attaining supreme fitness, hair loss, hair removal or completing a marathon. There is no doubt that this niche has always been incredibly popular, but with the advent of social networks and the accessibility of smartphones, the speed of results is off the charts.

If I asked you how long it took L'Oréal's Lancôme cosmetics to reach $1 billion in revenue, what would you think? The answer is 80 years. What if I asked you how long it took for a Kardashian to achieve the exact same result in the same industry? Would you believe me if I said less than 3 years? Yes, incredibly, Kylie Jenner of Keeping Up with the Kardashians fame stands to be a billionaire by 25 because of linking a power house niche with the phenomenon of social media. Her makeup company made $420 million in sales in just 18 months since launch. It is another example of how RETHINKing social media has completely turned traditional business on its head; the big companies are no longer the sure things they once were.

Kylie Jenner is currently selling about 5 products per second, and by the time you read this book that number could have doubled or more. Fortunately, you do not need the fame of Kylie Jenner to become very successful and profitable with social media yourself.

Weight loss is another part of the "health & beauty" niche that receives a lot of focus, and it's one that really does cause people pain, making them willing to spend money to find a solution. The interesting thing about the health niche is that people are often looking to celebrities rather than qualified experts to get their advice. People want to look a certain way and will often look for the shortcut rather than going through what they might actually need to do, like hiring a personal trainer, for example. It used to amaze me how much money is spent in this area, especially because every person I have ever met already knows the three-step formula for weight loss:

Step 1: Eat less

Step 2: Move more

Step 3: Drink water

Yes, that's it ☺! Every weight loss program ever sold is based around these three basic pillars. As humans, we know what we need to do, but what we want is very different. We want a quicker, less difficult solution. This is why the companies that know how to market the solutions better are the ones making the most money. It is not so much the expertise that is the determinant of your success, often it's how well it is packaged up.

If you consider the entire concept of Weight Watchers is based on you having to watch what you eat, to make a note of it and then show up weekly to get weighed, it's not rocket science! However, it is what people want. They want the accountability, they want to be part of a group facing the same pains and struggles, they want to feel normal, they want to find people with common likes and dislikes and they want to compare themselves to people much worse off than they are! There is much more at stake than the actual loss of weight itself; it's about community. Community is something that social media can certainly provide if handled in the right way.

One of the main beauties of this niche is that there is no shortage of products that you can promote. Within the product selection section later, I will discuss the process involved in selling other businesses' products, but for now, you can just take me at my word that there are literally hundreds of thousands of products that you can promote in this niche.

2. Wealth

The pursuit of money, and later wealth, is of varying degrees of importance to all people on the planet if they want to live a healthy, fruitful life. Without getting into discussions on how it is possible to live off the land directly, etc., I am speaking in more general terms about most people. Every family will have their goals around lifestyle and how much money they need to fund it. Once they have reached that level of lifestyle, human nature will generally dictate that our standards will increase and that we will look for more.

Money is a topic that evokes strong emotions in many; just think about when you meet up with your family. It's only a matter of time before the hot topic of money comes up, and the advice around what you "should" or "should not" be doing with yours. The number one cause of relationship breakdowns is apparently arguments over money. In its very simplest form, most people would agree that they could do with more money in their lives.

This provides a huge opportunity for education, as we are quite simply not taught in schools how to grow money or invest it, for that matter. Robert Kiyosaki's Rich Dad Poor Dad financial educational books, which are specifically aimed at this niche, have sold over 40 million copies, not to mention all the additional training seminars that followed on from this. Learning how to earn more money can be in a multitude of different areas, each providing its own educational opportunity. For starters, you can show people how to save correctly and the importance of compound interest. You can show people how to trade the stock markets and how to invest. This is a huge opportunity alone.

People can learn how to trade with any of the following

- Forex

- Long term buy and hold

- Spread betting

- Swing trading

- Leaps

- Options

- Iron condors

- Butterflies

- Crypto currencies

- And many more…

Mastering the science of extracting money from the stock market is definitely an area that people really want – and need – to know about. Educational programs are available in this area, ranging from being completely free to costing literally tens of thousands of dollars. It is also a great area for marketers to become involved in, as there are tens of thousands of products available to sell for other businesses, any of which are "high ticket" or more expensive products, which means more commission for you.

Many people look to the internet to solve their financial problems. Creating an online business and learning how to sell online, whether you have a business or not to begin with, is an area that has huge scope in terms of a niche. There are multiple areas within this that people want and need to know about in order to grow a business, such as:

- Email marketing

- Database building

- Digital marketing strategy

- Facebook

- Twitter

- LinkedIn

- YouTube

- Snapchat

- Instagram

- Google advertising

- Social media advertising

- Opt-in pages

- Content creation

- Video marketing

- Live streaming

- Product creation

- Podcasting

- Affiliation

- Funnel creation

- Simplification of a little understood arena

- And many more…

Once again, this is a great place to focus on when starting out, as it is an area that very few people know much about, but it's one that you can learn a lot about in a very short space of time, that has tens of thousands of products that you can sell for other businesses. Just like with the trading niche, many of the products sell for tens of thousands of dollars, and in some instances, hundreds of thousands of dollars; in terms of commissions, that's ideally something you want to be looking out for. I personally promote certain high-ticket products in this arena, as it is extremely profitable for little effort, especially when you know what you are doing. You can learn more about this by going to http://resources.rethinksocialmedia.com.

3. Happiness

An entire industry has been built around our pursuit of happiness. It is not generally known as the "happiness niche"; most often it comes under the umbrella of "personal development". This is an area that has been around for thousands of years, and in modern society it is an area that can generate serious wealth because of how well it lends itself to educational products.

Personal development is a very broad field, covering the areas of physical well-being, financial health, family life, business success, spiritual development, social relationships and mental stimulation. In fact, the first two niche areas we discussed could fit under the umbrella of personal development, as it is generally looking to assist people in becoming successful and happy in all areas of life.

Although it's been in existence for millennia, this field has really only become mainstream since the late 20th century, and more specifically with the launch of the book and subsequent movie The Secret. The author Rhonda Byrne, with the assistance of Oprah Winfrey, made personal development a much more accepted norm and brought with it a huge business opportunity for many to capitalise on. In this area, products and services can be corporate focused or aimed at individuals, with a slightly different focus for each audience. The education can be delivered via books, audios, video courses, workshops, talks and seminars, in person or online.

Many of the "motivational" seminars could be seen as potential solutions for this void in people's lives; the Netflix documentary of Tony Robbins' program "Date with Destiny" will give you a good overview of this area if it's completely new to you. Some of the very well-known experts of years gone by, who have since left us, include Jim Rohn, Wayne Dyer and Zig Ziglar. More recently, Tony Robbins, John Assaraf, John Demartini, Brian Tracy, Bob Proctor, Les Brown, Rhonda Byrne, Eric Thomas, Mark Victor Hansen, Judymay Murphy, Mike Dooley, Jack Canfield, Lisa Nichols, Robin Sharma and many more have become household names around the world.

Within this niche comes the opportunity to promote these experts' vast ranges of products without ever having to become the expert yourself! I will explain this in full a little later, but once again the concept will be the same. This niche has hundreds of thousands of products available for marketers to promote, with the potential for some high-ticket programs, also with the back-end seminars that are provided.

Beginning with the end in mind is important with any business, but within these three areas, there are hundreds of thousands of products to choose from, so the products as such are not critical – they have already been created for you! This means you no longer need to think about creating amazing products and the associated customer support, at least until later when you can add your own, if you wish.

You can focus on one main thing: learning how to market some of the readymade solutions to readymade problems to a very hungry market. You become the matchmaker. It frees you up to really learn how to master the art of using social media correctly rather than being distracted by the operations of your everyday business and its associated headaches. This is why once you have selected the right niche, we can really start to think about social media the way it should be from the outset. Without a niche, we are lost; we don't know who we are looking for to purchase our offerings or where they might be.

Social media by itself is not the solution to business or money problems. It is bandied about as if it's the perfect solution to all problems, especially with business. Learning how to use social media, however, is only one part of a much bigger puzzle. It enables you to find the people who have a problem within the right niche. Having chosen your niche you can confidently move onto various social networks, looking for the perfect prospects for your business. In finding the right niche for you, ask yourself these two questions:

Which of these three niches do I have no interest in pursuing as a business **1. health & beauty, 2. wealth or 3. happiness?**

Of the two that remain, which one would I like to know more about 6 months from now?

Go with your first instinctive answer! If you are still not sure, go with 2. wealth, as I know you want to know more about this if you're still reading this book!

Congratulations, you are ready for the next step. Let's now work out who exactly those people are!

Summary:

There is no such thing as the perfect niche. Looking to make your wealth from your passion could end up being a futile and stressful search. Other people have your money right now, and if you want it, you need to give those people what they want in exchange for it. The odds are in your favour, as people love to spend their money. Your job is to present the products or services you are promoting to a prospect in a way that they feel they are better off with that product rather than keeping the money. It's therefore best to choose a niche where people are spending money already, and lots of it, such as in 1. health & beauty, 2. wealth and 3. happiness. You decide which one is the right one for you and stick with it until you at least match your salary.

Traditional Thinking:

You need a great idea about what people need to have a great business. If you pursue your passion, the money will inevitably follow.

RETHINK:

People buy what they want, not what they need. The focus of your business is not you, it is the people who are potentially going to buy the product. If they don't want it, you don't have a business.

Chapter 7: Evaluate Who Your Ideal People Are

*"Problems can become opportunities
when the right people come together."*
- Robert Redford

Once you have chosen the right niche, finding the right people and understanding their perspective on the problem you are solving is THE most important aspect of this entire operation. Individual tactics like Facebook and YouTube will come and go, but the fundamentals that drive people's buying decisions will be around forever. Your future fortune may rely significantly on your deeper understanding of people. Now don't worry, I'm not going to ask you to sign up to a psychology course or anything like that. I will cover more than enough for you within this chapter, at least to give you a very good grounding.

If I was to offer you a consistent strategy that if you apply the learning properly will guarantee a consistent and ever-growing income over time, would you be interested in learning it? I certainly hope so. The strategy I refer to is understanding your and other people's mindsets. What is it that makes you instantly like or dislike somebody you just met? What is it that makes you instantly attracted to something and immediately repulsed by something else? Why can you remember some people's names and instantly forget others'? When you begin to look at the underbelly and uncover what it is that makes you do what you do, it will unlock an incredible opportunity for your business. That might sound like a big claim, and indeed it is, but let me start you off with a quick statement to consider.

The money that you have in your bank account right now is a direct representation of the level of value that you provide to other people and how that value takes people closer to a buying decision.

If you look at the wealthiest people in world, they ALL deliver value to LOTS of people. The value in many cases is not even very high up the value chain. Some of the products and services they provide are very low down in Maslow's hierarchy of needs.

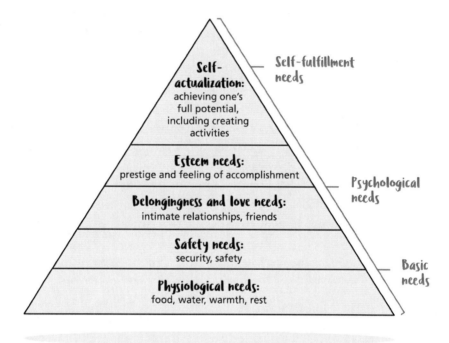

Fig 7.1: Maslow's hierarchy of needs

What is the value oil billionaires provide, for example? Well, heating and transportation would not be possible (at least with current technologies) without oil. Software is another big money maker, and in general we are not talking about sophisticated software, we are looking at Microsoft's basic tools that allow people all over the world to work their way around a computer and make some kind of sense out of it. Real estate is another of the other key components of the basic needs that we have for shelter, for either domestic or commercial purposes.

Finding the value is rarely the difficult bit, it's finding a significant volume of people that most businesses have the challenge with. The solution, of course, lies within social networks with over 3 billion people at your fingertips, and with this book as your guide, you should never again have to worry about finding lots of people to help!

Drilling deeper

What is it that makes a person tick? What are the right signals that will indicate if a person is a good fit for what you have to offer?

Let's go back to the drawing board and review people and the beliefs that drive their emotions, feelings and buying decisions. Having studied many sources about the different components of one's life, the model that I like best is my good friend and mentor Dr John Demartini's seven areas of life. They are as follows:

Physical:

This is your attention to your physical body, your fitness, your interest in your appearance, your weight, your clothing, your exercise routines, your eating habits and anything at all related to how you look and feel. You will also be interested in the physical underlying systems that control your appearance and how it all works.

Financial:

In this area, the main focus is money – cold, hard cash and how to earn it, save it, grow it, invest it, compound it and use it effectively. It also involves having a good understanding of the systems related to finances, such as the economy, trading, stock markets, company returns, choosing good companies to invest in, indexes, cryptocurrencies, foreign exchange currencies and basically anything related to growing money.

Spiritual:

Your main focus is your spiritual being. This can mean different things to different people. In many cases, it is associated with aligning to particular religious beliefs or dedicating one's life to a specific religious group. This doesn't necessarily have to be the case, but traditionally it has been intertwined with different types of religious groups. Your connection to a higher being or source is a major priority.

Social:

In this area, your focus is on your impact socially, ranging from your immediate social group of friends to your network of business relationships and, on a bigger scale, the influence you may have on a global social movement, perhaps on people's rights or for a cause that focuses on improving specific social issues.

Mental:

This is an area you may associate with knowledge and education and dedicating as much time and effort and focus to specialised knowledge in any particular field of your choosing.

Vocational:

In this area, your vocation or career is your highest priority. Many associate this directly with their place of work, their career or business, but this doesn't necessarily have to be the case. Your vocation is your overall calling, and what you dedicate yourself to.

Familial:

This is one of the easiest areas to understand and one of the most popular of all areas, the focus being on your family. This begins with your immediate family unit of parent and children and extended family. It may go beyond this too, but the primary focus is on the people closest to you and your relationships with them.

These are the seven areas and each and every person alive has a different perspective on the world relating to their relative prioritisation of each of these areas.

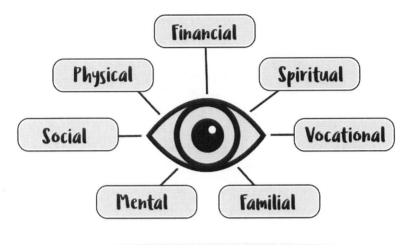

Fig 7.2: The seven areas of life

Now that you are aware of these different areas (and as I said, you can add in a few more depending on your studies), we now want to figure out what area is a priority in a specific person's life; we work this out through their values. The study of values, known as axiology, is the science behind understanding what it is that you prioritise most in your life, and understanding this is fundamental to understanding yourself and why you do what you do. This is the first prerequisite to even attempting to work out anybody else's values, as you first need to be aware of your own bias towards particular areas.

How do you work out your values? Can you change your values?

Two great questions. The intention of this book is to cover this in enough detail to get you started. However, I do strongly suggest that you take the time to read The Values Factor by Dr John Demartini in order to complete this exercise in full. There is a series of questions you can ask yourself to work out your values, and this is one of the first exercises I carry out with my more advanced students. I am going to limit the questions to five here; there are many more you can ask, but these five will be enough to get you on the right track.

Question 1: What do I spend most of my time on? In which area do I spend my time more than any other?

To help you with this, bring awareness to a typical day and assign roughly how much time you spend in each of the seven areas. Trends will appear very quickly. Let's say for example that from morning to night most of your time involves getting your children ready for school, then minding the youngest at home for the entire day, and your day involves mostly cleaning the home and organising meals for the rest of your family when they return. At this time in your life, family would be your highest value. You can then look at what you spend the rest of your day doing. For example, when you are making dinner or out walking, do you find you constantly think about your health, food and exercise and are listening to audiobooks on the topic of health and fitness?

Value	Most Time Per Day
1.	
2.	
3.	

Table 7.1: Tracking time spent

Just write them down – don't judge, there is no right or wrong answer. As we go through the questions, your answers will become clearer.

Question 2: What do I like to speak about with other people?

What topics of conversation light you up and what topics completely shut you down? Imagine you are at a party and you don't know anyone there. You are completely bored and about to nod off, when suddenly the topic of conversation changes, and you light up and become a completely new person. You know what the topic is, write it down.

Value	Conversation Topics
1.	
2.	
3.	

Table 7.2: Tracking topics spoken about

Question 3: What do I surround myself with at my place of work?

This is a very telling one, and it usually results in a few giggles at my workshops. People can immediately think of work colleagues who fit this acid test perfectly. You can't get into their cubicle without being surrounded by pictures of all of their children or maybe all their qualifications – for example, the half-day diploma they received for communication skills in the workplace from 9 years ago. Someone could just as easily have religious images or perhaps their gym and eating plan for the week. All of these signs are very telling.

Value	Images I Surround Myself With
1.	
2.	
3.	

Table 7.3: Tracking pictures in proximity

Question 4: How do I introduce myself to other people?

Self-labelling can be a great way of beginning to understand what your values are. When you meet somebody new, after you tell them your name, how do you next identify yourself? "Hi, my name is Paul and I am a professional investor" or "I am a personal trainer" or "I am a priest" or "I am a father". Each one will give a different indicator of what value may be your highest.

Value	How I Introduce Myself
1.	
2.	
3.	

Table 7.4: Tracking self-appointed labels

I will also include as part of this, what do you wear on a regular basis? You can often quite easily spot people who are more polarised in their values because they spend significantly more time on one particular value, just by being aware of their physical appearance. For example, if a gentleman enters a room and needs to turn sideways to get his muscular frame in the door, it is very clear that he puts a lot of time in at the gym and is committed to his physical appearance. Perhaps you may know someone who has long grey hair and wears a particular type of jewellery and they almost float around. This person might identify themselves as being quite spiritual and introduce themselves as "I AM..." followed by no label at all ☺. Alternatively, the person always found in a suit and tie, even on a Sunday, is creating an impression that business or vocation is important to them.

Once again there is no judgement here, in case you find that you are reacting negatively to any of the above. Yes, I agree 100% they are stereotypes but I am purposely using examples that will make me more polarised to get the point across.

Question 5: How do I spend my M"ONE"Y? What is MY ONE?

I have left what I found to be the most valuable question of all to last. It is possible to fudge the answers in the first 4, but this "ONE" is the acid test to find out "M___Y" top values. What you can do is to pull out your bank statements from the last 3 months and go through each item one by one, putting a letter beside each item to identify which area you spent the money on. Physical (P) Financial (F) Spiritual (S), Social (So), Mental (M), Vocational (V) and Familial (Fa). This is a phenomenally powerful exercise, as it truly gives an insight into your daily behaviours, which add up to demonstrate the values that you live out in your life. You will always spend your money in line with your values.

Value	Most Money Spent
1.	
2.	
3.	

Table 7.5: Tracking spending of money

Imagine for a moment you are hanging out with your friend at their house. You were just watching an advert on TV that was promoting an audio and video training set on financial mindset and investing strategies, and the product was $1,000. Your friend immediately pipes up, "Oh no, I can't afford that, in fact there is no way on earth I could afford that". You suggest that you are interested, and you get the response "Are you crazy? Are you seriously considering this, spending $1,000 to learn how to grow your money? You've no money to grow!" Finance is clearly not the highest of your friend's values, and naturally they are looking to influence you based on their value systems. Five minutes later, you speak to the same person, and they have just received the bill for their child's summer camp, and after a sigh they immediately start writing the cheque. Either way, it is the same money, but in one case it was deemed affordable and in the other not. It all depends on your individual values.

When you complete this exercise, you will be able to determine rightly or wrongly how you spend your money and how you currently have your values prioritised. Other areas that you can explore are what you think about the most, what you are grateful for, what areas you are most organised in and where you put most of your energy. Look for common themes in the top three across the five areas we are looking at. An interesting exercise would be to pull up your bank statements from 10 years ago and to do the exact same exercise; most likely, you will find that your spending patterns are quite different now.

The vast majority of society dream of one day winning the Powerball or the lottery equivalent. How often have you found yourself in discussions at work or with friends relating to what you would do if you won $30 million, or whatever the latest jackpot is? What would you spend it on? Let's reduce the number a little so that you actually can get more realistic about it. Let's say it's $3 million. How would you spend it? A typical answer might be:

"I would immediately book an exotic holiday with family or friends to have a think about what I would do. Then I would probably buy houses for my children. I would move my parents out of where they currently are and buy them a home by the sea. I would obviously get ourselves a brand new home and upgrade our car; actually we'd upgrade both cars to brand new top of the range Mercedes or BMW. Clearly all of my family's wardrobes need upgrading, so we would go to NYC and buy new clothes for us all. I would probably clear the mortgages of my brothers and sisters too, and help them with some of the debts that they have. Thinking about it, I have a few friends too who could really do with a dig out, so if I did have any left over, I would give them a gift or a partial loan. I would probably give 10% maybe to a charity. Whatever is left over after that I would put it into the bank until I needed it."

Sound familiar? I remember these conversations very well! I also remember the responses of the group to my answers. In my early 20s they were all about the dream house, the dream car, etc., and everyone would smile and nod their heads in agreement. Not long before I left my final job, the answers changed. Here is a fairly accurate response that I provided in my late 20s:

"I would hire a mentor in finance and invest in them to show me how I could invest the money to make it grow. I would create a property portfolio and one in stocks, bonds, commodities, etc. I would also pay to go on masterminds with people who have huge success from a financial perspective. I would look to build a business where I could create employment and help others learn about finance and how to manage their own money to remove the financial stress and pain in their lives. I would set up a training organisation to teach children how to become financially independent before leaving school."

The faces in the group were not so agreeable. "Christ, how BORING is that", or "Seriously though, what would you do with all that money that you are making, what would you spend that on?" These comments were really interesting to me. It immediately made me aware of others' values, none better or worse by the way, just people's values. Saving money is boring but spending money is exciting!

Let's look at the statistics of lottery winners. About 70% of people who win a lottery or get a big windfall actually end up broke in a few years, according to the National Endowment for Financial Education. These numbers are from the US, where the sums involved in some cases are over $1 billion! The percentages are even higher as the winnings get smaller. Many people are shocked by this, but when your plan your entire life was to spend all of your winnings, why would it come as any surprise? You will spend in line with your values, no matter how much money you have. Did you ever notice that no matter how much you earn, or no matter how many promotions you get at work, your expenses don't take long to increase to match your new income? Only when you value "finance" more than the others will you start to value the process of having money and keeping it. John Demartini says "If you are not a millionaire by 40, you can be certain that finance is not in your top two values".

Most people I knew in my 20s had planned out exactly how they were going to get rid of all of their money in advance of it hitting their bank account each month. Their direct debits were set up to immediately pay their mortgages, car loans, debt payments, Visa cards, Master Cards, Amex bills, TV bills, electric bills, gas bills, etc. The money doesn't get much of a chance to get comfortable sitting in your account; in fact, the truth is you rarely get to see, touch or feel it.

When I was first introduced to this concept, it really woke me up to my own behaviours and how my financial results were a direct outcome of my values, specifically the value I placed on money. The more I had, the more I would spend it on having a "good time" and being out with friends. Any promotion was more of a reason to go and celebrate and spend even more – "easy come, easy go" attitude! Let me reiterate, there is nothing inherently wrong with this behaviour. It all comes down to values. However, with more awareness of the topic, more financially educated decisions can be made and a situation that may be causing a lot of stress can begin to be adjusted, firstly by working on your values.

Right now, you may well be asking: How do I "fix" this, how do I hold onto money? Is there a process? The answer is yes, but let's remember the purpose of the book... to RETHINK social media. I will show you how, for sure, at another location: http://resources.rethinksocialmedia.com.

There is a clue in this quotation:

"Investing in yourself is the most important investment you'll ever make in your life... There's no financial investment that'll ever match it, because if you develop more skill, more ability, more insight, more capacity, that's what's going to really provide economic freedom... It's those skills that really make that happen."
- Warren Buffet

Now that you have gone through the 5 questions about your own values, you will have a much better appreciation of your personal priorities and spending behaviours and how you choose to allocate your time, thoughts, energy and space. Every single person has a unique value system fingerprint; no two people's values are exactly the same. If you look hard enough, you will find someone with exactly the opposite of your values, and more than likely you would not agree with this person on much! Often, people end up marrying someone with different values to theirs, so they can delegate low priority tasks to each other.

Like people, businesses have different values too, as do cultures within different countries. Just look at the ever-increasing levels of terrorist threats because a clash in values has led to a very polarised situation of right and wrong, black and white. The values of the Western world are very different to those of the Middle East, and depending on where you were brought up, your values, and as a result your views, will be influenced to a degree by the "value blinkers" of your country and culture. It's all a matter of perspective. Understanding your values gives you an enormous insight and advantage when it comes to marketing, as you can immediately spot your own biases. You tend to like people with similar values to your own, while you dislike those who have very different values.

Enough about you, though, for now; what about everyone else? Remember, they have your money! The degree to which you become aware of other people's values, and in particular your potential clients' values, the more likely you are going to be a very successful marketer. As soon as you notice the tell-tale signs of someone's values and as soon as you can describe your product or service in terms of their highest values, you often don't need to do any selling, as the product becomes such a natural fit. When you market well, selling becomes almost unnecessary.

As we saw earlier, the feedback from someone that they "can't afford it" is a clear indication that at this particular moment what's on offer in the way it's described is not in line with their highest values. Let's return to the example used above about the training program on finance and investing, and your friend's feedback that it was not something they could afford now and possibly ever. Assume that your highest values are finance and mental growth; you love to learn, specifically about anything related to making, growing and investing money. You can clearly see that your friend's perspective actually dooms them to a lifetime of financial struggles.

Knowing this, how do we start to categorise the people who will be potentially buying from you, or at least to begin with might be considering downloading your free guide? The better you understand yourself, and understand how the average person thinks within your niche, the more successful you will become. While there is no such thing as an average person, in that everyone has their own unique traits, attributes and values, we do tend to have similar behaviours as different people in a group. I suggest that you think deeply about what your "ideal" client looks like; this process is sometimes known as creating your "avatar". We will provide you with a full checklist of this later in the book, but for now you can consider the following to get you started:

- Age

- Demographic

- Where they live

- Sex
- Marital status
- Children / Grandchildren
- Spending ability
- Key pain points
- Interests
- Values for age group

A useful exercise I find here is to go to google.com/images, type in the age and sex of the person you are thinking of, find the image that most looks like your ideal client and print it out. It may be one female and one male. Give them a made-up name, consider where they most likely live and start to (as much as possible) think like them, consider their day-to-day pains and areas of their lives that are probably the most important at this time. Look at the image over and over, really get into playing the role, just like a method actor. The more you can relate to how they think, the easier it will be to market to this person and people just like them.

When you can understand their highest values, your job is to position your marketing so that your product or service is a very natural fit to fulfil their highest values. As we discussed, people will always spend in line with their values, so you are maximising your chance of doing business with this person. Your marketing material and your social media messaging will also follow suit, appealing to the values of your audience. From now on, your messages will be aimed directly at your imaginary avatar, ignoring everyone else. Remember, too, that you are never going to please everyone – it is just not possible, and the more "vanilla" you become, the less appealing and more generic your message will be. If this happens, you can potentially lose out on the benefit of having a "tribe" of followers, as explained in the now infamous book Tribes by Seth Godin.

We are all unique. Yes, that is true. However, we do also behave in packs on occasion. Going back to the 7 areas of life in figure 7.2, we can trace a typical life path through these areas. People's biggest problems depend on many factors, including age, location, etc., but often we can group people by age to simplify the process. As we move through life, our problems change.

Let's start with teens: their main priority is "Social" and hanging out with friends. Their main problem areas are looking good in front of their friends and hatching a plan to escape from their parents' clutches as soon as possible! In their 20s, this need increases further as they really want to move out from home and support themselves, and the focus is on getting a good enough job to support this goal, which is "Vocational". In their 30s, having children of their own usually becomes a focus, bringing all the issues and problems that arise with this – namely "Familial".

In their 40s, there is a fork in the road where men and women tend to go in different directions. If the average life expectancy for someone today is 92, that would make 46 the half-way point, or in other words, a mid-life crisis! Us men get very confused. We were very clear in our focus 'til now but suddenly we become very unsure, so we buy Porches and wigs and look to reclaim our youth in any way possible. We start to do crazy things like running marathons – "Physical". Women, on the other hand, in many cases have just spent 15 years raising what started as little angels but have become devils! They seem to suddenly decide almost en masse to "reintegrate into society" after a long hiatus, ready to learn more, be more, do more and get their message out there – "Mental".

In their 50s, men and women unite again with their highest value, which becomes "Financial", as they realise they can no longer procrastinate on their finances – their primary source of income is about to expire, yet their expenses are not, and they start to look for solutions in this area. In their 60s, people's thoughts tend to start drifting to the next life and taking out some "Spiritual" insurance in case it might help soon. Unfortunately, if finances have not been organised in earlier life, often we must resort back to "Familial" in our 70s, when there is no alternative other than having our children take care of us. Until a few decades ago, in many developed countries, having lots of children was people's pension – the parents would be shared among the children without any major burden on any of the children. This is still the case in many developing countries, but in the developed world, there are serious issues when there are only one or two children to meet the needs of elderly parents.

While these are generalisations, this guide should help you start to get into the mindset of your target market and see how they view their world at different times in their lives. A 70-year-old man is unlikely to be drawn to an advertisement for an app that can make you rich overnight with Forex, but a certain type of teenager or someone in their early twenties looking for a quick financial fix might be just the right target!

The trick is to be able to get a message across that has mass appeal to your audience but does not lose the personal impact. Using social networks in the correct way can allow you to facilitate this apparent contradiction. From an individual perspective, it will also help greatly if you have an understanding of at least some of the basic psychological profiles that are used to help you segment and target certain types of your people with certain messages.

There are numerous strategies used when profiling personality traits, such as Myers Briggs Type Indicator, The I Ching, Kiersey Temperament Sorter, iPersonic Personality Type, DISC Personality Types and Profiles, INSIGHT Inventory Personality Profile Test, Holland's Theory of Career Choice, NLP Meta Programs and Wealth Dynamics Personality Profile. If you operate in the corporate world, you will have come across some of these already. While they are not necessary in completing this exercise, the more knowledge you have, the better prepared you are.

Our personalities can also be divided into colours, which I find another useful categorisation in day-to-day marketing, especially on a one-to-one basis. Each colour has particular traits. Not only will this help you to psychologically understand the person better, but it will also aid how you

Ref: (http://www.abbyeagle.com/nlp/what-is-my-personality-type.php)

interact with them. If you know how to get the best out of a person, you will see great results – and better still, if you recognise what colour YOU are, you'll be able to advise people how to get the best out of you, your likes and dislikes, your strengths and your weaknesses.

Red personality: They are usually leaders, energetic, full of drive, impatient and very competitive, and not afraid of risk.

Yellow personality: They are generally very sociable and love being the centre of attention and around people. They can be very optimistic and informal, and quite animated.

Blue personality: These are the people who like to focus on the detail and are very systematic in their approach. They are usually very keen on being on time and wanting things to be where they should be, and they think things through to completion rather than giving rash responses.

Green personality: These people are quite relaxed in their approach and very informal. They are also quite social and agreeable in nature, and naturally empathetic.

The more you know about your target market, the more it helps you ultimately. Knowing this assists you in knowing what type of personalities are more or less likely to find your messaging appealing or repellent, but getting started within the seven areas and identifying your avatar is a great starting point. Now that we know who they are, it's time to go find them.

Summary:

In order to consider who the perfect people are for your business, you need to delve deeper into the psychology of the people, and even into understanding what makes them spend their money the way they do. The first step towards this is to perform a self-assessment on what your values are and how you currently spend money in line with those values. Completing that task enables you to understand your target market in a very clear, coherent way, allowing you to craft a marketing message that meets their immediate wants and fits their desires. Once you know who they are and what they look like, we can then go find them on social networks.

Traditional Thinking:

One size marketing fits all; let's get the message out there and see what happens. There are lots of different people who need what the business has, so let's target them all at once. It's impossible to work out the needs of all of our clients individually, as they are unique and so you cannot market to them separately.

RETHINK:

Our message should perfectly match the right people for our niche. Our wants and needs change as we get older, and understanding what these are is hugely important for your marketing. People face the same problems worldwide as they age throughout life; they can be targeted as groups and also as individuals through remarketing.

Chapter 8: Target the Right Traffic

"Stop waiting for the right person to come into your life.
Be the right person to come to someone's life."
- Leo Babauta

Now that you have a much better idea of who you are looking for, you are officially granted a license to go forth and conquer social media! Finally, you have a real focus that will allow you to laser target your marketing and advertising moving forward, potentially both saving and making you a fortune.

With any book that has social media in its title, it is inevitable that the topic of traffic must come up in various forms at some stage. In this chapter, I'll walk you through a number of different areas that you need to be aware of when it comes to targeting the right people, how to target them, where to target them, the most commonly made mistakes and the journey we wish to take a complete stranger on, in order to help turn them into a lead, then a prospect, a customer, a client and finally an addict! Let's kick off by fixing the most common mistakes being made before setting you on the right path to online wealth through building a loyal and profitable list of followers.

Part 1: The Social Media Paradox

"It's not me, it's you!"
- Anon

You might need to read that one twice! Why do most people use social media? We can safely assume that it is mostly for personal use. What about those who specifically use it for the purpose of business?

There are a multitude of possible answers, such as:

- To build a following / tribe / community

- To engage with potential clients

- To brand a business

- To access almost half the world's population

- To build relationships with potential clients

- To find prospects for your business

- Because everyone else is doing it

- To avoid being left behind by competitors

- To create an online presence

- To be found through Google and other search engines

- To provide an alternative online engagement tool to your website

- To provide value to your community

- To promote products and services in order to make sales

- To provide customer service support

- To find out what your community are looking for / market research

- To recruit new hires

- To facilitate the running of paid online campaigns

- To network with similarly-minded people

- To build a database of relevant people for your business

This list is certainly not exhaustive, but these reasons are among the most typical as to why business owners use social media. If I were to narrow all of these reasons down to just one main priority, which do you think it might be? Please go back and reflect on them and consider what you would choose if you could only select one.

My selection is the very last one: "To build a database of relevant people for your business". In my opinion, your primary purpose for being on social media when in business is to use it to gather as many possible leads for your business as possible. Many of the other factors come in to play, but the main driver that must be behind your social media activity is to have more and more people become aware of what you do, and to leave their details to find out more. I will discuss the specifics of how this is done later. I find that once this priority is clear with business owners, it makes everything else a lot easier for them to grasp to realise that there is indeed a very tangible benefit to their social media activity.

Much of the time wasted on social media comes down to a lack of awareness of its overall purpose. You may hear about the importance of delivering value, etc., but you can provide value all day every day and be completely broke. There needs to be an overriding purpose behind all of what you do. The value you provide is to assist in moving your audience closer to firstly leaving their details and ultimately making a buying decision.

Now having established this framework, let's take a look at some of the mistakes most commonly made by business owners on social media so that we can a: become aware of them, b. reduce them, c. eliminate them, d. replace them with a much more effective alternative, so that e. you stop wasting time on social media. There are many more than this, but these five will be a great place to start.

Mistake #1: It's not you, it's me…

The ultimate paradox of businesses using social media is that the vast majority of their focus is on themselves and not their followers. Each user wants to focus on "ME". Our first subconscious thought is "What's in it for me?" Even the words Soc"I"al "ME"d"I"a contain both a "ME" and two "I"s and nothing about a "you" ☺. The focus on "me" rather than "you" is certainly how social strategies tend to be played out in the real world, and this results in many damaged reputations and ineffective social media campaigns.

In any relationship, be it business or personal, one of the keys to being successful is to ask questions and then listen intently to what the other person has to say. In fact, at relationship or "pick up" conferences for men, one of the main topics of discussion is learning how to ask a question and then learning to just shut up, stay quiet, nod your head and agree every once in a while, saying "yes", "ahem" or "oh right" (or at least so I am told ☺). While the man is sitting there wondering if he has made it too obvious that he isn't fully tuned in, the woman may be thinking that she has finally found the perfect man, full of empathy, compassion, a great listener and so interested in knowing everything about her! Now this is clearly a stereotype and a bit of fun, but it's not a million miles away from the truth.

As the commonly-used saying in relationship breakups goes, "It's not you, it's me". It's time for a RETHINK here. It needs to be all about your potential client, the "you" and not "me" the business.

Look at how we are designed as humans: we have two ears and just one mouth. In theory at least, we should be listening twice as much as we speak!

> *"We have two ears and one mouth so that*
> *we can listen twice as much as we speak."*
> *- Epictetus*

In 2006, Louann Brizendine, founder and director of the University of California, San Francisco's Women's Mood and Hormone Clinic, published

The Female Brain. In this book, she makes a comment that women use approximately 13,000 more words a day when speaking than men, coming in at a whopping 20,000 words per day – almost three times the 7,000 spoken by men. While Scientific American later disproved this, clearly it is completely off the mark, but for a bit of fun, I still like to reference it to make you aware of how much listening you need to do if you are using 20,000 words a day on average ☺. Regardless of these numbers being totally unfounded, I think we can all agree that we need to listen more and the same is very true on social media. Social media might be better thought of as social "YOU"dia within your business.

Fig 8.1: The new social media strategy for business

The social network communication plans employed by either an individual or a business must incorporate the other person in the relationship, the YOU.

RETHINK Workaround #1:

When deciding what to post about, begin by thinking about the type of prospect you are looking to attract. Understand their point of view, their pains, their needs and their values, as we discussed in chapter 7. You need to care more and to let your audience know that you truly care. You can do this by requesting more information from them.

Once you have established the "voice" of your prospect, ensure that you now switch to stop talking about your business incessantly. Ask for comments and feedback on your posts. Use surveys from time to time to gauge interest in what you think your prospects want. There are excellent free tools available to do this, such as www.surveymonkey.com or http://www.wofuu.com that will give you priceless information in your pursuit of serving your potential client better from the start.

Mistake #2: The "social media thing"

One of the things that I most enjoy doing as part of my work is to consult with individual companies and assist with their social media strategy. While every company and situation is different, the similarities are quite startling. Most often I am called into an organisation that has "done" or is "doing" the "social media thing", using their own words, but the results are not what they expected. This immediately raises alarm bells with me.

The "social media thing" is usually the same thing from entrepreneur to entrepreneur and company to company. With most businesses, and you may have been guilty of this yourself in the past, the tendency is to follow the most "affordable" social media marketing advice of the time and get started by setting up a Facebook page and Twitter account for your business as your first step. Step 2 involves putting your branding and logos on the pages and then step 3 is to start to grow a following by whatever means is in fashion at the time. Step 4 is when it all starts to unravel.

When most businesses start their "communicating" process over social networks, it usually involves the following: post a couple of times a day (if you can), let people know about your products and services and of course offer them discounts intermittently to encourage them to take action and buy from you. They basically pick up a megaphone and start to preach about themselves and how great they are.

Does this sound familiar? It doesn't take a social media consultant to realise that this is what 90% of businesses do on social media, yet it should be the role of a social or digital consultant to discourage these practices, as they quite simply don't work. This strategy of one-sided communication has never worked.

RETHINK Workaround #2:

It is very important that when it comes to getting social media marketing coaching and advice, you get it from suitably qualified people. What does it take to become a social media "expert" or "guru" nowadays anyway? Well generally, you just need to have a profile page on your social networks that says you are a "Social Media Expert"!

There are quite a few problems with this. Many business owners will go to the lowest bidder in an attempt to save money, and in a competitive industry, many social media "experts" will be happy to work for very little. You get what you pay for in most instances. Just because they know more than you, that does not make them qualified.

"In the land of the blind, the one-eyed man is king."

Be sure to do your research. Look for case studies and previous clients of theirs, and do your background checks. Make sure they walk the talk, or at least at a minimum can prove it with their own social media presence. You may be surprised how many experts out there have just a couple of hundred followers, yet are happy to spend your hard-earned money on advice that's outdated at best or severely damaging for your business and reputation at worst. Don't get me wrong, there are some amazing experts out there too, but make sure you do some research if you're hiring.

So, let's put down the megaphone, and let's agree that social network communication plans should not in any way resemble a one-way conversation where you constantly talk about yourself and your business. Hopefully that ends today, ok? Agreed? I certainly hope so ☺.

Mistake #3: Treating social media like a business networking event

Let's leave the online world for a minute and look at an equivalent offline example that has many parallels: the world of business networking. Imagine for a moment you are attending a networking event. People are meant to be there, in theory at least, to meet others, exchange ideas and make people aware of who they are and what they do. However, if you have attended any networking events in the past, you may have noticed that it usually follows a familiar pattern. A bunch of people get together with the same goal: to get rid of as many business cards as they can in the 30 minutes or one hour that they have ☺. I'm not suggesting that everyone at networking events does this, of course not. There are the astute few who know exactly what they are doing and are there to build a relationship first and foremost, not to hand out business cards.

Nobody likes the pushy salesperson, or the person who does nothing but speak about themselves at these events. It's rare that this strategy results in getting any business, and you also harm your reputation, as others in the room start to give advanced warning to keep clear of you. With an attitude of "I am here to make money from you and I am going to tell you all about me", you are missing some of the key components of any relationship: the social engagement, the getting to know each other, the building of a bond. This behaviour is all too often carried over to its online equivalents on Facebook and LinkedIn. It may not come as a surprise that it does not work there either.

RETHINK Workaround #3:

This might be a little controversial, but I am of the opinion that business cards are next to useless nowadays, as they do not set the scene for a two-way conversation. Whenever I'm asked for a business card, and it doesn't matter who is asking, the response is always the same: "I've actually run out, but may I add you on Twitter, Facebook and LinkedIn right now so that we can carry on our conversation there?" You immediately show your intent, which is to build something meaningful right from the outset.

As soon as you hand out a business card to someone else, you have just given away control in the relationship. You are now relying on someone else to firstly remember who you were and why you are important to them, and then to show the initiative to go find your card among the thousands they may already have and THEN pick up a phone to call or maybe email you. What is the likelihood of this happening? You may already know the answer to this. How many business cards have you handed out in your lifetime, and relatively speaking, what percentage of those cards has resulted in any kind of follow-up later? I can guess almost zero, unless you drove it from your side or you know how to leave a great impression.

We are all very busy. We are too busy to go back through stacks of cards in order to find the person we think is the contact we made at event x, etc. Alternatively, you can do a couple of things. I will certainly happily take someone's business card and make it my business to reach out to that person, either via their social media if referenced on the card or via email. When one of the key purposes of any business is to collect leads, why do people always try so hard to give them away rather than collect them?

Your second option is one I talked about earlier. Connect with that person at that very moment on at least one social network and strike up a conversation immediately. Don't wait. With every minute that passes after that first engagement, the likelihood of any follow-up drops dramatically. If, however, you do add social networks into the equation, it stacks the odds in your favour and you are in control of the level of engagement you wish to pursue afterwards, depending on who the person is and how valuable they may to you as a contact moving forward.

One last comment on this is advice on how to handle B2B (business to business) as opposed to B2C (business to consumer) relationships. Treat every single relationship as P2P (person to person), as Chris Ducker often says. In B2B relationships, you ultimately still need to convince a person to do business with you, so the usual rules continue to apply.

Mistake #4: Treating social media as if it is completely separate to the rest of the business

If you are in business already, it is very likely that this is a trap you will have fallen into. This is something that you won't have come across just yet if you are looking to get started on your entrepreneurial journey. With the amazing possibilities that social media provides, it is easy for the expectations of what it can do for your business to get completely out of hand. If it's to be deployed in a manner that allows for ongoing success, it is important to consider what success actually looks like. What are the key performance indicators (KPIs) for you to understand if what you are doing is working, and where should you invest more of your time and effort?

There are many books on this topic, and I won't get into it in detail here, but needless to say, the KPIs of your main business should align with the KPIs of your social media marketing. Its successes and failures can be measured just like any other marketing strategies that you may have run in the past. The key is that you do measure it so that you know when you are achieving what you planned for, and if not, how to adapt to get there. The more integral it is to your overall business, the more successful it is likely to be.

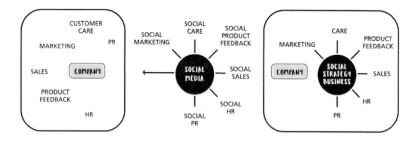

Fig 8.2: Integrating social media within the overall business

RETHINK Workaround #4:

First of all, this only applies if you already are in business. Find out what the overall key performance indicators for your business are. If you are just starting out, it would be a very useful practice to work out what these are. Some books to assist you with this are Key Performance Indicators (KPI): The 75 measures every manager needs to know by Bernard Marr and Scaling Up by Verne Harnish. Once clear on those, get clarity on what the specific goals are for your marketing activities and how they feed into the overall KPIs. When you know your marketing goals, it is very straightforward to fit in your social media marketing goals and align them in the same direction as the company. If you are using social media for other purposes, such as HR, recruitment, PR, sales, market research or customer care, just as before, make sure you align the overall KPIs in each of these areas with the expectations of the social media "wing" of that department. I highly recommend Keith Cunningham's The Ultimate Blueprint for an Insanely Successful Business for the integration of these metrics into an ongoing process for your business.

Mistake #5: Breaking the circle of trust

Most people on social media are just bored! They are looking for a break from the mundane – the job they hate, the life they complain about incessantly – and what better way to do this than to pop on board their favourite social network to spy on their friends and family? This is key. Time for another RETHINK here. People on social networks are generally not expecting to be sold to. They are there to be entertained, to laugh, to cry, to judge, to react, to participate and to share. As a marketer, this is amazing news. The typical person on their cell phone on social media has their "guard down", so to speak. They are not expecting to be sold to. With this lies great opportunity and great risk at the same time for a business.

If someone has followed or liked your page, or whatever term is relevant to your social network, they see your posts among those of their friends and family. Subconsciously, you are within their circle of trust, you are among their circle of friends. Awareness of this is really important.

You need to realise that while the benefits here could be great, all of this goodwill can disappear the moment you become "salesy" and annoying, telling them about how great you and your products and services are. It doesn't take much to be cast out of the circle of trust forever.

RETHINK Workaround #5:

Keeping your audience in mind and how they act during a typical day will be essential to managing your social media correctly. Later in this book I will elaborate on this in much more detail. For now, keep in mind that your social media posts should be more focused on entertainment and education rather than promotions and sales. Don't worry, I will shortly provide you with an alternative – a strategy that has stood the test of time and one that works no matter what the social medium.

Also, be very aware of consistency in your posting. It is very easy to spot the people who have just attended a marketing seminar for their companies and are super eager in their posting for a few days, only for that enthusiasm to disappear and then perhaps reappear intermittently in the future. Once again, you are breaking the trust of your audience here as a lack of consistency subconsciously leads to a lack of trust.

Ok, with the mistakes out of the way now, let's dig a little deeper into the decision making of our target market so that you can dig a lot deeper into their pockets to reclaim your money ☺.

Summary:

When it comes to business, social media can be thought of as Social "YOU"dia. Its primary focus must be on the user that we are looking to engage with, if we are to encourage them to join our database at some point in the near future. In order to serve them as well as we can, we must give them what they want. Too many businesses, under bad advice, think of social media as an amateur networking event, where everyone is just there to pick up some business without listening to the others at the event.

There are some clear RETHINK workarounds that can be implemented to fix these mistakes. Social media marketing within a business should ideally have its goals and objectives aligned with the overall KPIs of the organisation for it to be sustained and in order to measure its true value. Finally, accessing people through social media gives you an amazing opportunity to be regarded by your followers as a "friend", as their guards are down when using these platforms; you are in their circle of trust, so be careful not to abuse and lose that trust.

Traditional Thinking:

Your business should post consistently on social media and offer discounts and sales to get people to buy. Provide lots of value and the sales will take care of themselves. Use social media in your business to see how you can increase sales. If someone likes your pages, then they are game to receive your marketing messages.

RETHINK:

Social media marketing should be focused on the user, encouraging engagement and serving their desires. The value content strategy must have an overall objective in mind that moves the follower towards doing business with you. Social media and its results should be aligned with the KPIs of the company as a whole, not independently. Remember that people are ultimately on social media to be entertained and educated, not to be sold to. Don't lose your place in their circle of trust. Social media is a very powerful tool that you can get the best results from when deployed as part of the overall RETHINK model.

Part 2: How do Emotions Lead to Action?

"If you want to charge people financially,
you need to first charge them emotionally!"
- Paul O'Mahony

One of the major concepts I hope to get across in this book is the idea that people make decisions based on emotions first and logic second. While you may know this in theory, using this information on a day-to-day basis can mean the difference between you having a highly successful business and having to struggle to get by financially. In order for you to master marketing of any kind, let alone social media marketing, it would be hugely helpful if you understood what makes you "tick". What is it that makes you decide whether to buy something or not, to procrastinate or to do something this very moment?

Many years ago, I was introduced to a concept that blew my mind. It was about emotions and understanding them beyond the obvious. It was, once again, Dr John Demartini at one of his Breakthrough Experience events that made me sit up and take note. The basic concept was that in studying the meaning of words, known as etymology, we can understand better the meaning behind a lot of words that we use every day, allowing us to see hidden truths behind them.

In the diagram below, you will see a line down the middle, a positive symbol on the right and a negative symbol on the left. The word "emotion" derives from the Latin "motus" meaning to move or movement. An "ion" is a charged particle. So you could look at emot-ions as the movement of charges. Life is, after all, a constant movement from negative to positive to negative and back again. Most of us feel that events happen to us, when in fact it is our react-ion to those events that determines what emotion and feeling we associate with them.

At a younger age, our emotions are a lot more polarised than when we get older and wiser. If you watch the reaction of a child who has their teddy taken away from them, it's the end of their world! If you study the reaction of a 95-year-old who is just made aware that their best friend of 90 years has just passed, there is usually a more solemn and knowing reaction, without a massive display of emotion. With age comes the realisation that it is not possible to have one-sided events. You cannot have a positive without a corresponding negative, and vice versa.

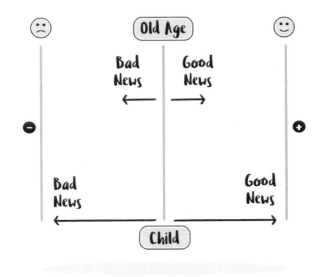

Fig 8.3: Emotional poles changing with age

This is the case in chemistry, physics or biology: you can't split a magnet in two, no matter how many times you slice it. It is these charges that dictate so much in our lives. We often refer to people who are quite erratic in the extremes of their emotions as bipolar while others who do not react as much as balanced or stoic.

Balance is the point at which the two charges meet. We sometimes refer to people as emotional basket cases when we find that they are "bouncing off walls" in their daily lives, with everything being a major drama. Once the emotional rollercoaster is in full flow, sometimes this person is happy regardless of the emotion itself as long as they feel "alive" and the tears are flowing!

As I'm sure you might realise, the level of emotion that we portray also has an underlying foundation in our cultural upbringing. In fact, studying cultures can tell us a lot about emotions. If I was to ask you to name some countries in Europe that you would consider the people to be quite "emotional", more than likely you would choose countries like Italy, Spain, Portugal and Greece. Outside of Europe, what other countries come to mind? The Latin American countries, perhaps?

What makes this so interesting to me is to consider this and see if we can somehow measure emotions numerically. One possible way of tracking people's emotions with a reasonable level of accuracy is to track how they spend their money on a day-to-day basis. As I said, people generally make buying decisions based on emotions. So how can we measure what a country's spending habits are? We can take a look at a country's overall economic performance. Now don't fret, I am not going to produce pages and pages of graphs and bar charts about GNP and GDP, I would rather just deal in generalisations for this purpose.

All of the aforementioned countries would often be considered to be "troublesome" economies, generally going through boom or bust scenarios throughout history. Some of the Latin American and European economies are even known as "basket case" economies, and it is not surprising when you look at the people's spending behaviours in those countries. Emotional people are generally more erratic in their decisions; in the good times people tend to spend, and in the bad times they don't. This is not meant as a judgement – it's neither good nor bad, just a reflection of the people's spending habits.

On the other hand, could you think of a few countries where the people would be considered to be more balanced or neutral in their views and day-to-day behaviours, or at least less emotional when compared with their Latin American counterparts? The Germans certainly spring to mind, the Swiss, the Nordic countries, perhaps? Their economies would be much better known for slow and steady growth year on year, which amplifies the cultural behaviours when it comes to emotions.

When you realise this, it should have a big bearing on your social media use, especially if you are a global company, as people will react very differently in different parts of the world depending on their cultural background and emotional makeup. While one audience can be quite impulsive, the other may need a lot more convincing and touch points with your product or service before jumping in and taking the plunge with your business.

While we're on the topic, let's delve that little bit deeper into the "ion" world. If you look carefully at words in the English language, almost all words that have an "ion" at the end are generally referring to a charged state. Now this is where it gets really interesting.

Consider the graph below for a moment; this time it has a trailing line from a central balanced position to negative and back. This reflects a day in the life of a regular person. At point 1 in the diagram, let's assume you wake up in a balanced state but quickly realise you have clicked snooze too many times! You are late, very late and you jump out of so bed so quickly you stub your toe at the end of the bed. You get into the shower, but all the hot water is gone. Things are not looking good and you end up at point 2 in the diagram in quite a negative state.

You quickly inhale a double espresso, the caffeine begins to kick in and things slowly begin to improve. By some miracle every traffic light into work is green and you somehow make it into work just ahead of your boss, who doesn't notice that you have just arrived. In fact, your boss takes time out to acknowledge your time keeping and in front of all your colleagues makes a point of highlighting how reliable you are. Now we are certainly moving through 3 and onto 4 in the diagram. You are in quite a positively charged space... A space, may I add, that will never last very long!

One of your colleagues, decides to make fun of you as soon as your boss leaves, commenting on how you are the boss's pet, that you get constant favours and that you are treated differently to everyone else. You start to feel embarrassed and perhaps even disappointed, and your "good" mood quickly moves through stage 5 into 6, where you just aren't feeling all that great anymore; in fact, you feel very poorly. Your best friend at work then chimes in and supports you, commenting that your other colleague is only jealous and wishes they have had the smarts that you have, and on it goes. The constant movement from one side to the next, up and down, up and down.

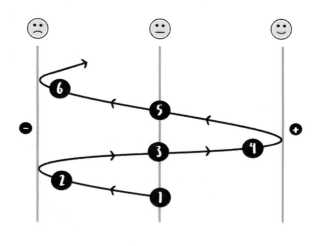

Fig 8.4: Daily emotional rollercoaster

When your partner asks you at the end of your day at work "How was your day?", the inevitable stories of the "up and down" day begin. As I said earlier, most people live in complete oblivion to this and truly have no idea that this journey takes place every single moment. In fact, a journey is exactly what it is. You could call it a "quest" perhaps, the continuous and ever-moving quest through life. The "quest of the ion".

Now what word does that remind you of? The clue is in the question ☺. Yes, "question"! You may have heard the much-used phrase, *"the quality of your life is determined by the quality of the questions you ask"*.

Your perspective when it comes to your mood, emotions and feelings on a day-to-day basis is often determined by the type of questions you ask, and this rolls up into a lifetime. As long as you ask questions of yourself that are disempowering, like "why do bad things always happen to me?", "why can't I lose weight?" and perhaps "why am I always broke?", it will continue to put you in a place mentally where it is difficult to see a solut-ion. On the other hand, when your quest-ions are solut-ion based, it puts you in a more empowering frame of mind, where you can focus on the real problem. Questions like "what can I do to bring more joy / money / health into my life starting now?" wouldn't be a bad starting point.

Let's take a closer look at the two polar ends of the diagram, where we have our highly positive and highly negative charged states, starting with a highly-charged positive vibration. What English word might we consider to describe a highly positively charged state? Let me give you a clue, it too ends in an "ion". This one may not come as a surprise initially. "Passion" is a highly-charged positive state. In fact, most often you are "pass"ing the "ion" from a highly-charged negative state to a highly-charged positive state, and with this comparison of polar opposites in place, you can become very charged about a particular situation.

If you have any interest in the personal development field, no doubt on numerous occasions you will have heard about the importance of passion in your life, whether that is finding your passion or living with passion. What are you passionate about?

It is a word I hear regularly from students and when consulting with clients, when they discuss how passionate they are, or at least were, about their business but their passion has disappeared. However, I am not a big believer in finding your passion or living with passion. If you have a spare moment, please find yourself a dictionary and look up what the word "passion" means. It might surprise you that one of the definitions of the word is "the sufferings of a martyr". In other words, passion = suffering. Yes, you read this correctly, passion means suffering. Now there's a bit of a shocker. Have you been chasing your "suffering" all this time and wondered why you don't feel fulfilled? It is probably more accurately defined in my mind, as being willing to endure suffering to achieve a specific goal. But most people never associate passion with suffering, quite the opposite in fact.

Let's explore this a little more before we draw any conclusions. Passion is a highly-charged positive state. The problem with anything in a highly charged state is that it is not sustainable, it always seeks its opposite to get back to the natural state of neutrality or balance. Have you ever had a passionate affair? I love asking this question to audiences in different cultures all over the world. In some countries, people can be acutely aware of the camera at the back of the room and very few hands are raised, while in Australia recently, we had an overwhelming "YES", with some participants even raising both hands in the air!

Ok, let's assume that you have at least watched a passionate affair on television or the movies at some point. What do passionate affairs have in common? To begin with, they start with a highly excited or charged state. Both people in the relat-ion-ship want to rip each other's clothes off to express their passion as quickly as possible. Patience, second guessing, rationality, and thinking it through disappear for a while. In most cases, the highly charged state eventually runs its course when one or both partners realise that their one-sided perspective turned out to be a fantasy. No, she wasn't single, in fact she has seven children. No, he wasn't just seeing me, and I wasn't the first affair he had! Inevitably, the equal and opposite negative charge comes in to end the suffering and bring you back to balance, ending with a BANG... boom boom!

This is a light bulb moment for many people I speak to. For their entire lives they have been chasing a one-sided fantasy, either in relationships or in business, only to find that it is never what they expected. Now, I should add here that I am sure some of you are asking, "so what do you want us to do- go around and live our lives with zero passion, like zombies?" That is a great quest-ion. People LOVE to be passionate. My take on this is to select a different word. Replace passion with enthusiasm. Be enthusiastic about you do. See both sides and embrace them equally and LOVE it. As Dr Demartini puts it so eloquently,

"Love is nothing more than the synthesis and synchronicity of complimentary opposites."

Are you in a relat-ion-ship? You would probably agree that there are times that you truly love your partner and times when you are ready to kill them. This is love, embracing both sides equally. So be enthusiastic rather than passionate – set yourself up for success.

Positive thinking is in a similar vein to this. I am certain that at some point in your life you have heard about the importance of positive thinking or been encouraged to see the sunny side of a problem or stop focusing on the negative, etc., and there are millions of dollars spent on books and courses every year on the topic of positive thinking. You are probably going to guess where I'm going with this, right? If you are a positive thinker you are chasing one side of the coin. You are chasing something that cannot exist without the complementary opposite. The more you focus on positive thinking, the more you draw negative into your life.

Look at the original father of "positive thinking", Norman Vincent Peele, who wrote the book The Power of Positive Thinking all the way back in 1952. His own wife admitted that Norman was one of the most, if not the most negative person she had ever met. He himself said he created positive thinking to balance out the negative in his life; how interesting! The first time I heard this, I really laughed out loud, it was so beautifully perfect. We have all heard of the public optimist and the private pessimist! Now at no point do I claim to be a psychologist, but I do love to study people and the way we think, and sometimes I think not having been channelled through the standard processes of thinking about these areas and instead exploring them based on what I see in real life has helped my marketing, and that of my clients, enormously. Look for the balance!

What about the other side of the coin? What is the opposite of passion? What is a highly-charged negative state? Have a think about this one and don't cheat, don't peek ahead ☺. Once again it ends with an -ion. The answer is "depress-ion". To "depress" means to push down or to hold something down, in this case pushing down the charge. A depressed state is when someone is in a mindset where they have a perspective that involves a double negative.

First and foremost, the person in that state can only see negatives in their current scenario. The best way to explain this is with an example. Let's say that you are depressed because you are broke, or have no job, or a combination of both. If you ask that person what are the positives of this situation, they most likely will have a very one-sided perspective, and at first glance they will tell you there are no positives. Now, you know better, that there is no negative without a positive. All it takes is a little reframe of the quest-ion to change the illus-ion of one-sidedness. What are the benefits of not having a job?

Please let me kick off, if you don't mind.

1. You don't have to get up on Monday mornings for work (the dream for most people)

2. You don't have to get up any morning for work, for that matter (truly living the dream!)

3. You don't have a boss to report to

4. You are not stressed out over your job

5. You can spend all the time you like with your family

6. You are not worried about how you will be treated by your colleagues

7. You don't have any colleagues that you hate

8. You are not worried about getting fired every day

9. You don't need to stress about being late for work

10. You don't have to concern yourself with the goals of a company

11. You are not exchanging time for money

12. You don't have any direct reports to manage

13. You have no performance review coming up that you are concerned about

14. You can spend the days filling your mind with great books

15. You can spend time watch training videos on any variety of useful training

16. You can sign up for government benefits

17. You can avail yourself of the various free training programs and get back to work schemes that are provided free of charge

18. You can start your business right away

19. You can run your business with wifi and a laptop, without leaving your house

20. You can study strategies for multiple streams of income and get started on building a few

21. You don't have the excuse of most employees that they "don't have enough time" to break from the rat race.

I could continue and add another 80 if need be! These are the benefits of not having a job, so what about not having money or being broke? Well the system remains the same, start with one and then keep going until you have added enough benefits that you or your friend truly sees that there is an equal number of positives to the apparent "negatives", and there may not in certain cases, be anything to be depressed about.

Well perhaps you are thinking, "well go on, enlighten me, what are the benefits of having no money? I sure as hell can't see any at all..." Ok, well since you asked so nicely ☺.

1. You don't lose sleep at night wondering what the stock market is going to do and if it will wipe out your hard-earned savings

2. You don't get stressed if you have chosen the right savings accounts and setup

3. You don't live in fear of the IRS coming to get you at any moment

4. You are not worried about your children being kidnapped for a ransom

5. You are not bothered by paparazzi day and night following your every action

6. You don't have every charity in your city, chasing you looking for handouts

7. You are not worried that your partner is with you only for the money

8. Your house is unlikely to be targeted by criminals to steal your safe

9. You are not concerned about the latest exotic disease carried by mosquitos in the countries you just visited

10. You are not concerned about a downturn in the economy that will put your houses into negative equity – and possibly you out on the street.

I hope you are getting the idea here. Sometimes the upside is not very obvious until it's pointed out. You won't often be thanked for attempting this exercise, and I don't recommend you use this with people who are suffering without firstly seeking out qualified professionals on the topic.

In addition to having an illusion that their current situation only has negative outcomes, the other element of depression is a partner fantasy in which they compare their life to somebody else's fantasy. Again, let's use an example: you are still depressed about your lack of money and you don't see any positives. You are also comparing yourself to someone who has $1 million in the bank, who you've seen on television, and to you that person's situation may be the idea of all your prayers and dreams being answered. You see only the positives of being wealthy, where you live a problem-free existence. The exercise to bring this into balance is to counteract the one-sidedness by finding the negatives associated with having $1 million. Oh, did I mention a "mill-ion" dollars – a thousand ions! There should be no shortage of negatives ☺.

Let's kick it off as before. Just like the benefits of being broke, many of them correspond with drawbacks of being wealthy, but let's add in a few more to complete the exercise. Ok, for starters:

1. You are suspicious of one of your cleaners who could be stealing jewellery from around the house

2. After you came into this money, most of your previous friends now think you are mean and that money has changed you

3. Your family constantly squabble over you and your money, all looking for their piece of the pie

4. Your children have become little divas, expecting everything to be handed to them on a plate

5. Your brand new car just got "keyed" by someone just because it was a nice car and they didn't have one. On and on it goes!

To summarise the depression side, it is a combination of missing the positives in the negative situation and comparing to a positive fantasy in which you don't see any negatives. I suggest if you do want to take this any further than just reading for interest and would like to apply any of the concepts, please refer to the Breakthrough Experience for a complete holistic perspective on how to handle this.

What if we go a little deeper with our ions? Are there any more nuggets that we can investigate that will give us an almost unfair advantage when it comes to dealing with people on social media in the future? Let's go back to our little diagram and add in some more very interesting plays on commonly-used words. If the quality of your life is determined by the quality of the quest-ions that you ask and you are one ever-moving ion on a quest, what is your mission? This is a term used not only in our work lives, but also in military and religious organisations, and many more.

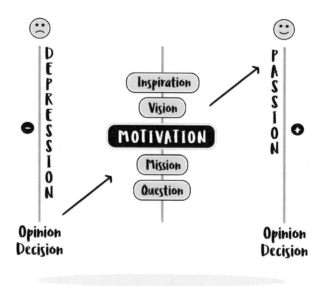

Fig 8.5: Moving between poles

Mission comes from the Latin "meso" or meeting point; the meeting point of the ions. In other words, your overall mission is where you continue to come back to regardless of your ups and downs; it is your core, your midpoint, your hinge, your purpose and focus in this life. Vision, similarly, has a deeper meaning from a root word perspective. "Visio" means to see. In other words, your vision is to see where your movement of charges is leading you, to see where you are going.

What about words like decision or opinion? Both are very important words when acting as a marketer, knowing what the person's view of the world is (opinion) and what likely outcome will result (decision) from it.

Opinion comes from the Latin word "opinari", meaning to think or to believe. In other words, having an opinion is to think or believe in one particular ion/charge or one side. I love this word, especially as it relates strongly to social media. When is the last time that you saw or read a beautifully poised and balanced post, with both sides argued to completion, that got shared or went viral? It simply doesn't happen. Rather it is opinions that get shared, as they attract supporters and challengers in equal measure, in many cases. You might call someone a leader when you agree with their stance, while you might have a tendency to call them opinionated if you don't agree. Sound familiar? The more black or white the opinion, the more interact-ion it causes, as it is a highly charged state; the higher the charge, the bigger the equal and opposite response.

Decision comes from the Latin word "decidere", or to cut off. Very similarly to opinion, it is to cut off or to believe in a side and go with it. Jim Rohn has a great quote on decision that is very appropriate here:

"It doesn't matter which side of the fence you get off on sometimes. What matters most is getting off. You cannot make progress without making decisions."

We have already discussed the importance of an individual's values and how motivation feeds into this. Motivation is what you need when what you "should" be doing is naturally low on your list of values. If you find yourself saying, "I should be doing this", "I should be doing that" – as Tony Robbins calls it, "shoulding all over yourself" – you know what you "should" be doing is low on your list of values. "Moto" and "ion" are present here too. Moving the ion from a really negative place to a hugely positively-charged space is how one can become motivated very easily. This is a tactic used in most motivational seminars to get people worked up and feel "charged", which inevitably ends up being quite-short term in its benefits, as you will never continue to do anything that is low on your list of values. As Zig Ziglar famously said:

"People often say that motivation doesn't last.
Well, neither does bathing - that's why we recommend it daily."

Inspiration, on the other hand, like the word enthusiasm that we discussed above, is one of the magic words of our existence as far as I am concerned. The word inspire means to instil great hope, joy or enthusiasm into others. BUT it also has a much simpler meaning: to inspire is to breathe in, the opposite of expire. When you inspire or feel inspired, it is because you are in flow with what is within you, what comes from deep within you. You will never need to be motivated to do what inspires you.

Taking Action

Let us return to our diagram again and study the polar opposites one more time. What feelings in our lives are represented at the emotional opposites? What are two feelings that we associate with positive and negative charges? Most often they are pleasure and pain.

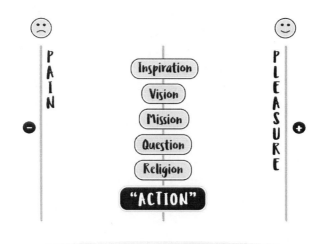

Fig 8.6: The meaning of action

On the negative left side, I have added pain, and directly across from this we have pleasure. Pain and pleasure are two of the most basic stimuli for humans. All of our decisions are based around avoiding pain or gaining more pleasure. Generally speaking, we react a lot more to avoid pain than to gain pleasure. Think about this, even in your life where you run through the ritual each morning to motivate yourself to get out of bed. It would be so pleasurable to sleep for another hour, but on the other hand, if you are late for work again, this time you could get fired, have no money to pay the bills and miss the mortgage payments, so you might have to move in with the mother-in-law. Before you know it, you are up and getting ready for work! I'm sure you've heard the saying many times that "bad news sells", and it absolutely does. We as humans are compelled to take more action as a result of bad news rather than good or neutral news. Numerous studies on email subject lines show the same results, with the top open rates being associated with negative subject lines, followed by positive subject lines, followed in the end with neutral or balanced subject lines.

This point may not seem overly important, but it is actually hugely important in the greater scheme of things. We do indeed react quicker and with more intensity to pain than pleasure. Let's think this through with another example. At the start of every year, a lot of people go through the same habit that they have each year of setting some short-term goals with almost zero expectation of meeting them. Do you recognise what I am referring to? Your New Year's resolutions ☺. What seems as a well-intended, "positive" exercise can have quite the opposite effect. Have you ever given up smoking on January 1st only to resume January 8th or 9th? What about joining the gym the first week in January, as this year is going to be different, only to forget about your big plans roughly 2 or 3 weeks later, despite your best intentions at the start?

As I see it, the problems with New Year's resolutions are three-fold. Firstly, as it is a habitual process, people are conditioned to set goals that are unrealistic, as they don't truly intend on keeping them long-term. This is compounded if you are setting the same goals from the previous year, as you proved to yourself once before that you could not stick to the goals and hit your targets. Secondly, New Year's resolutions are generally focused on the person setting them, so they are personal goals. We are conditioned to let ourselves down; we do it all the time and never get overly bothered if we once again do not meet our personal targets. However, many of us will do our very utmost to make sure we don't let others down, like our partners or family members. Thirdly, many resolutions will involve going through pain to bring about some unguaranteed pleasure, like having to eat less and move more in the gym and sweat a whole bunch to maybe lose a measly kilogram or two that no one will notice and will probably come back again. People tend to avoid pain and seek pleasure, so if you set up your resolution to lose weight around seeking pain and avoiding pleasure, you are truly setting yourself up to fail. You are going against your nature!

In order for you, or anyone else for that matter, to take ACT-ION, (incidentally one of my favourite words in the English language), or to

"ACT" on the "ION", you need to create the ion to act upon. In other words, you need to create a situation that gets the individual charged!

People can only act on the ion if they are charged in the first place. We need to get SUPER charged. The best way to do this is to charge up the pain and the pleasure involved in the decision. If, for example, you really needed to take action on something, you could firstly stack up all the amazing benefits of doing this and the associated pleasure that will result. You then look at all the negatives associated with you not doing it. Look at all the drawbacks, downsides and pain points of not doing it. Moving this pain from you to the ones you love is even more powerful – what levels of pain will you add to their lives if you don't do this now? Organisations have known how to make use of this inherent human reaction for many years. As such, some of the richest organisations in the world today are set up in a black and white manner, where you are punished if you are bad and rewarded if you are good. Can you think of what they might be?

Relig-ion rolls in with a big ion attached ☺. "Relig" comes from the word "religate" or to "bind"; to connect or bind the charges. In essence, religion is meant to explain to us the meaning behind all the ups and downs, the negatives and the positives that happen on a daily basis, to join the dots for us, so to speak. Is it any wonder religious organisations are so wealthy when these are some of our biggest questions: "what is it all about?" and "why are we here?" The pain/pleasure aspect in religion is most commonly going to hell or heaven, or the equivalent, depending on how well you obeyed the rules of the particular group you're associated with. Churches are one of the earliest forms of social media, where communities would come together for a joint cause.

This is a lot to take in, especially in just one segment of a chapter, but think about its implicat-ions! The entire purpose of an online business is to move people through the journey of Interaction to Conversion and ultimately Monetisation.

Interact-ion:

On social media, through our posts and ads, we want to create a response to charge people up enough emotionally in order to interact with us through a like or a share or a comment.

Convers-ion:

Reaching the mecca of online business involves charging people sufficiently so that they wish to converse with us. In order for them to converse, we need them to provide us with their contact details – in other words, their email addresses! We can bring about this conversion through our marketing and advertising.

Monetizat-ion:

The focus of this book is that you can learn how to charge people so that you can charge people! There was a big WOW from me the first time I spotted this! When I realised this for the first time, it made me very enthusiastic about sharing it with the world, as it all made so much sense. As Dale Carnegie famously said:

> *"When dealing with people, remember you are not dealing with creatures of logic, you are dealing with creatures of emotion."*

Summary:

People are emotional creatures. Where you are from and how old you are both have a strong impact on how emotional you are. This has major implications for how people spend their money, and understanding this emotional cycle can help enormously when it comes to marketing and sales. Learning how to charge or "ionise" people to make them take action sooner rather than later is vital in attaining financial success.

Traditional Thinking:

Your goal is to do whatever it takes to get your prospects to take the appropriate action.

RETHINK:

In order to have your prospects take action, there are a number of emotional factors at play; when you get them right, it will make an enormous difference to your marketing results. Focus on moving people from the interaction phase to the conversion stage and then into monetization. You must learn how to charge people so that you can charge people!

Part 3: The Social Youdia Journey

"The journey of a thousand miles begins with a single step."
- Lao Tzu

People want to be listened to! That is one major reason why people use social media in the first place, so that they can vent, complain or boast. More often than not, people on social media are on one side of the polar chart we described earlier. Let's look at the chart again here, but this time with superimposed aspects from one particular social network. Let's use Facebook as the example this time.

On the left-hand side where we have the negative charges, we have people on Facebook who go there to complain about everything from their lives to their kids, their partners, their jobs, the traffic, the weather and even their boss, who they forgot could see what they were posting ☺. I sometimes refer to these people as the "poor me, please feel sorry for me" people. These people want to vent their frustrations and have somebody listen to what they have to say. They are certainly not going on to Facebook to hear about a company's latest great offer and discounts.

On the other side, we have the positive charges, or the "boasters", as I like to call them; the "poor you for not being me" ☺. Generally, these people only show the amazing things that happen in their lives. They could be very quiet for a very long time, when suddenly, over a period of one hour, 235 photos of them in the Maldives appear, with their perfectly tanned body, beautiful partner and three gorgeous children, who appear never to have cried since they were born and seem to all be top of their respective classes and sporting events. These two types of people are the polarised "poor me" and "poor you" complainers and boasters.

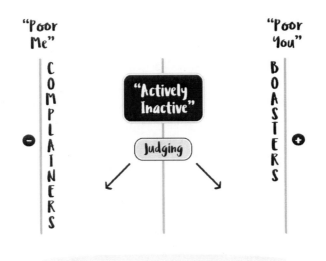

Fig 8.7: Poor me vs. poor you

There is a much larger group of people on Facebook (and the other social networks too) – the group that sit somewhere in the middle. I call them the "actively inactive" or "stalkers". They are there just to keep an eye on others, looking at who they are feeling sorry for and who they may be jealous of; their equal and opposite friend types ☺. You may very well be in this group, sitting, watching, judging without engaging so much. Now who am I to judge this behaviour ☺? These are the three prevalent groups that exist, and it is up to you to decide which you are in, or if you float between them at various times depending on your emotions.

The groups I am interested in the most are the complainers and the boasters. My social media advertising campaigns are mostly aimed at them. People who are charged are most likely to take ACT-ion, and I will utilise networks in a variety of ways either to find the charged people or go where it is most likely that people will be charged. I will elaborate on exactly how later in the book.

Now that you are aware of the different types of people you are dealing with, what is the journey we wish to take them on? I recommend that you use a five-stage system to follow, which helps enormously in planning the management of your relationships moving forward. One of the best comparisons to explain how these five stages work is to once again bring the idea to the fore once more ofbusiness and personal relationships being merely a different form of the same thing to the fore once more.

Imagine or take your mind back to a time when you were in a job and you were single. One day a new girl or guy joins the company and holy cow, they are seriously hot, just your type, and you are feeling confident in your chances. What is the first thing you would do? Well maybe that's the wrong question, that very much depends on your tact and skills in this area. Let me rephrase it, what is the first thing you should do?

Stage 1: Awareness (getting attention)

Your first objective is to GET NOTICED ☺. I don't necessarily mean getting noticed at all costs or by falling down the stairs in front of them accidentally because of your nerves. The key is to get noticed, because unless they know you exist, the game doesn't even begin; they MUST know that you exist, so you need to exist in their awareness. Competition may be very high, as this person has just joined the company and there are lots of potential suitors all vying for attention. What can you to do get his or her attention that makes you stand out from the rest without making a complete fool of yourself? A great place to start would be to study that person's habits and their movements, so you can start to plan where to find the person based on recent behaviour. What does this person do every day at roughly the same time?

Perhaps it is as simple as noticing that they go to the water font at roughly the same time every day. If you just happen to be at the water font at the same time on more than one day without getting creepy about it? and without even putting in much effort, that person will inevitably become aware of you because you are in the same place at the same time.

Stage 2: Like (encouraging interaction)

What if you continue to do this every day? At some point, the ice needs to be broken, and what better way than with humour! Humour is always the best strategy to break down the initial barriers of unfamiliarity. We would then ideally have the person LIKE us. How can we get this person to LIKE us? Well that generally happens by giving something first. A great book on this is The Go-Giver by Bob Burg and John David Mann. If you are continuing to meet at the same spot every day by the water font, obviously you are limited to doing something in that general area, unless you have learnt something else about the person's hobbies or interests during your initial light conversations. Let's assume you have learnt nothing else, what can you do?

One option would be to be there in advance and as they approach, have the cup filled and ready for them. You need a certain amount of familiarity before you can do this but it doesn't take too long, and you could even make a joke about it. The key here is that you are not going to propose marriage on your first meeting at the water font, right? You might be smiling at this, as it seems so obvious! You are not going to ask them what their preferences are for their children's names on your second meeting either. Yet this is exactly what businesses do on social media a lot. They immediately go for the sale or go for the kill, so to speak. It simply doesn't work; in fact, it will frighten away the potential client, and most likely they will also warn similarly minded people to avoid you – a double whammy.

Stage 3: Trust (leads to conversion)

Assuming that the water filling trick went as planned and now you know that there may be a little bit of "like" in the air, there is still no commitment on either side. At this point we need to move into building TRUST. How do we do that? As human beings, we begin to trust people after they have proven to be consistent in their behaviour over time and perhaps have demonstrated on at least one occasion that they can be trusted with a secret, or something similar. In the little meeting by the water font, showing up consistently at the same time and eventually winning the person over, and even not putting roofies into the water, would be a step in the right direction, right? If, however, you show up on Monday full of jokes and the joys of life but on Wednesday, you pick up the water font and throw it to the floor in anger, it probably isn't looking good for furthering your relationship.

Stage 4: Buy or refer (monetization)

I am joking, of course, but familiarity will eventually lead to trust developing, and then over time stage 4 may be reached. There are no guarantees with stage 4. Stage 4 is sealing the deal or making the sale. You need to move the person out of the work environment in order to move things along, unless you want to get fired! So how will this happen? In your case, it's moving to a first date away from the water font so that you can further research the person's wants and needs. Are they single, first and foremost? Are they straight or gay? Do they have a particular type? Are they just out of a relationship or perhaps have no interest in a relationship? Over time you will be able to ascertain the answers, either directly or through finding other sources where you can learn a little more about this person, perhaps through colleagues or some simple stalking on social media ☺.

Let's assume that everything works in your favour and the first date goes ahead; well then fantastic, you have made the initial sale successfully. Another option may be that timing is not quite right now, that there is a time gap required before such a sale can be made, perhaps as they have just come out of a previous relationship. However, if it turns out that they are not a potential suitor, that may not be the end. If you have taken care of the first three steps correctly, they will refer you to a friend who is looking for your "services", just like in business ☺. Now you might find this funny, but it is definitely a good way to start to think about how you move through your social "dance" with your new prospect.

Stage 5: Relationship (ongoing communication)

As we've seen, although you may have done all of the "right" things at this point in time, the stars may just not be aligned for you right now. It is a "no" for now, but potentially not forever! Alternatively, you may have received the initial "all clear" or "yes" from your prospect, who has now clearly let you know that they want to progress things to the next level whether that is dating outside of the working environment! The final stage is to take this initial relationship, regardless of whether it resulted in a "no" or a "yes", to continue to nourish the seeds that have been sewn. This takes place by firstly continuing the conversation and ensuring not to suddenly turn "cold" and neglect this person after all the initial groundwork is already in place.

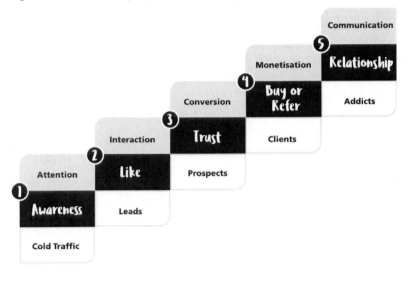

Fig 8.8: The ascension model of cold traffic through an evolving relationship

Ok, enough about the water font; let's bring this back to social networks. Stage 1 is to build awareness by grabbing attention. Start by having your basic social media presence in place; let's say a blog, Twitter account, Facebook page and YouTube channel. Start by running ads on those, to at least let your potential lead know you exist. This is where you start, setting up the pages on each platform. Get the name of your business for each, if possible, and add your logo, branding and any links to a website that you may have. You will then need to get this new account or page in front of potential suitors. To do this you will go where they most likely hang out and place your ads. Where is their water font? Where do they hang out on a regular basis? Refer back to the segment on avatar creation where necessary.

If you know the type of person you are looking for, and depending on your budgets at this point, you can go directly to your competitors' accounts on Twitter and start to target their followers who you know will be interested in what you do too. You can look for groups that discuss these topics on Facebook or LinkedIn and build engagement there. Alternatively, you can cut to the chase and ask Twitter and Facebook to lead you directly to where your people are hanging out – this is done by running paid ad campaigns. What a phenomenal opportunity, where you have the potential to leverage access to millions of your ideal clients by paying a social network to do the hard work for you! Ideally, you need to match your message with your audience, and they will start liking your content and perhaps even sharing it with others.

In order to move them to the trust stage, you need to be consistent in your posting. We mentioned earlier that inconsistent posting was one of the big mistakes that businesses can make on social media. When you continue to show up and offer them incentives to leave their email address with you, usually it will be only a matter of time before the people who are interested will take things to the next level and provide you with their details to continue the conversation. Once you have their email address and they have joined your database, you can contact them on an ongoing basis. You now begin the journey of building a trusting relationship with this person over time. Just like in the example earlier, we will build this trust through consistency in behaviour and continuing to live up to any promises made and, where possible, over-deliver on any expectations that were pre-framed at the start of your relationship when you collected their contact details.

The 4th stage is to move towards making the sale. If the marketing is done correctly at this point, selling becomes almost unnecessary. Purchasing the product or service should appear to be a complete no-brainer to the prospect at this point. We would start by testing the waters with an immediate upsell, which we will discuss in greater depth later, and then follow up over time with content and shortcuts to their solutions that are available to buy. At all times, we will continue to move them through a process of why it is a completely natural decision to invest in this product or service.

The final stage of "ongoing communication", as the title suggests, is not a one-off process. This is the key step of forming relationships and building them into deeper trusting connections over time. There will be many items offered to your database over time, and the more they trust you, the easier the sales take place. Building ongoing relationships is a process in itself that deserves further discussion. Considering that most of your future sales are dependent on this stage being managed well, building relationships through ongoing communications is the most important of the 5 stages, in my opinion. If you have any experience in online marketing at all, I'm sure you will have heard many times before that the "money is in the list". This implies the more people on the list, the more money you make, almost on autopilot. I would suggest to you that the **money is not in the list itself but in the relationship that you have with the list**.

Relationships are a complicated business! One minute, things can appear to be rosy in the garden, but before you know it they can be completely toxic, and you may not even know why.

There are multiple "Rs" to keep in mind when it comes to the communication plan that you have to nurture your "relationship" with your list.

1. **Retain:** First and foremost, after going to all the trouble of getting people onto your database, you want to be sure to keep them there. It can be a tricky balance to maintain. People will only stay provided that they see the value in staying subscribed and that you are not making yourself an annoyance by being in contact too much.

2. **Remind:** For the majority of your list who are your non-buyers, you want to remind them from time to time of what change or result they are missing out on by not taking your relationship to the next level and purchasing your core product. You also want to remind them who you are. It is all too easy to become a distant memory in today's environment. Just think about musicians who take a sabbatical for a year or more – how quickly you can forget their names! There is always someone ready and waiting to jump in and take your place.

3. **Reinvigorate:** From the moment you first spark your audience's interest with a particular idea, there is an inevitable decline in interest, as some other priority in their lives takes its place. One of the key purposes of your communication plan in the relationship phase is to reinvigorate your database by showing them why what they signed up to learn about is just as important as it was when they began your relationship.

4. **Relevance:** Your list is made up of a particular segment of people who are looking for a solution that you provide. Within that group,

however, there will naturally be smaller micro segments that have particular niche interests within the overall niche. For example, if your niche is social media marketing, for some segments of your list a programme on "Ranking your business on the front page of YouTube" is relevant, while for others a programme on "How to find other businesses' products to sell" will appeal more. By following up with different free gifts in these different areas you can increase the average transaction value of your clients while unveiling more potential goldmines within your current database.

5. **Refresh:** Within any niche, regardless of the one you choose to go with, there is an inevitable injection of new ideas and new products and solutions over time. Keeping your list abreast of these latest changes assists in not only reminding them of your ongoing relevance but refreshes their interest, and of course, gives you the opportunity to sell other offerings.

6. **Renew:** As you become more experienced, you will inevitably start to look at making offerings to your clients that involve some form of a renewal program like a membership site for a weekly, monthly or annual subscription fee. This gives your higher-end value clients the opportunity to retain their close relationships with your business. Even if the charge is automatic, it is a good idea to remind your client of the importance of the renewal and what they are gaining with the membership – and accordingly, what they would miss outside of the programme.

7. **Rethink:** Ideally, you want to be somewhat disruptive in what you do with your relationship with your list, so that you stand out from others. Always look to do more for your list than others would. Give more for free than others would. Use examples of your clients as testimonials

and showcase them to your list. Make videos for them regularly and really let them know that you care about them more than others. For example, I look to create at least two brand new videos per week exclusively for my email list so we keep the relationship fresh and keep my business top of mind. This will build a very strong community around your brand and will lead to the next "R"

8. **Referrals:** One of my mentors, Keith Cunningham, asks business owners: *"what would you do differently in your business if you could only get new business through referrals?"* It is a very powerful question! The relationship you build with your list can encourage the building of an army of referrals. If you encourage your list to recommend you to just two more people, that can increase your business sizably. Make it easy for your clients to refer you. Create a system that encourages them to easily perform this task, resulting in them being rewarded.

9. **Reward:** In order to create a list of prospects and clients who are very loyal to you, it can be a great idea to have a rewards system almost like an airline's frequent flyer programme. If they hit certain targets, for example, you can reward them with Amazon vouchers or something small and then showcase them to the rest of the database, which reinforces the reasons for being on that list and continuing with the relationship in the first place.

10. **Regular:** This "R" is a catch-all to ensure that regardless of the intention behind each message you send that you keep your communications regular. This means your leads become familiar with you and trust you more with each and every contact.

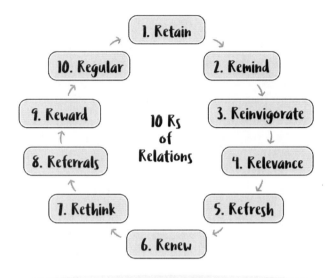

Fig 8.9: The 10 "Rs" of relationship management

Summary:

Engaging with people on social media is no different than in real life. We don't start a conversation with a new person by asking them to marry us and naming our future children ☺. We must take people on a journey from complete strangers to trusted friends. This happens through a 5-stage journey: 1. Awareness, 2. Like, 3. Trust, 4. Buy or refer, and 5. Relationship. Each stage is managed differently in terms of your marketing, as you have different micro goals at each point. Selling is not attempted until stage 4.

Traditional Thinking:

Your key focus on social media is to make sales so that you can see the direct impact on the bottom line. You can worry about the relationship side of things later!

RETHINK:

Social media is not for selling products or services in most instances. It's about creating awareness and building up trust over time through consistency in advertising and marketing, ultimately resulting in the person agreeing to move your relationship out of the exclusivity of a social platform and into another means of more personal communication such as email.

Part 4: Your Traffic Options

"Be patient, everything is coming together."

- Anon

The world of social networks, let alone social media, can be extremely confusing and overwhelming.

There are many roles that social networks can play, including:

- Customer support

- Communication

- HR

- Sales

- Marketing

- Internal staff communication

- Forums

- Education

- Events

- Live streams

- Video

- Instant messaging

- And many more…

Where do you even start? What follows is a breakdown of some of the main social networks that you may consider using as a traffic source and the RETHINK philosophy for each network.

Twitter (Est 2003):

Twitter is used to share short, succinct messages about you or your business with other people who are interested in what you do and have decided to follow you as a result. Its initial intent was to be used as a group text messaging system, where you could text all of your friends at once, hence why the initial restriction on message was only 140 characters, although this has since been lifted. People really struggle at times to understand why anyone would use Twitter. It certainly is an amalgamation of people who like to share with the world what they are thinking about at a particular point in time for no particular reason.

Traditional Thinking:

- "Why would I care that Jenni just had a coffee in Starbucks? I don't care!" is a common type of remark that I hear.

- It's used only by teenagers following celebrities.

- It's almost completely dead as a network.

- Twitter ads don't work.

RETHINK:

- You shouldn't care that Jenni is having a coffee if you use social media the way most users do, which is to just pass some time and keep an eye on what's going on. However, as a marketer who owns a coffee shop just up the road from where Jenni tweets every day about her coffee, you become very interested as you are not a "user", you are a "marketer" who sells coffee and you have just found an addict for your product!

- Twitter can be used to literally hand pick individuals from all over the world who are expressing that they have a specific problem and can take less than seconds to do this search.

- It is also used by businesses not only to find potential clients, but to keep their followers posted on updates.

- The advanced search feature allows you to track people not only by what they say but where they are located.

- You can target people who are watching specific television shows and advertise specifically to those people who are in a charged state.

- You can build a database by sending someone directly from clicking an image on your home tweet to your lead magnet.

Facebook (Est 2005):

Facebook is a network that allows individuals to connect with friends and family to share their life experiences and other titbits of funny or interesting information with each other. It is also used by businesses to find their ideal clients based on the behaviours of these people while on Facebook.

Traditional Thinking:

- It's for young people who just want to show off to their friends any time something "cool" happens in their lives, and a tool for their parents to show off their holiday pics or those of their children.

- As a business, your first objective is to set up a page and constantly tell people about your products and services and offer discounts. You should also include the odd motivational quote or picture of a cat to keep your audience engaged.

- If anyone puts up a bad comment about your business, you will delete it, and if they do it again, you will block them from ever posting on your page again.

- Every single business seems to be using Facebook ads.

- If you continue to post every day 3- 4 times a day, you won't need to spend money on ads.

RETHINK:

- It is the ultimate tool for marketing available today. With its capacity to engage almost everyone in the developed world and track their likes, dislikes, interests, hobbies, relationship status, buying behaviours, where they live, work, etc., when used in the correct way, finding people to buy from your business (assuming you have good products or services) should never be a problem! The average age of a Facebook user continues to get older with time.

- It is not about talking about you; it is about asking what your consumers want and listening to them and showing that you care.

- You can use it to upload any database you may already have to target your own people with reminders about your business and to keep your brand top of mind.

- Any visitors that come to your website can be retargeted on Facebook to help them on their journey by becoming more familiar with your business and how you can help.

- It's about moving people through the awareness, like, trust and buy lifecycle.

- It can be used to handle any customer service issues that arise via that channel and used as a reputation enhancement tool.

- You can build a database without the person ever needing to type their name or email address – they just need to click a button twice.

- It is used by people who often openly express the charged state they are in, so are more likely to take action.

- Instant messenger, Instagram and WhatsApp provide even more amazing opportunities within the Facebook family.

Blogger (Est 1999):

The concept of blogging predates some of the more commonly known social networks like Facebook or Twitter. It is not a social network as such, but it is a form of social media. It allows anyone to set themselves up with a base on the internet and share information, thoughts and knowledge on a specific subject.

Traditional Thinking:

- You need to write all your own blog posts.

- You need fresh original content that no one has ever seen before three times a day.

- You need to be an expert in something to start a blog.

- People might love your hobby that you blog about and you will definitely get rich from it.

- Blogging is very difficult and time consuming.

- You must use Wordpress to have a good blog that will rank on Google.

- It costs money to set up a blog.

RETHINK:

- This might sound very harsh, but at the beginning you do not need to write any of your posts because quite simply nobody cares what you have to say ☹… yet! Until you build up your social media presence and brand, people would rather listen to people that they already know and trust (by the way, this is a good thing!).

- The blog is used to position yourself as an expert, even if you are not one to begin with. Whatever business area you choose to be in, it is quite probable that you are aware of many people and businesses that will command a lot more, if not infinitely more, respect than you do. The reason why you still can command respect is that you can share other people's content (provided it is available to share), and by default you become the one-stop-shop in the industry for all the best information, saving people a lot of time and effort searching for themselves. Remember: nobody was born into this world an expert, they had to learn the skill over time. There is no time period required.

- Your blog posts for a whole week can be scheduled in advance just once. You could organise up to 14 posts for the week in less than half an hour. It can take less than 30 seconds to share a post from

YouTube on your blog. You do not need to do this daily; organise it just once a week.

- In my tests, Blogger can work just as well as, if not better than Wordpress in terms of getting organic traffic. My thought process is simple here: Blogger is owned by Google and Google is GOD ☺.

- You can set up a blog completely free of charge at blogger.com with no hosting or domain costs required.

- It is very unlikely that you will get rich from your blog alone. It can be done, but you will need to be experienced in marketing and not just writing or blogging. You can certainly use it to build your database and drive people to your funnel or make money from advertising and promotions. You can set up links to affiliate products, like many great marketers such as John Chow and Pat Flynn, but just having a blog in itself where you write your musings will not generate you a lot of money until you upskill yourself to market with your blog.

- Your blog can be an excellent tool to generate leads, build an online business, provide great value to people and to make a lot of income once you learn the skills of marketing, not writing.

YouTube (Est 2005):

More and more, the content creation strategies of individual entrepreneurs and business owners are taking the form of video. Video has so many advantages in that it portrays a message without the consumer having to read and give their full attention. You can obviously watch and listen and read too, if it has subtitles. It generates a completely different level of engagement compared to a picture or an article. Saying that, so many businesses are slow to adapt as they don't know what to do with it. YouTube is owned by Google and is the biggest of the video hosting networks. More and more people now go to search engines like YouTube rather than Google, as they would rather "see" a solution in video than read about it. Their paid adverts are very powerful, as they work differently to Facebook and Twitter ads. Twitter and Facebook target people mostly based on what they like, do, how they behave, where they live, etc. – this is known as disruptive marketing, as the recipients are not expecting to see it. On YouTube, the focus is on behaviour-based marketing, as the person has already typed in what they are looking for, so they are ACTIVELY in action mode looking for an immediate answer to their query. This makes the prospect much warmer to begin with, as they are already in search of what you may have.

Traditional Thinking:

- Creating videos is expensive if you do them well.

- Videos are very time consuming to make.

- YouTube ads are as expensive as Google ads as they are run on the same platform.

- In order to have a successful video, it needs to be clever or different enough to go viral.

- It's impossible to have your videos seen when your competitor has been in #1 ranking for years; you can never compete.

RETHINK:

- Professionally-created videos can be relatively inexpensive if you organise them in the correct way. Green screens can be purchased for less than $100 and the same goes for perfect lighting. Any decent HD quality phone or SLR camera can now produce high-quality video. Top class video editors from the UK, Ireland and the US can be hired at minimum wage (when you know how ☺).

- Videos do not need to be time consuming. Proper organisation in advance, with scripts ready and a clear plan organised, means you could create six months' worth of top quality content in one day ready for editing.

- YouTube ads are probably the best value for money ads you can invest in at the time of writing this book. They can also be combined with

Facebook ads to double the impact. In many cases, unlike the other major networks, you can have your ad appear for free.

- You do not need to have the next viral video in order for your video to be seen. There are several clever strategies that can be employed to have your video get huge traffic without it being overly clever or different.

- You can run ads on your competitors' videos so that anyone looking at the video will have to watch yours first, to save you the time and effort of trying to shift a video from its perch on YouTube search.

LinkedIn (Est. 2002):

This network is designed for and used primarily by professionals. Since its acquisition by Microsoft, there have been some changes but overall the fundamentals remain the same. It is used to a large extent as a hiring portal for recruitment companies, but it can definitely be used successfully to build great relationships and do business.

Traditional Thinking:

- People only use LinkedIn when they are looking for a new job.

- To find business partners or clients, it is a good idea to message all my connections regularly, telling them about what I do and that it would be "good to connect".

- It is really only useful for B2B (businesses selling to other businesses) people.

- It is just one big "spamathon" of untrained or poorly-trained entrepreneurs pitching for business.

- I can't build a database from LinkedIn.

- By having my employees up on LinkedIn, I am basically putting them up on the shop floor ready to be taken by the highest bidder.

RETHINK:

- While LinkedIn is certainly used for recruitment purposes and some of its professional features help recruitment companies enormously, there are also millions of people using LinkedIn for networking and business opportunities.

- One of the worst things you can do on LinkedIn is to start sending messages to all your connections telling them how impressed you were with their profile and that you own a web design agency or a VA company that is perfect for them. This does not work and generally really annoys the recipients.

- LinkedIn is renowned for being the best network to go to for B2B contacts, and that still stands. However, never forget that every account on LinkedIn is owned by a person. Person to person marketing is always the most important of all. The average person on LinkedIn earns over $100,000 per year. They are all consumers of products. You just need to match the right product to the right consumer.

- There is a certain amount of truth in the "think" about the spam fest that goes on within LinkedIn. This is and will continue to be addressed by LinkedIn; however, this is just one minor issue and should certainly not take away from the massive opportunity within the network. Using LinkedIn groups can be a very powerful way of building your credibility as well as your relationships with peers and potential prospects.

- LinkedIn is one of the only networks where you can access all of your connections' details, such as name, email, job position and phone number, and instantly download them.

- If you are a business owner, efforts on LinkedIn from your employees should be focused on the company's LinkedIn page rather than their individual accounts, as you are in control of the page while the account will always remain with the person who created it.

Google+ (Est. 2011):

The owner of Google+ is pretty evident from the title. Of the networks listed here, it is the one most likely to disappear or at least change title. The reason I am choosing to include it is that you do need to have it if you are a local business, as I will explain.

Traditional Thinking:

- It is a completely useless network that nobody uses anymore.

- It is just a copycat of Facebook.

RETHINK:

- Google+ has a huge number of users, primarily because you can be forced to open an account when using certain Google tools. Posts shared on timelines do get quite decent engagement.

- While in many ways it looks like Facebook, it does have unique features that make it worthwhile using. Creating a Google+ page will allow you to have your business verified and then show up on Google Maps for people searching for your particular business in a local area. This is probably the biggest advantage of Google+.

- Google+ removed the Hangout feature, which was very popular for businesses, and now has more focus on communities.

Pinterest (Est. 2010):

At certain times in its development, Pinterest has had the most impressive rates of sales conversions from posts of any network. It has a demographic of mostly women, and it allows people to create boards like you might have in your kitchen to pin your reminders and shopping lists to. Users create boards for different parts of their business and use them to share primarily pictures but also articles and videos.

Traditional Thinking:

- It is only for businesses that sell B2C products like jewellery or a local business that sells cakes.

- Advertising is not possible.

RETHINK:

- Can you graphically represent what you sell or provide? It doesn't necessarily mean that you have to be product-based with an attractive looking product. Can you use visuals that will show the benefit of what your business does or the outcome it provides? If you can say yes to any of the above, Pinterest is definitely worth testing. Engagement is high and people on Pinterest tend to buy sooner than people coming from other sources.

- Although slow to launch, the Pinterest advertising model is gaining momentum. If your business is well suited, it is definitely worth testing to measure cost per lead and the value per lead that comes from new ad platforms like Pinterest.

Instagram (Est. 2010):

Instagram is a photo sharing network owned by Facebook, primarily used to give quick photo updates of what is going on in someone's life that may be interesting. It works in a similar way to Twitter in that you follow others to see their posts and they need to follow you back to see yours.

Traditional Thinking:

- It is for teenagers.

- It is only for companies similar to those mentioned for Pinterest.

- It's not worth advertising on it.

RETHINK:

- Instagram is used more and more by an aging follower base with each year that passes.

- The engagement levels are through the roof on Instagram, hundreds of times more powerful than either Twitter or Facebook

- While it certainly can benefit companies similar to what we mentioned with Pinterest, if you can use visuals to explain the benefit of your company, Instagram is worth a look.

- Instagram ads are bundled into the Facebook ads platform. It is therefore very easy to track and measure and easy to compare with your Facebook ads. Generally, the engagement is a lot higher and ads cheaper than their Facebook equivalents.

- Instagram stories are a powerful way of telling your story in an engaging manner.

- Facebook is likely to put a lot of investment into making this work even better for businesses, as it could be an extremely profitable model for them as the Facebook timelines become busier with ads.

Snapchat (Est. 2012):

Snapchat is a social network primarily used by teens that is mobile-based and allows its users to share video "snaps" with each other that disappear after a limited time. For a while, it looked like Snapchat from Snap Inc. was really going to be the next big thing! Facebook responded by introducing filter and story features into Facebook and Instagram, which seriously impacted on the initial expectations for business use.

Traditional Thinking:

- It is for teenagers only.

- It doesn't really have any business applications.

RETHINK:

- It can be worth testing if your demographic is in its teens to mid-20s.

- Use it in tandem with Instagram to find if it is worth using this separately or confining your efforts to Instagram for this style of messaging.

Livestreams:

As with all of the examples above, there are a variety of networks that do more or less the same thing. In the case of livestreams, there is no point in segregating them out so instead I will treat them as one. There are many of these with Periscope, YouTube Live and Facebook Live leading the way.

Traditional Thinking:

- They are not worth putting in the effort.

- If the first couple I test don't work, it's not worth pursuing.

RETHINK:

- When done correctly, livestreaming can be very powerful. The reach can be very good, obviously depending on your levels of connection to begin with, but they make sense to do when leveraging something else that you are doing at the same time – this can only add to the results. For example, if you are running a podcast, why not put this out over livestream at the same time. If you are running a presentation within your business or about your business that could be educational for your audience, it is worth considering livestreaming on multiple platforms using different phones.

- It is unlikely that that you are going to nail it right from the start with your livestreams! It is definitely worth becoming consistent in order to build a fan base who become familiar with you and the times you speak at. Keep testing this, as it is an amazing way to have real, live and interactive sessions with your potential clients – and it shows that you care.

- Be consistent in the timings of your livestreams and your audience will start to dramatically increase (of course, if your content is up to scratch!).

Instant messenger (Est. various):

Instant messenger sites take many forms, such as Facebook Messenger, Viber, WeChat, WhatsApp and many more. There is a huge consideration here for your marketing based on what happened in Q1 of 2015.

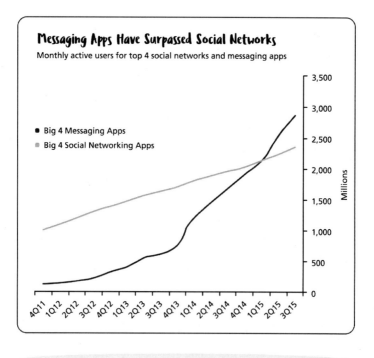

Fig 8.10: Messaging app vs. social network app usage

Ref: BI Intelligence

On that date, for the first time more people used instant messaging apps on their phones than social network apps! This has huge implications for us, because as marketers we want to follow people – they do have our money, after all ☺. Later, we will discuss the implications of instant messenger and how it has revolutionised the open rate of messages as well as potential game-changing automation features with chatbots.

Traditional Thinking:

- Instant messaging means spamming people with unwanted text messages.

- They are therefore extremely annoying.

RETHINK:

- People are now using IM apps more than social network apps.

- The average open rate of instant messages is 80-85%!

- Facebook allows you to run ads in a number of ways with Facebook Messenger.

- There are strict controls in place that will only allow you to send messages to people who have already engaged with you previously on that network.

- You can build a list directly within messenger apps without ever having to collect emails.

- An entire automated system can be built out taking people through the stages of awareness, like, trust and buy.

That should give you an overview of the major players at present, with some of the "dos and don'ts" for your business and how you apply them in each instance. I find that the easiest way to start is to have a good understanding of some of the mainstream social networks that are used initially, like Facebook and YouTube. Once you know what they do for your business and how they are differentiated, you can then look at which other networks can assist you with what you specifically wish to achieve. Only add new networks once the initial social networks you are using are being managed well.

When and where to use the various social networks – a case study

In order to help make it clearer when and how you can use the social media sites we have just reviewed, I will use a real-life example to make it easier to grasp the concepts. I assume that you currently own a coffee shop on High Street, London and that you are thinking about how you can best use a variety of social networks to help grow the business. In an ideal world, as the coffee shop owner, you should know how much on average each customer is worth to you when they come through the door. When you know this, you can really start to work out the value that social networks are bringing to you, based on how many new people they bring to your coffee shop. You can treat it almost like an online business, and facilities are there to assist you in measuring its effectiveness. Later in this book, I will walk you through exactly how you would do these calculations and find out what the right metrics are for your particular business. For now, this exercise will give you an indication of how the networks all slightly differ in their use and application.

Twitter:

As a coffee shop owner, you would generally use Twitter to post out regular short messages about something interesting that is going on in the coffee shop that day. Perhaps someone famous just walked in. Maybe the brand new fridge / oven / coffee machine just arrived. When a little more advanced, you can use it to find local coffee lovers in the vicinity and encourage them to pop in for a coffee or two. You can also add images and gifs to the posts, and you would also retweet items of interest from other Twitter accounts from around the local area, showing that you are a part of the community.

Facebook:

You can use Facebook in a number of ways, but to keep this simple we will use it as a Facebook page. You can think of your Facebook page as if it was the website for your coffee shop. People will find everything in there, including opening hours, where to find you, contact address, phone number, website, email, and any other content that you are willing to share. The difference to a website, however, is that as soon as a person "likes" the page you can now engage with them as you choose through their Facebook stream. As a coffee shop, ideally, you would post 3 to 5 times a day with images or heart-warming stories of regular visitors. You would also look to personalise the shop by sharing some details about the staff behind the scene, acknowledging various celebrations that might be occurring in their lives, like birthdays, engagements, marriages, births, etc., with photos of the team. You could just as easily share similar updates on your regular customers. You can also run competitions to increase engagement and encourage your likes to share the post with others to get more and more people engaged on your page.

YouTube and Livestream:

As a café, there are many ideas that you can use to put on your YouTube or other livestreaming channels. Obviously, you can have a promotional video for the coffee shop that might take some time and effort. It would be easier to have some simple regular videos that show "Claudine" creating one of those amazing images on a latte that she has just made, or of anything exciting that may have happened during the day, like a celebration that was taking place among staff or customers. If you can make if funny, then all the better, as more people will be likely to share. You could build up a personality profile of some of your staff members to once again make the brand more personal, and even have the staff come up with new sandwiches or ideas that the consumer can connect with. You can also select certain videos that may have a greater appeal if streamed live, to do exactly that while recording the video. Of course, keep an eye on the level and the degree of engagement and if it is worth doing. If you have a special event, or a book reading or something similar, this lends itself well to livestreaming.

Blog:

As a coffee shop owner, you can use your blog to position yourself as an expert when it comes to your core subject of expertise: coffee. On the blog, you can share information about all the different types of coffee, such as Arabica and Robusta, or discuss the types of beans from different countries and their differences, etc. At each point, of course, you can mention that this particular type of coffee is available upon request in your shop. You can also discuss the different types of coffee machines and how they affect the taste and so on. It doesn't stop there, either: you can write about anything that shows your passion for coffee, which makes you stand out from the rest, especially the big chains.

Pinterest, Instagram and Snapchat:

In a coffee shop, you are surrounded by content for your photo-sharing social networks. While so many businesses struggle for content, most don't realise that they may be surrounded by it all day. Everything from designs on coffee and where you can invite your viewers to vote for their favourite, to cupcakes and cake designs, to meals, to staff and customers – your surroundings are flowing with imagery that will make your coffee shop come alive! Snapchat can be used in a very similar vein, especially when appealing to a younger audience. Taco Bell became legendary as being one of the very first big companies to run successful Snapchat campaigns aimed at teens.

At the start of this exercise I mentioned that ideally you would look to measure the impact of what you are doing with each of these social campaigns as much as possible. The least complex of these is to offer separate coupon codes on each network offering incentives like 10% off or 2 coffees for the price of 1 when someone uses a coupon code. The codes would be different with each network that you use. At the end of the day, you can simply add up how many of each type of coupon came in. You can then work out how much you paid on each network, either through advertising or through the time spent posting, to have those coupons come into the shop. The final component is to look at the average spend of that customer when they came in. You can assume that they spent the average of your regular consumers (taking account of the second coffee that may have been free) or if you want to get really focused, you can tag each sale with the particular coupon code that was used, to give you even more accurate readings. This would be how you can instantly measure ROI on up to 8 to 10 social networks in an offline business. To make it easier, you might just offer a coupon on separate networks that can only be used on a particular day of the week.

Just to add, you are not selling here, as at no point are you looking to collect money over the social network; instead you are inviting them to come see you in person as the next step.

Google+:

As a local coffee shop, Google+ is quite important to you, as you do wish to get found on Google searches when people are looking for coffee in your area. As a business, you would open a page on Google+ and register your business, its address and all the other contact details it requires in order to complete your registration. You generally need to verify shortly after that your business is indeed located where you say it is by postcard. Once registered, you will show up on Google Maps. You can always have a coupon code on your Google+ page with a discount for the first time they come to the café to test and see how many people are coming in to your shop as a result of having found you on Google+.

LinkedIn:

LinkedIn can be a bit of an unusual one for a local coffee shop. If there is a big company across from where you are located and many of the employees are using LinkedIn, it may be worth looking at, but it is probably not the best use of your time. If, however, you were considering franchising your coffee shop, it may be the ideal place to engage with others looking to set up franchises in your area or nationwide.

These are the main sites that are most commonly used. This is not meant to be a recommendation that you need to use all of these, even if you happen to own a coffee shop; this exercise was mainly for illustration purposes, so that you can understand the differences between the networks and how they are used differently. What you need to decide is which of these are the right ones for your business. Are you offline or online, or both? Are you just thinking about starting an online business and don't really know what you should look at? What networks to most of your ideal clients use, if any?

When you start to ask yourself these questions, you can then start to figure out which of these is most likely to give you the highest return on your investment for time or money or both. Remember, if you are not seeing a real return, then it is probably not worth doing! There is no point in being on a network just for the sake of it, we need to have a RETHINK, and work out in advance what the purpose of this is: what are you expecting to see? What does success look like, and how are you measuring it? What are your cost per lead and lifetime value per customer numbers? I will assist you with this a little bit later so you can continue to RETHINK everything that you did once upon a time ☺.

How to post and when to post on these networks in an organised fashion is clearly something that also needs to be looked at, and we will come back to this in more detail in the social media plan section of the book.

Now that we know where to find the people we are looking for, we can start to focus on what it is we do with them that makes this a very profitable venture. Learning how to take the people who are "interested" in what we do and finding out who is "committed" to taking things further are critical for our success. This is the element that most people lack awareness of on their social media journey: namely, what to do when we have matched the right message with the right people. How do we take complete strangers on a journey to wishing to hand over their money?

Summary:

There are thousands of social networks being used today, and figuring out which ones to use and which to leave out of your marketing can be very tricky, cumbersome and time consuming. It is usually a good idea to look at the biggest, such as Facebook, YouTube, Instagram and Twitter, and assess as you go if the expense of using them is worthwhile. Each has a different purpose and use or slight variation of a theme. Your niche and the people you are targeting very much dictate which social networks you should be using.

Traditional Thinking:

Have a go at them all and see what sticks and if you can make more sales. Avoid spending money on social media advertising at all costs! It's a waste of money, because you can do it for free!

RETHINK:

Only choose the networks where your ideal avatar hangs out. As you have mastered one, move onto mastering the next. Measure everything in relation to what you are doing and the direct impact it is having on your business. Use advertising to get results in a fraction of the time so that you can adjust and react quicker and get profitable sooner.

Chapter 9: Help for Free

"Our prime purpose in this life is to help others.
And if you can't help them, at least don't hurt them."
- Dalai Lama

Without a doubt, one of the single most important elements of this system, and the one I'd like to speak about now, is what you need to do to collect the contact details of targeted groups of people. Without this, the entire system falls apart. Doing this in the best way possible involves understanding human psychology and combining it with the most suitable technological solutions. Let's consider for a moment why building a database is so important as a key fundamental of our business, starting with the statistics of some of the big guns.

Facebook is worth well over $500 billion and Twitter about $15 billion – and possibly a lot more when you are reading this book. But why? The value stems mostly from the size of their databases of users, and even more importantly, the knowledge they have gained about their databases. They know pretty much everything about their users: their likes, their dislikes, where they live, their purchasing behaviours, their age, the number of children they have, the ages of their children, their net worth, their income, their discretionary spend, their relationship status, the number of credit cards they have, the type of car they drive, and so on. The value that these companies have is that they can sell this data to you and me so that we can target our perfect avatar, which means you have access to this knowledge too! It's our job to build our databases from their databases, as they have done all of the hard work already; we just need to hand pick who we would like in our list. I am so grateful for this opportunity every single day because one thing's for sure, I would never have had the desire or ability to create a Facebook... lol! I would much rather piggyback their work for my purposes.

About 99% of regular people using Facebook, Twitter, Instagram and other social networks are spending hours every day keeping up with their "friends" and favourite celebs. These are the people we can often judge as to whether this is the most valuable use of their time in the first place. However, they are also the people who we want to help – and get rich doing it. Often, they themselves have no idea that they could be using this time on the same networks to literally make thousands of dollars every month, like you can!

The reason I love utilising social networks so much is that Facebook, Instagram, Twitter and many others will allow you as a marketer to target the perfect people for your business by clicking just a few buttons. This is a complete game changer even from when I started, when this quite simply was not possible; targeted traffic is now a commodity. You can now go directly to the source and request to place your ad in front of your ideal people, and then repeat over and over again at a profit! It is simply amazing!

You can target people by their language, sex, age, demographic, post code and more, as mentioned earlier. Why run an old-fashioned business that has a 90% chance of failing in just a few years, when you can find out if your business will work in just days with social media?

The concept of "helping for free" is certainly now new. The squeeze page and opt-in page and lead magnet page, which are all designed to get people to leave their details in exchange for a free gift, have been around for years. Something that has changed dramatically, however, is that you can now collect people's email addresses without them even having to type their own name and email address! Yes, it's true, with no more than a couple of clicks, and in some cases with a single click, you can collect all the information that you need! For now, don't get too hung up about any of the technicalities, as it's all very simple to do and I will be walking you through it one step at a time. In fact, I will make videos for you that you can refer to so that no matter when you read this book you will be able to watch the most up-to-date method for doing this on the most relevant social network at the time. For now, I just want to give you an idea of the basic steps involved with this contact capturing and email building tool, because by building a list of targeted people in this way, you are well on the road to great success.

This will probably be obvious to you if you've ever studied any marketing experts or know successful people in business – you'll be familiar with phrases such as: "The money is in the list..." or "You need to build a database to make serious money..."

Building a targeted database is a must. However, with the RETHINK Social Media Model I use in my businesses, and as I will explain later in the "Nourishing the relationship" segment, the list in itself is not everything. That said, as I mentioned at the start of the book, current estimates show that most businesses or successful entrepreneurs, as a rule of thumb, should make at least $1 per person on their database per month. Think about what that means for a moment. If you have 1,000 people on your email list, that list be making you a minimum of $1,000 every month – and this will only continue to grow; I emphasise the word minimum. However, by using the fully leveraged system that I will explain to you as we move on through the book, you can easily make between $4 and $5 per person per month from your list. Now think about that, it means you can average $4,000 to $5,000 per month from a tiny list of 1,000 people. Once you know how to 'harvest' people from social media sites using the system I'm teaching you, getting 1,000 people on your email list isn't exactly difficult!

Why it isn't good enough to keep people on social media?

Once you are clear about the type of people you are looking to attract, the next part is to secure a more definitive means of communication. You want to find out more of their details like their email addresses, and collect them to reuse them as a means of contact later. Although somebody may "like" or "follow" you on a particular network, regardless of how much or how often you post on social media, there is no guarantee that those people will see your message. You need to have their attention while they are on the phone or laptop, not while you are sending your message. The trick to doing this successfully is taking control of the message. Once you capture somebody's email address, you now know that your message will arrive in their inbox the next time they check it – quite unlike social networks, unless you are using their messaging services. This is the difference between the traffic you don't have any control over and the traffic you own. Once you own the traffic, you own the message! Your goal is therefore to give someone an overwhelming reason to pass on their contact details to you, their email address in particular, so that you can follow up with them later, on your terms rather than theirs.

Step 1: Creating an irresistible lead magnet

Ever since I started on my online journey, many of my teachers liked to use a fishing analogy when explaining this. First and foremost, once we selected our niche, we decided what type of fish we wanted to catch. We then need to work out are they fresh water or salt water, shallow swimmers or deep swimmers and then we decide what particular bait we need to use in that environment to attract the fish we want. Watching "Finding Nemo" what must be over a hundred times with my daughter Jess has certainly reinforced this with me more recently!

It is very much the same with finding our ideal clients, except we don't really apply the "catch and release" policy so easily! As discussed in chapter 7, while creating your avatar, until you understand the wants of your clients, you can find it very difficult to find them, let alone have them provide their contact details.

Setting the bait, the gift or the "bribe" is key to this exchange. You want to start off this relationship by offering something completely for free in exchange for contact details. You are not looking to sell; remember we do not sell directly from social media, in most cases. This means that the bribe needs to be something that a person would really like to have in order for them to give away their precious email address.

The key to a great bribe is to make it irresistible; quite simply too good to say "no" to! Now the natural reaction to this can be to overload the free offer with lots of content, and make it very lengthy. But these are often left aside into the dreaded "free gifts" folder on the desktop, never to be seen again! What tends to work a lot better is to be more specific, making it more attractive for your avatar. Ideally you are looking to solve a specific problem rather than multiple problems, with a specific solution rather than many more general ones. As soon as the person accesses the gift, they get straight into the meat of the solution in just a couple of minutes. There are a number of options available to you when it comes to encouraging people to join your database, and I will give you plenty of choices here.

Competitions:

You could run a competition, for example, where you must provide an accurate email address in order to enter some type of prize draw. You may see this strategy employed at hotel receptions quite a lot where they ask you to leave your business card in order to enter a draw for a free night. This is an excellent way of securing somebody's actual email address as opposed to a "made up" one, as they will want to be notified if they win!

Discounts:

Another option that works well is to provide a discount coupon that only has value if used to purchase something else, or alternatively provide free shipping with a product as the coupon.

Free book:

You can offer your prospects a chapter of a book, or even an entire book, for free. All they need to do is provide their details and pay for the postage and packaging, or the book can be delivered free as an online version.

Reports, guides and checklists:

You could also provide a report or booklet of some kind that is related to the problem that you are providing the solution for. There are many options here. You can create your own, you can give away somebody else's free reports or products or you can do a combination of both. This could also take the format of a checklist, cheat sheet or list of "hacks". They can often take the format of a list of resources that are freely available, but all aggregated in one report.

Swipe files:

A swipe file is a bundle of ready-made samples that serve a specific purpose for your audience and can prove extremely useful. An example of a swipe file could be a selection of pre-written emails for the launch of a new product, which can help the person who downloads them by either using them for their own products or helping promote an affiliate product.

Video or webinar training:

Providing free video training or series of videos is a good strategy. My favourite strategy for a free gift is to invite people to free training online so they get to learn more about the problem and the solution; this has a much higher conversion rate overall. You can maximise the effect of a live interactive webinar by recording it to be replayed when people access it as a free gift.

Audio files and interviews:

Being able to access information by listening to it is becoming more and more popular, and certainly has a high value perception. Free mp3 files are very easy to provide, yet add significantly to the value of the guide. If you are brave enough to produce your own, you can use the free software Audacity. An example of a free audio gift could be the recording of an interview you performed with an expert. It is very high in value, and the better known the expert is within your niche, the more irresistible the free gift becomes.

Free trials:

If you own software, you could provide a free trial, or if you have a membership site that you are looking to promote, you could provide free access for a limited period of time so that people can get a "feel" for it before they decide to invest. And even if they don't invest, you still have their contact details.

Questionnaires:

Surveys, questionnaires, quizzes, audits and assessments are another grouping of free gift options that can be provided. These can prove particularly useful as you can find out a lot more information about the prospect through a series of questions so that you can better serve their needs later on.

Email training sequence:

This is where the emails themselves are the gift. You might offer a 7-day intensive training series where you email your list each day with access to a specific training program. This can also be bundled together as a community exercise, in which everyone works together to complete a specific task, like building their online business in 30 days.

Case studies:

Using success stories framed as case studies can be an excellent idea for a free gift. When you can refer to a particular success story, not only is it educational but it can act as inspiration to encourage others to follow a similar path. It really comes into its own when you show a very specific result that was achieved, as this becomes very appealing to the right target market.

Other people's products:

Another option is to give away something that is not yours. Believe it or not, there are millions of products, books, e-books, reports, videos, articles, audiobooks and even software that are available to give away completely for free. Many of the old classic books are freely available to give away, such as Wallace Wattle's classic book The Science of Getting Rich, which most people are unaware of. There is an additional approach that you can take that allows you to give away much more recent up-to-date products and software called "private label rights" products. This is where the product creator freely gives away the rights to people to give away their content, provided that it is untouched and given away exactly as it was created. You can also pay for the rights to label these as your own if you wish, and even to sell them. Best of all, with these free products, the graphics for the covers are already created for you so it is quite easy to stack a few together and give them away all at once. You might wonder why people would create a product only for it to be given away at no charge, and it's a fair question! The reason is usually because the free gift will contain links to products that people can purchase, and the links are tracked back to the product owner so that they make commission on any sales made.

Live events:

If you really intend to up the ante, you can always offer free seats or tickets to live events, either online or in person. Not only do you then build your database, but your opportunity for a higher converting upsell has improved too. This is a topic deserving of a book in itself (maybe someday!).

Step 2: "Never judge a book by its…"

Oftentimes, the most obvious thing for people to do when creating their free gifts is to write their own report or book on the topic of interest, but this is by far the most difficult way to get started, especially when you have never done anything like this before and your experience is minimal. It is very natural to start getting concerned about the content and ensuring that it is top notch and original. If you are starting out on this journey, without a huge amount of experience, my suggestion is that you first and foremost create a cover for your free item that stands out and really looks like it is hugely valuable. You can create covers for your book, cd, dvd, training course or software completely for free with a number of different programmes! This is where you can maximise the results for your bribe, by making sure it looks amazing. We all judge books by their covers, so let's make sure this really looks amazing, even though it is going to be given away for free. Here are two websites you can use immediately: www. myecovermaker.com or www.place.to. These are some examples of the type of imagery that they produce for free without ever having to hire the services of a graphic designer.

Fig 9.1 Product cover options creating a high perception of value

Once the cover is created and looks great, you are more than half way there; now you can start to think about the content and specifically what you want to put into this report. One of the best uses of your time in this area is to leverage the work of experts who have gone before you and are only too happy for you to share their content, especially if you are not yet at a point where you have that knowledge. This allows you to overcome a very common sticking point for many people starting out on this journey – overthinking it. My perfectionist friends especially will know what I mean ☺. The thing is, if you don't get this done, and done quickly, you will never get to the key parts of your business and may freeze all activity.

Please allow me to put your mind at rest! How many free gifts have you downloaded over the years and stashed away in a file on your desktop, intending to get back to them at some point in the future but never have? If only 10% of people read past chapter 1 of the non-fiction books they purchased, what are the odds of them reading through your free report? Now we are going to do everything in our power to get people to read them straight away, but this may be a challenge! That is the reality of the situation. As I say to my students, "Don't worry, your free report will not be read out at your funeral unless it is particularly entertaining!"

The reason why I emphasise this is so that you realise that the cover is the deal breaker, and the content just needs to be good enough for the person to read through and appreciate. If it is very good, all the better of course, but it shouldn't be the deal breaker that slows you down from getting to the next steps in your business. It does not have to be out of this world, and you can always come back later and continually improve the content.

I would much prefer you to share the content of others, as I mentioned above – at the beginning, at least. Here's a RETHINK idea for you: what if you opened a Microsoft Word document and started to copy in only the very best videos from YouTube from the top experts in your field and collated it all into one convenient document for the reader? To do this you need to use publicly available videos on YouTube, which are free to share, and the snipping tool from MS Word to take an image of this video and pop into a document. Ensure the images are linked back to the original files so they can be played within your document, save it as a pdf file and the gift comes alive! Place your cover on the front and you have a brand new, completely unique free gift. When choosing the videos to include, rather than watching them all through first, filter them by view count to let the viewers make the decision for you rather than wasting time watching them yourself. It's all about leverage! You can watch a video of how to do this here: http://resources.rethinksocialmedia.com.

The days of "Get your free e-book" having any real value in the mind of the viewer are now long gone. Neither of the words themselves – "free" and "e-book" – create a concept of real value. The way you word your offerings is critically important, so that there is a massive perception of value associated with them. Rather than "free e-book", you can use terms like "strictly limited latest report on topic x". Make sure that the language reflects the specific end result that it is going to provide, rather than the detail of what it is. So how can you make your free gifts a complete no-brainer for the right avatar?

Traditionally, the thought process was that when you are encouraging people to leave their details in exchange for some type of gift, raising the "free bar" was key. The free bar refers to the amount of content that is being given away for free – the higher the bar is raised, the more content you give away, the more enticing the offer is to sign up for. This still can be the case in certain instances, but as mentioned earlier, it seems to be that a shorter, more specific key offering is much more powerful than causing overwhelm and inaction with too many generic offerings. The beauty with all of this, of course, is that you can test it immediately by running your traffic and finding out which has the better results for your specific business.

Please remember, though, that the imagery and headline you use to present these products is even more important than the actual content itself in terms of initially enticing people. Your traffic is making decisions based on the perception of value, which in turn is based on how the products look to them. Let's assume for a moment that you have three products ready to go that you wish to bundle and give away. What's next? It's now about ensuring that whatever you are offering is a really good fit for the specific problem you are looking to solve. There is no point having a mix-and-match of different products outside of your niche. You must make sure that you clearly focus on the benefit of each freebie and ensure they fit cohesively together as a solution, as opposed to seeming like a haphazard collection of free gifts that you managed to put your hands on.

Assuming, then, that you have the right products for the right people and they are a perfect match for the problem being solved, what is the next part of the equation? We really would like for the person to make their decision immediately rather than procrastinating. We tend to naturally put off the things we can get away with and prioritise the more urgent and pressing tasks. Your job as a marketer is to ensure that the person who comes across your offering really, really wants to take action now and not later. You need to create some serious urgency around accessing the reports right now. You will certainly see this on social media, whether they are ads or just posts, all the time attempting to inject urgency into the matter.

One of the key elements to think about when you are looking to create urgency is you should NEVER lie about it! You would not believe how many times you can see offers online about only having 100 e-books to give away; I think we all know that is not true! E-books by their very nature do not have a limit. But there are a number of options available to create urgency, such as limited time to access the products, or a limited number of combinations of products, or adding extra bonuses for the first few people to access them. The more real and believable the urgency, the better it is. The countdown clock has almost a hypnotic effect to get you to take action immediately. Think about the last time you went to ticketmaster.com just to see if tickets were available, and it notifies you that your tickets are on hold, but you have just 5 minutes and 59 seconds to guarantee them before they are released. Your hand immediately moves towards your credit card!

You may see this tactic being misused online from time to time where the countdown clock never seems to expire, and when it does it just resets again. You might get away with this once, but considering it is so easy to organise around this, it really is not worth taking the chance.

Whatever you decide to do, whether it is scarcity in numbers or time-limited, please make sure that you keep two points to the forefront:

A. **Marketing is "caring".** The more you show your people that you have their best interests at heart, the more they will trust you and the more likely they are to do business with you. If your marketing does not create trust, you are fighting a losing battle.

B. **Maintaining your integrity.** Funnily enough, this can make you stand out like a shining light. Be sure that whatever you say, you can back it up. Treat your audience with the respect they deserve, speak to them as you would wish to be spoken to yourself.

Here are some ideas that will allow you to maintain your integrity and at the same time create real urgency around your offering. Use countdown clocks to create urgency. In the next chapter, I will tell where you can find software that will help you create one of these. Once the clock expires, you can no longer give away the gifts as you had them, so change them up completely! Create new covers and new gifts for your audience to access. Not only does this allow you to keep your integrity and trust intact, it also presents you with the opportunity to test various offerings on a regular basis against each other and learn what your target market really wants. When you have the correct lead magnet to attract your perfect audience, which looks very enticing graphically, and you add in a level of urgency, you are a long way down the road towards having a really successful database builder. You can continue to use the same idea when you have an established database to work out what particular interests the people in your database have, and you can segregate them based on the new lead magnets that they choose to access. We will delve deeper into this idea later in the book.

Watch out #1:

There are many legal implications when it comes to email addresses, which we will discuss later in chapter 15 on GDPR requirements. For now, there are some non-legal issues, but important nonetheless, to look out for. One thing to be careful of when you are building databases is that sometimes people will naturally try to get access to your free gifts without giving their real email address the first time. You may even have tried this yourself from time to time ☺. I feel sorry for whoever owns the email address paul@gmail.

com! There are a couple of ways to counteract this. The first is to ensure that when people type in their details and click on submit they are brought to a congratulations page which makes it clear that their gifts are now on their way to the email address provided. Sometimes opt-in page owners send people directly to the free gifts, which is what the viewer is hoping for in the first place. Another option is to request a "double opt-in", which is where a person is automatically sent an email to open and click a link confirming that they do wish to join the list which they just signed up for. This has the inevitable downside that quite a few people will not click on the follow-up link within the email for different reasons, such as not having checked their emails in a while or not recognising the subject line email address. Ideally, on the congratulations page, you could have a personal video explaining exactly what is going to happen next and what to do to close out the process.

Watch out #2:

Your email may never get to its intended party! Given the added security that email management software has in segregating spam and expected whitelisted email, your email may end up in your potential client's trash or spam folder. Depending on which email provider your client uses, there are different methods of whitelisting the email. In your welcome video on your congratulations page, it would be good practice to either show the person how to whitelist your email address or at least send them to a video or article that shows them how to do it. If you wish to find an instruction guide that you can use to show your traffic how to whitelist your email address, please go to http://resources.rethinksocialmedia.com.

Let's turn this into a convenient checklist for the key things that you need to consider for your lead magnet to be as irresistible as possible.

Lead magnet checklist items:	Yes/no
Is it succinct, to the point and specific?	
Have I just one clear result in mind?	
Is it easy to implement for quick win?	
Have I built in a success story around it?	
Have I created a high perception of value through the description?	
Did I use imagery to add to the perception of value?	
Did I use it as a precursor for the next "big solution" which will be sold?	
Have I ensured the content is fresh, relevant and useful?	
Is it easy to implement?	
Does the content back up the promise?	

Table 9.1: Lead magnet checklist

Now that you understand the concept of using the right bait to attract the right "fish", we now need to invest in the right gear, i.e. the fishing rod, the reel, the line and any additional equipment needed to bring the "fish" home. The next step is to work out how we do this from a technology perspective. What are the tools that the top marketers use to build these databases from social media on autopilot?

Step 3: Qualifying the traffic

It's time to find out how well your bait is going to work! You need to take the free gift and present it in a way that makes it a truly irresistible offer to others. You must qualify the people you are targeting by distinguishing between those who have a passing interest and those who are willing to take this to the next level by providing their contact details and indeed spend their money. This involves using either software or a web designer, but please don't freak out! When I started on my online business journey in 2009, my greatest fear was that I would have to learn how to do things like coding and software programming in order to make a success of this business. I was forced to take a module on Fortran 77 in college once as part of my degree, and I remember thinking that I never wanted to return to having to work with anything related to it! Fortunately, I never did – and neither will you!

The easiest way to get started here is to learn how to create a simple one-page website, which is called a squeeze page or an opt-in page. There are many different options that can be set up in order to capture email addresses, such as the following:

- Opt-in pages

- Popup opt-in boxes

- Opt-in boxes within your blog or website or Facebook page

- Floating bar opt-in boxes

- One-click popup opt-in boxes

- Exit pops

- 1 and 2-click auto options within networks such as Facebook

- Webinar registrations

- Free account registration

At this point, it's not all that important to know the slight differences between all of these; however, their focus is still the same: collecting an email address. The opt-in page is the foundation to start with, while others can be added later, using the same technology in many cases. The opt-in page is the portal between social media and your database. It is a one-page website that presents the free gift(s) that you have to offer and encourages people to leave their name and email address in exchange for the gifts. It has multiple purposes:

- To graphically show the free gifts on offer

- To provide you with the opportunity to explain the free gifts through text or video

- It allows people to leave their name and email address

- It connects to your email service provider (ESP) or autoresponder, which collects the email addresses and sends out the free gifts automatically

- It contains links to your privacy policy, terms of service, contact details and income disclosure statements

When I was first told that I needed to get one of these in order to have an online business, it definitely caused me a degree of distress, as I had no idea how to build a website, which in essence is what it is – a simple one-page website. Things have moved on dramatically since then, and all the tools you need to create such a page are readily available, with free trials to boot! What my business partner and I did back in 2009 was hire a web designer, as quite simply we had no other option based on our skillsets. As much as I loved my first web designer Jac, it was very much a case of the blind leading the blind, as I wasn't exactly sure what I was looking for and he was naturally looking to me for instruction. He could build anything I wanted, I just wasn't sure what I should be looking for.

Today however, every conceivable tool that you need to use is available at a fraction of the cost of a web designer. Before I give you some options for what to use, please allow me to elaborate a little more on the makeup of the opt-in page. It is made up of a number of separate components, as you can see below.

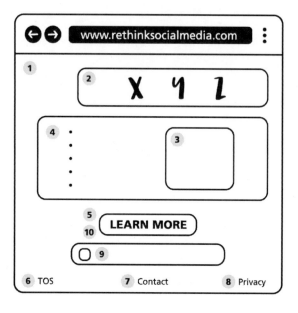

Fig 9.2: Standard opt-in page template

1. **Frame / template**

2. **Headline**

3. **Image or video**

4. **Description**

5. **Call to action button**

6. **Terms of service**

7. **Contact**

8. **Privacy notice (or "privacy policy" or "fair processing notice")**

9. **Consent wording**

10. **Link to autoresponder**

Now let us take a look at each of these aspects in turn so that you understand their purpose.

1. Frame / template

This was traditionally the most difficult aspect of the opt-in page to create as it required the involvement of a web designer. The template of the opt-in page is absolutely key to the success of the page itself. When discussing an opt-in page, success refers to how many people leave their details after visiting the page. The success of the page is measured as a conversion percentage, which is the number of people that joined your database divided by the number of people who visited the page. So, for example, if 100 people visited your opt-in page and 22 of them joined your list, that would be considered a 22% conversion rate.

How does one determine what the template should look like? Obviously looking for examples on the internet would be a good place to start, but you probably have no idea of the conversion rates, i.e. the success, of these pages. Thankfully for you and me, there are at least two amazing software tools available that not only have great templates designed by marketers for marketers, but they also allow you to organise them based on how successful they are in terms of clients' results.

The two software tools that I use are available at http://resources. rethinksocialmedia.com for completely free trials. These allow you not only to create beautiful, professional templates that convert very well, but also to integrate these pages into more elaborate online systems called funnels, which will be explained later in this book.

2. Headline

The headline appears on the top of your opt-in page and is what immediately grabs the attention of the person looking at the page. Usually making it specifically about a particular result is powerful, for example by stating the exact amount of weight lost or money made – the more specific the better. Starting the headline with "How I" or "How to", where the implication is that you are showing somebody how they can learn to do something, is a very powerful way of creating engagement from the outset. It is a good idea to start to set up a file where you store various headlines that you come across online, in particular those that your Facebook ads are sending you to, so that you can learn from the efforts of others and model these accordingly. Capitalising The First Letter Of Each Word Will Help In Making It Easy To Read!

3. Image or video

The focal point of any opt-in page is naturally the video or the image that you use on the template. There is no one-size-fits-all answer here as to which is best to use, as it depends very much on what the video looks like and how the imagery looks. Sometimes you will find opt-in pages that have neither an image or video and just use a description; these can also work very well. This is something that you will start to test to find which works best for your market.

4. Description

The description should focus on the main benefits or outcomes associated with the free gifts. Don't be drawn into explaining too much detail, keep it at a high level. People buy results as opposed to the exact details of how to do it. The higher the level you can keep it, and getting straight to the key result that the person will achieve, is critical. For example, if I were promoting a program through Facebook ads, a badly-written description would discuss the detail of each type of ad, such as: "You will learn how to run to maximise your CPC, CPL, CPM and ROI". A better description would be: "How I managed to create a huge profit from Facebook ads in 3 simple steps". While both are correct, one is a lot more attractive than the other.

5. Call to action button

This is the button that the person is going to click to confirm that they are ready for the next step. Ideally you would like to keep these buttons as little "agreements" to move to the next step, which seem almost insignificant commitments, making it easy to keep them on the journey. Amazingly, something as seemingly minor as the colour of the button and the words used on the button have a sizable bearing on your results. In general, I would use the colouring of the box in the suggested template within the software, but I would be more careful with the wording. In order for you to collect the person's email address, they will need to click on the button, so the less threatening it is the better. Often you will see the word "Subscribe" or "Join Now". Both suggest a longer-term commitment and relationship that will result in you receiving lots of emails in the future, so they would not be an ideal choice of wording.

Likewise, the word "Download" is often used, especially in corporate ads, but when you consider that most traffic is now on mobile phones and almost everyone I know is running out of space on their phones, the commitment to downloading something may mean that I need to delete some photos that I really want! It is very important to keep in mind the person who is reading the page and the thoughts that are at the forefront of their mind. Words like "Learn More", "Submit" and "Click Here" are a lot less foreboding and threatening.

6. Terms of service

Your terms of service tell the user what they're allowed to do when they get to your site and are an opportunity for you to give the customer information that you're obliged to tell them. There are some bits of information that you're required to give regardless of your subject area, and others that are specific to different niches. Looking at the main points:

a) Every online business is required to provide the following things:

- Company name/number/registered office (if you're trading as a company – or details where you can be reached if not)

- Vat number (if you are VAT registered – no need if not)

b) If your niche is regulated there may be rules that apply to your niche, for example – are you giving financial or legal advice? (In which case you'll need to give details of your FCA or SRA registration, or you might find that you're breaking the law.) Are you acting as an estate agent or travel agent and therefore bound by codes of conduct that require you to provide information? If so, your terms of business are likely to be the place to include that information.

c) If you're selling products then you're likely to find that there are mandatory consumer terms that you need to provide (e.g. a cooling-off period for certain goods and services).

This might look a little overwhelming, and I agree it can be without the right guidance! But you don't need to worry, as I'm providing you with some standard templates that will be constantly updated based on legal requirements right here: www.resources.rethinksocialmedia.com.

7. Contact

As long as you've set out your name (or the name of your company), then providing an email address to contact you at the end of your opt-in page may suffice for this requirement as it stands. But if you're using the site to sell physical goods that your customers are allowed to cancel, then you will need to provide a way for customers to return those goods to you, so bear in mind that you'll need an address or other process in order to comply with that obligation.

8. Privacy notice (or "privacy policy" or "fair processing notice")

A privacy notice (sometimes referred to as a "privacy policy" or a "fair processing notice") is a statement that sets out how you will gather, use, share and manage your customer's data. It's a statement to your customer of what you will do and it doesn't require (and nor should it ask for) a response. Your privacy notice sets out the purpose for which personal data is collected and what's done with it (including certain required terms). If you're tracking your traffic using cookies then you'll need to set out what these do as well, and you're going to need a privacy notice. The point to note is that the requirements have become a lot stricter with the advent of GDPR in May 2018. We will discuss these later in chapter 15. I know you just can't wait!

9. Consent wording

As well as telling your customer what you're going to do with the data you collect from them, if you're going to do any sort of meaningful electronic marketing then you're also going to need consent for that marketing. This means you have to ask them a question and get a response to that question (by them ticking a box or clicking a button). That is what the consent wording does – it's designed to capture the consent required for the purpose that you intend to use the data. Clearly this wording needs to be tailored for your own business, as once you've captured the email addresses or personal data, it's too late if you then want to use that same data for purposes that aren't covered by your consent wording. So you need to consider what you want to use the data for before you need it. Ask yourself what you're likely to want to do with that data in the future before you ask for consent from your customer.

10. Link to autoresponder

The opt-in page would not be complete without connecting it to the email service provider (ESP) or autoresponder – the tool that collects the email addresses for your business.

Once you have all of the opt-in page elements in place, the next thing is to ensure that you have it connected to a tool that will do the automation. Your email service provider such as mailchimp, convertkit, aweber or Infusionsoft creates the little opt-in boxes that you will sometimes see in an opt-in page as shown in the graphic below.

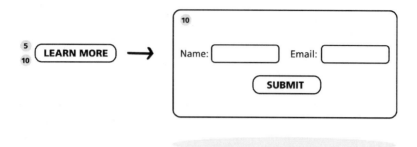

Fig 9.3: A basic opt-in box

It serves multiple purposes in your business and is completely non-negotiable when it comes to running an online operation. Some of the functions include:

- Storing all of your email addresses

- Allowing you to segregate your database into multiple lists

- Allowing you to have your database stored outside of your laptop or PC in case anything happens to them

- Sending your free gift automatically to your list

- Allowing you to email certain lists and exclude other people

- Preventing you from uploading people into your database who are already there and will only send one email per email address

- Automatically allowing people to unsubscribe from every email you send

- Automatically adding your contact details to your emails

- Letting you organise your emails to be sent out on autopilot for years in advance

- Creating your opt-in boxes

- Allowing you to create popup opt-in boxes to place in front of your website or blog (see figure 9.3)

- Allowing you to segregate people into different lists depending on what links they clicked in the email subsequent to joining your list

- Allowing you to resend emails to people who did not open the email the first time

- Giving an in-depth breakdown of all the statistics you require such as how many people opened the email, who they were and how many people clicked on the link and who they were

Some of the more advanced options can be integrated with an online shop for complete management of sales and deliveries.

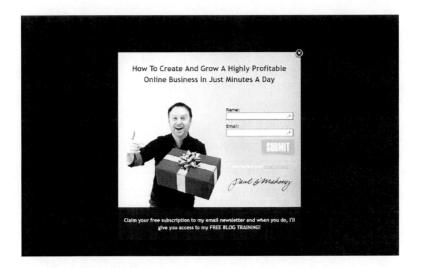

Fig 9.4: Pop up opt-in box

When it comes to selecting which autoresponder to use, it can be a tricky business. I have tested more than 20 of them to date with varying degrees of success and always continue to use more than one at any time. Your choice can be simplified based on your requirements and your budget. If you really have no budget whatsoever and need to get started on a shoestring, that is not a problem – mailchimp.com is the best option for you. It is free until you grow your database to a certain size. If you are middle of the road, which I would suggest is probably where most people would start out, I would consider using convertkit.com or aweber.com. If you are looking for all-bells-and-whistles solutions for an established business that you already have, and are looking to integrate mobile marketing follow-up as well as ecommerce and affiliate systems, you could consider using Infusionsoft.

Our businesses use 4 different autoresponders concurrently but with all things considered my personal favourite is convertkit. If you would like to learn how to use these in more detail, feel free to check out the training videos that I've provided on our RETHINK social media training site at www.resources.rethinksocialmedia.com.

Once you learn how to use the autoresponder to create your opt-in box, you can then place opt-in boxes wherever you like – your blog, your website, even within Facebook and your opt-in page. It is important to be aware that there is a huge difference between the opt-in box and the opt-in page. The opt-in box merely allows you to collect the emails, but it does not in itself entice people to leave their details. The reason why an opt-in page works so well for collecting people's data as opposed to a blog or a website is that the person on the opt-in page is presented with a simple choice, to leave their details to continue further or to leave without leaving their details. This is why the conversion rate on an opt-in page is vastly superior to what you would get for an opt-inbox placed anywhere else. Opt-in pages are not the only way to collect data at this point in the model. There are many other means by which we can help for free, although the opt-in pages remain the most popular method.

Before we leave this section on building your database, it is important to let you know the strides that Facebook has been taking in order to remove the need for your traffic to ever have to leave Facebook itself. There are some alternatives now available within Facebook that allow you to completely bypass the opt-in page. Facebook can collect the email address for you, and store it for you, without people ever having to leave the confines of Facebook or even type in their email address; now there's a concept! You might wonder how this is even possible. Firstly, if you are going to have Facebook collect email addresses for you, they will need a link to your privacy policy, as mentioned in number 8 of the opt-in page requirements above.

Facebook has a particular type of advertisement that you can select, known as a "Lead Generation" ad, which is a two-step process from ad to email collection. In the example in figure 9.5 you can see what one of these looks like. They have the look of a standard traffic ad with either an image or video to attract attention, but when the button on the ad is clicked, you are not directed externally away from Facebook. In fact, a second page pops open that has already prepopulated your name and email address for you, just in case you don't feel inclined to type it in yourself! This vastly reduces the chances of somebody leaving a fake email address, as all the person needs to do to join the database is to click on the button once more and that's it! Facebook has the email stored for you ready for you to download whenever you choose, or you can set it up to automatically connect Facebook to your autoresponder so that the whole process is automated.

Paul O'Mahony
Sponsored · ⊕

 👍 Like Page

Would you like to know how to use Social Media the RIGHT way to drive sales and leads for your business?

Join me on this free training class where I will walk you through step by step how you can use Social Media to launch your online business to drive sales and leads.

[FREE TRAINING] Learn How to Use Social Media for Growing Your Business

Grab this easy step by step guide on how you can launch an online business in the time you already spend on your Social Media platforms

GO.LEFTCLICKRIGHTCLICK.COM

Learn More

Fig 9.5: Example of lead gen ad from Facebook part 1

Paul O'Mahony   ×

FREE TRAINING

GROW A SUCCESSFUL
BUSINESS LEVERAGING
SOCIAL MEDIA

Launch a Successful Online Business With
Social Media

- The 4 Key Components of ANY Successful Online Business

- How to Create Multiple ˙   ˉtreams Using Social Media

- How I Have Created Financial Security Using Social Media in The
Last 9 Years

Sign up by providing your info below.

Email   ••••••• @gmail.com

Full name   Gregor *******

Nothing you share will be posted on Facebook. This info is sent to Paul O'Mahony.

Cancel   Next

Fig 9.6: Example of lead gen ad from Facebook part 2

In this option the name and email are automatically populated by Facebook!

There is another option that Facebook has introduced to leverage another platform of theirs, not only to make the database collection process easier but also to drastically shorten the speed of engagement in the follow-up sequence. By using their Messenger system, which has well over 1 billion users, Facebook has made it possible for marketers to run ads to people that directly appear with their instant Messenger. Once the person clicks to engage with the marketer, it is then possible to engage with the person over Messenger, cutting out the requirement for email completely. We will discuss this in more detail later in the book. This will provide all kinds of amazing opportunities, as you will see very shortly – including directing people immediately into a pretested sales process as soon as they have requested more information.

Once we have collected our contact details, whether through email or Messenger, the goal is the same: how do we make our money back as soon as possible by providing an irresistible offer with an immediate upsell?

Summary:

A major theme of this book is that in order to kick off a new relationship with a stranger online, we initiate it on our terms by offering some form of help for free in exchange for contact details. We are happy to bypass the possibility of immediate gratification temporarily, with the view that we can gain a customer for life if we focus on the relationship, not solely on the money. Traditionally the best way to set this scenario up is by driving traffic to an opt-in page or squeeze page, which offers a specific solution for free. There are many different offerings that can be provided, from free reports to discount coupons and free trials. The template that you use for the opt-in page itself is key, and there are at least 10 separate watch-outs to keep in mind with its setup. Some social networks, such as Facebook, now offer alternatives to this traditional model of taking someone to your own opt-in page by allowing people to subscribe within Facebook directly, or even through their messaging system, without any requirement for email addresses.

Traditional Thinking:

Your main goal with social media is to make direct sales. If creating a free gift, it must be completely unique and the more you add into the free offer the better. "Free e-book" offers are great at building your list. In your marketing, limit the number of free gifts you are giving away. Once you get an opt-in box on your blog and website, your list will start to build organically. Popup boxes are annoying, so you refuse to use them. Your web designer built your website and that is what you plan to use to get more business. All autoresponders are pretty much the same, so if you can get it for free, that would be the ideal one to use. People don't want to deal with automated bots.

RETHINK:

Your main goal with social media is to build a database. Keep your free gift focused on one key specific result that is easily actionable. The "free e-book" wording no longer has any real impact in terms of value. Although the content may still be great, how you market it is key. A great way of adding urgency is to have a cut-off time after which the gifts are no longer available. An opt-in box in itself is completely useless in terms of "attracting" opt-ins. It's the framework around it convincing people to leave their details that determines the success or failure of an opt-in box. Pop up boxes dramatically increase opt-in rates and can be set up so that they are not frustrating the viewer. Sending your traffic to an opt-in page created with a tried and tested template from established marketing software is a much more efficient way of building a database. The opt-in page forces the person to make an immediate decision on whether they want to learn more or not. Giving more information on products like a website does is not the goal; the goal is to collect contact details. Depending on your budget, it may make a lot of sense for you to invest in an autoresponder that has ease of use, superior deliverability and marketer friendly, so doesn't charge you per email sent. Investing in chatbots will be a very smart move for your business as it will save a fortune on customer service and allow you to cut your cost of lead acquisition and increase open rates to 80-85%+!

Chapter 10: Immediate Upsell

"Ultimately, the business that can spend the
most to acquire a customer wins."
- Dan Kennedy

This opening quote from Dan Kennedy is of crucial importance to your business. Clearly, if you can pay more for your customers than your competitors can, you will get them. But the speed at which you make back your investment to get them, I would argue, is just as important.

Let us think about this for a moment to ensure you fully understand it. The faster you make back your costs of lead acquisition (email address collection), the more certainty you have in your business model and the more you can reinvest into marketing, with the confidence that you will continue to make a profitable return. In other words, if you can prove the concept immediately, you have almost no risk as you continue to scale your business. This is why the "I" in the RETHINK model is immediate upsell; the goal is to get money from a new lead as soon as possible.

So first things first, we need to work out how much it costs to collect someone's email address, and after that, how much it costs to find a buyer. Let's assume that with your current marketing campaign, it is costing you $2 to collect an email address. Is this expensive or is this cheap? It very much depends! Firstly, we must have an offering in place to sell to these leads to allow us to make back some money as soon as possible.

Secondly, we need to know what the "quality" of this new lead is. By quality, I mean the likelihood of that person deciding to spend money with you. The more they will spend, the higher the quality. You can work out immediately if you have found a "buyer" with a cleverly set up "front-end funnel", which we will review in this chapter.

Thirdly, we need to find out if this is a "hyper buyer", i.e. once they start buying, they just keep buying; like the Pringles tagline "Once you pop, you can't stop!" We also find this out at the "front-end funnel" stage.

Finally, we want to know what this client will be worth to us over an extended period of time. This assumes that we have more products to offer over time and can be structured in terms of a "back-end funnel". This is where the majority of the income is made through higher-value offerings.

From a high-level perspective, we want to know what it is costing us to get the lead and how much we will make back from that lead over time.

Fig 10.1: Your online business in a nutshell

Our goal is to spend less on the left-hand side than what we make on the right-hand side of figure 10.1. As the business scales, we focus on continuing to reduce the cost per lead on the left-hand side and increase the value per lead on the right-hand side with our sales funnel. Let's break the sales funnel down into its individual components. To begin with in part 1, we will review what a "value ladder" is, where we structure our sales offerings, then in part 2 we will review how a front-end funnel works. In part 3 we will review what a back-end funnel looks like and then in part 4 we will consider what your options are in terms of finding products to sell.

Part 1: Setting up a value ladder

Once you have collected an email address, your immediate goal is to find out if you have you found an "interested" lead or a more "committed" buyer. This is the process of "qualifying" your leads. To make things easy on yourself, what you really want to have here is an automated process that will work this out for you immediately! This is why there is a need for something called a "funnel" or "sales funnel". Of course, in order to do this, we must offer something to sell. We will discuss your options for this in part 4 but for now, to make this easier to understand, let's take a specific example: let's assume that we own a book writing training company that helps people to write their first book called "Bank For Your Book Ltd".

Our core offering is a 3-day online workshop on "How to write a bestselling book" that retails for $2,997, and our target market for the business is people who wish to write their own book and have the money to get educated on how to do it. The traditional thought process would be to start off by targeting people who wish to write books with Google advertising or traditional media and send them directly to our website, which offers our 3-day program for $2,997.

However, this is definitely not the best approach; this requires a complete RETHINK! When you use such a relatively high price point as the initial offering and the trust is not yet established with these leads, the likelihood of success (making a sale) is low. What we need to focus on instead is establishing a "value ladder" between the starting point of a complete stranger finding our website and encouraging them to purchase our core offering. We can do this by setting up a series of bridge offerings to our core offer. Let's look at the image below – the value ladder of potential offerings we can provide with increasing value and cost.

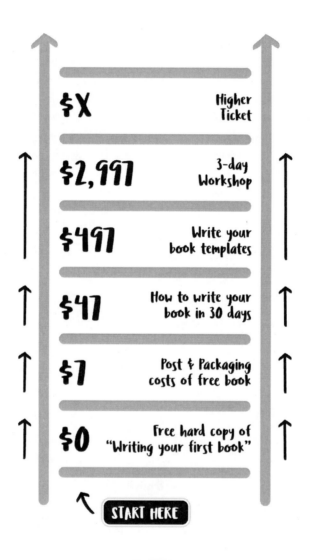

Fig 10.2 A value ladder

This value ladder lays out one potential method of delivering our core offering after firstly offering a free gift, followed by a series of low-cost products that lead to the higher-priced core offering. By having this tiered product offering, we can position these later into a sales funnel that can automatically move people through the purchasing process. Using the value ladder in this way provides a convenient and powerful method for structuring your businesses offerings so that you can clearly see what the natural progressions are for your customers to move through the various options available. In general, you position this with the cheaper offerings on the bottom rung of the value ladder and the more expensive offerings higher up the ladder.

In this example, we start by offering a free book that can be downloaded digitally for free. The book is about writing your first book, so we know that it will only attract the attention of people who are interested in this topic. If someone wishes to receive a physical copy of the book, this can only happen if they pay for the postage and packaging, which is the second rung of the value ladder.

The next rung of the value ladder is a video training, "How to write your book in 30 days", which is set at $47. This is a more interactive training, as the client can now watch on videos how this works in real terms, which has a higher value proposition than having to read a book. After this, we have offered a series of "plug and play" templates for $497 that will allow the budding author to write a book very easily by adding their content straight into the templates to produce a professionally finished looking book.

It is only at this point that we come to the core offer of attending a 3-day online "How to write a bestselling book" workshop. Now the value of $2,997 makes a lot more sense to the client. Firstly, they have had access to various levels of your services at this point, and assuming the products have been of high quality, the chances are the trust levels are very high with your client. There is also now a high probability that the client will want some additional hands-on support and will be willing to pay for this if they are truly committed to the outcome of completing their first book. The value ladder does not end here! We can add subsequent offerings, where each is priced above the $2,997 mark, all the way up to $49,997 – this will feed into part 3 of our back-end funnel.

Summary:

Beginning with the end in mind is a really powerful concept when it comes to your online business. Knowing in advance the potential sales journey that you wish for a new lead to be introduced to will help enormously in setting yourself up for success. The framework used to make this a reality is called a value ladder. It allows you to think it through and visually represent what the ideal customer path is. You can easily identify gaps and where the value leap is quite large you may need some intermediate offerings. Generally speaking, you should be delivering at least 10 times the value that you are charging for at each level.

Traditional thinking:

I have my core product and it is available for sale on my website. This is where I will send any potential leads.

RETHINK:

When our core offering is relatively highly priced, it is a big challenge to move people straight in to purchase it, especially when there is no previous history or trust built with the lead. This is overcome by offering much cheaper products or services to begin with, where the level of outlay is minimal for the level of value received. As the journey continues, progressively higher value offerings can be made, each more likely to be purchased as the level of trust increases with time.

Part 2: How to set up the immediate upsell with a frontend sales process

Once we are clear on the value ladder, we can now take these various layers of value and turn them into a systemised method of delivery. It's not much use having lots of great products if we don't have a system whereby the customers are offered the products in a clever, efficient and profitable manner. This is where funnels come into their own. A sales funnel may be something you have heard of before reading this book, but the likelihood is you may not have implemented one, or you may have one, but it doesn't quite work for you.

The problem I find with businesses and the people that tend to complain about funnels most often, is that they simply don't have them or only partially use them. I myself was guilty of not having a highly -tuned online funnel for many years in my business, but as soon as I got it implemented, it changed everything! The primary reason was due to the difficulty in portraying what I wanted to a web designer, but this issue has now been eradicated, as you will soon see.

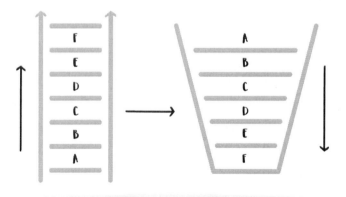

Fig 10.3: Turning a value ladder into a sales funnel

The sales funnel can be split into two components, the front end and the back end. In order to explain the differences, we first need to take a look at the product offerings a little more closely. Let's go back to the specific example of Bank For Your Book Ltd. At present we have two offerings under the $50 mark, the postage and packaging (sometimes called "free plus shipping") offer of $7 and the "How to write your book in 30 days" video training for $47. These two offerings serve different purposes, but both make up part of our front-end sales funnel.

The first goal of the front-end sales funnel is to check if our new lead is a buyer. We determine this by immediately offering something we want to sell. There are many ways that you can do this, such as:

- Free book but pay for postage and packaging

- Offer a reduced-price free trial on software or membership site access

- Offer a cheap "trip wire" product, which is a small part of your core product

- Immediately offer a higher-priced product aiming for a self-liquidating offer

Of all of the above, the easiest one to start with is the free gift but pay for shipping offer. The reason this is so clever is because you can ask for the person's contact details in stage 1 of the opt-in page so that on the subsequent landing page they are asked for their credit card details for the shipping costs. Even if they do not leave their credit card details, you have at least received their contact details, which allows you to follow up later. In part 3 of this chapter I will recommend some software that will make this process very easy indeed – and the good news is they're the same tools we have already recommended!

Once you drive your traffic to this first lead magnet and automatic upsell, you will then have a very clear picture of who your buyers are. At this point, we have received enough money to cover the cost of shipping, and possibly a tiny amount left over, but not enough to cover the cost of collecting the email address itself. The second goal has a dual role in finding out who our hyper buyers are as well as covering the cost of the lead immediately.

Let's go back to the example where we said it cost us $2 to collect the lead's email address; how can we make that $2 back as quickly as possible? Do you offer them something for $2? Well, not exactly. This is where the higher-priced offering comes in of approximately $50. Once the client has paid for shipping, we will instantly offer them the training video offering for $47. If our overall cost per lead is $2 and we are charging approximately $50 for the video training, only one in every 25 sign-ups need to buy this higher-priced product in order for us to break even! This is what is known as a "self-liquidating offer", where the cost of the lead is covered by the immediate upsell.

As you already have the person's credit card details, it is now possible for them to upgrade with simply one click, so it is even easier to get them to upgrade at this point. Now you are really in the gravy! In fact, if any more than 1 in 25 people purchase from you, that means you are in profit right from the outset! What more could you ask for than being paid to build your database? This is where you really want to be! We now know who our hyper buyers are, and we have a self-liquidating or even profitable offer. This might sound like it is undoubtedly going to be quite complex to set up, but it really is quite straightforward, as you will soon see.

Fig 10.4 Webpages for basic front-end sales funnel

Summary:

Once your value ladder is clear, the next stage is to work out how this material can be delivered efficiently and ideally automatically to our leads. This is achieved through the creation of sales funnels. These are split into two parts, front and back-end funnels. The front-end will determine which leads are buyers and which buyers are hyper buyers. Software is available to build these in just a few clicks!

Traditional Thinking:

Let's target people who wish to write books with Google advertising or traditional media and send them directly to our website, which offers our 3-day program for $2,997.

RETHINK:

Let's firstly find out who is interested by collecting their contact details and then immediately work out if they are a "buyer". Then let's build up to our core offering by building trust with smaller tiers of lower-priced products that continue to increase as we gain an additional step of commitment each time. After we provide our core offering, let's add even more value and charge significantly higher amounts based on the value being delivered.

Part 3: Setting up a profitable back-end sales process

I certainly hope you are still with me at this point! It can be difficult to fathom that you can be making money while building your database, that's for sure. As I have said many times before, just because you don't know about it doesn't mean it isn't happening; it really is time to rethink what you may be doing currently. Now is the time to get really excited! It's time to step up our game and start looking to make some serious profit from our business; it's time to introduce our back-end sales system.

In figure 10.2, we looked at the value ladder for Bank For Your Book Ltd. At the top of the ladder, we had left it generic with "High ticket" but let's get more specific now. The back-end really kicks in on the value ladder where we have the $497 product. This is where the numbers increase and the sales messages, whether they are videos, sales copy or webinars, need to be that little bit longer and more convincing. What would the back-end value ladder look like?

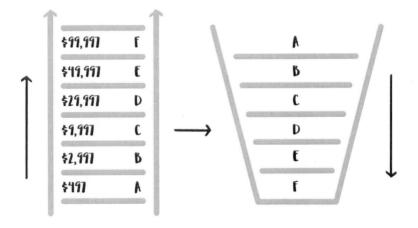

Figure 10.5: Value ladder and back-end sales funnel

Now this is the part where you may have to really take a leap of faith with me in terms of suspending belief. It may seem beyond reason that there are products in this value ladder and funnel selling for $100k, but please allow me to explain with this specific example. Let's assume that our client has upgraded to Product C, which is the 3-day online workshop for $2,997, and then at the end of the workshop, they are very excited. The book is now planned out and there are clear instructions in place about what to do next. Like many people, however, they are very busy and realise that without dedicating some significant chunk of time all at once, this book may never happen! That is why there is an offering of Product C for $9,997, which is a 7-day "Writer's Bootcamp" in person in NYC later this year, where the goal is to come and meet the trainer and write the book with their support and guidance in person.

Alternatively, they can choose Product D for $29,997, where the book will be written and edited by expert writers and editors with complete book cover designs provided by Bank For Your Book Ltd. Now you can probably see why this is tempting, provided of course that you had the money! There is more, however: Product E for $49,997 comes with entire front and back-end sales funnels for the new "done for you" book built out on webpages by the design team at Bank For Your Book Ltd and guarantees the sale of at least 1,000 books and a number 1 ranking on Amazon.com! Once again, the value has significantly increased, and it gives the budding author the certainty of a number 1 ranking, which brings with it all kinds of credibility.

We do have a Product F for $100k. What could that possibly add? Well, like anything here, we can continue to stack the value. This time the company adds a guaranteed 2,000 book sales, a major book launch in two cities worldwide, a promotion to their database of customers and number 1 rankings in multiple Amazon segments. They could also offer a top 10 ranking in the New York Times bestsellers list. Now $100k might seem like a bargain, because if they have a back-end sales funnel all done for them and guaranteed exposure, the outgoing of $100k should disappear into insignificance when compared with the profits that should ensue.

Moving people through the back-end funnel is not as simple as a couple of sales pages and videos. When the numbers are as big as those in this example, somewhere along the line at a bare minimum, sales calls are required. But most likely, in-person events are going to be needed to allow people to apply to be accepted for the next level.

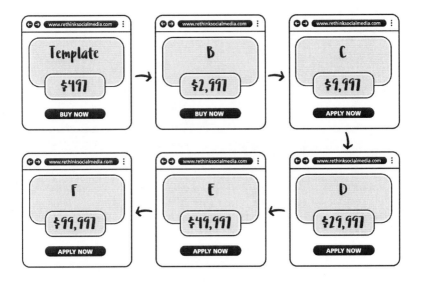

Fig 10.6 Web pages for basic back-end sales funnel

You may notice that I have used the word "basic" in the description for both the front and back-end webpage images. This is not an error! The reason that they are basic is that it is also possible to add various sales at each point, in case the client decides against upgrading. They can be provided with one time offers, or OTOs, where they can receive a discount, but only if they purchase there and then. For the purposes of this book, we don't need to add more on this, the awareness of them is more than enough for now. They would be the icing on the icing of the cake.

In figure 10.7 we have taken the diagram of the first value ladder and defined where the funnel changes from a front-end to a back-end sales funnel.

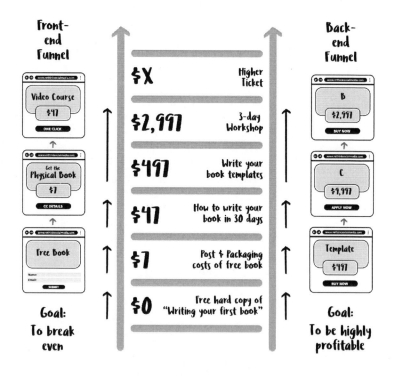

Fig 10.7: Front and back-end funnels and a value ladder

Regardless of what you label them as, the plan of action is hopefully very clear. But two main questions remain:

1. Where do I even start to build something of this complexity online?
2. What if I have nothing to sell?

To answer the first question, you are reading this at a very fortunate time where there is software available that can build your front and back-end funnel for you with ridiculous ease! There are all kinds of funnels that you can build, and Russel Brunson, who is a master of the creation of sales funnels, lays them all out very clearly for you within his software, including training videos on each type of funnel regardless of level of complexity that you may require.

You can sign up for a free trial of the software right here http://resources. rethinksocialmedia.com. The reason that it took me so long to finally get my own online funnels up and running was because I was waiting for a software like this to be created. I could not explain to web designers how to create what I was looking for. In fact, all of the funnels linked to this book are built using the same software, so it is definitely worth signing up for the free trial.

To answer the second question about what to do if you have nothing to sell, well, that is exactly what we'll discuss in detail now in part 4 – you have lots of options..

Summary:
Once your front-end funnel is in place, then the fun really begins from a money perspective… It's time to ratchet things up! The back-end funnel refers to the higher-price offering products from approximately $500 right up to hundreds of thousands of dollars. The sales process used will need to be more convincing and will require some in-person sales as the numbers increase. The key thing to keep in mind is you don't need to know how to do all of this to get started; just build out a funnel in line with your current experience but have the awareness to always look to add more.

Traditional Thinking:

Once I have sold my core offering to a customer/client, I need to focus on getting more people in the door as leads to keep my business profitable.

RETHINK:

Unless you have a back-end sales funnel in place, you are leaving the vast majority of your profit potential on the table. Set up a value ladder that allows you to add many high-value ticket items. There is software now available to facilitate the building of sales funnels and simplify the entire process.

Part 4: Where do I find products to sell?

In 2009 when I created my very first online "business", and believe me I use that term very loosely, I made my first two sales from Twitter on my first day of trying. The money had come in on autopilot while I had been asleep, it blew my mind! Making money while I slept was no longer a dream. Earlier in the book I mentioned how I started initially without any products of my own and that to begin with I was very uncomfortable at the thought of selling other people's products without having tried them myself. That was until my mentor reminded me that all I had to do was to check the reviews of the products online first from people who had paid already rather than going broke myself working out if I liked the product! Sometimes it is something as simple as this that makes you realise the importance of having the right people around you. From there I went on to create my first product – the first of many, which eventually turned into entire sales funnels that my students can now promote as partners and make money from, which is the ideal place to be. Imagine being able to promote something that you have used yourself and completely trust; it makes it even easier to market and sell with enthusiasm. Later in this chapter I will let you know how you can do this yourself.

If you don't have a business right now, you are not alone! You are in the vast majority of people alive and readers of this book. One of the most common questions that I receive at public talks is "Paul, I get the social media stuff, sounds great, but can we just cut to the chase here, I don't have a business so what do I sell?" It's a fundamental question that needs to be answered. It can be answered with a dismissive "anything you like", which doesn't really help someone who truly is keen but doesn't fully appreciate the entire picture just yet. To simplify this as much as possible, I will group what you sell into three primary areas, depending on where you are currently.

The three main options are:

1. You can sell your own products or services if you are already a business owner

2.   You can create your own products and services to sell

3.   You can sell other peoples'/businesses' products and services

Let's discuss each in turn.

OPTION 1: Sell your current products or services (as a current business owner)

For the purposes of the next stages, I am going to assume that your products are of high quality. The reason I bring this up again is to remind you that if your products are not good, social media is only going to let a lot more people know this, so please ensure if you are going with option 1 that you are very happy with your level of products or services to begin with. If this is the case and you implement a highly successful "upsell", that happens immediately after social media has done what it was intended to do in finding the contact details of a prospect, the news is very exciting! You are really getting to the point of nothing but profitable returns!

As a current business owner, you already know what you sell. We discussed in chapter 2 why 9 out of 10 businesses fail in their first 5 years. With those odds, why would you even consider creating one? In my experience consulting with hundreds of businesses, much of this failure rate comes down to firstly the lack of knowledge of the business owners and secondly the lack of deploying tools like the internet, social media and sales funnels that could assist enormously. As a business owner, the smart thing to do now would be to initially look at your current product and service offerings and decide which of these are easy to sell online. Then ask yourself some questions:

Is this price point too high, acting as a barrier for my potential customers?

- If so, how can I create a value bridge to offer incremental steps with lower-priced products that can support the customer journey?

- How can I add more services that are of much higher value to my clients than I offer right now?

- How do I create a more targeted source of leads to begin with?

- How do I take my new value ladder and turn it into a new front and back-end sales funnel?

You may require help in creating these bridges to lead up to your core offer and also in creating increased value bridges beyond your core offer. If so, let's make sure you take note of option 2 next, which will assist greatly with this.

OPTION 2: Create your own products and services to sell

This option can certainly appear daunting, but it can be a very profitable undertaking when done correctly. Where do you start? How do you even go about creating your own products?

Firstly, to be clear, I am not talking about creating a widget of some kind here or some sort of physical product that can be sold on e-commerce sites. I want to use this example for more information or digital products. The statistics around the level of digital products that are being sold on a daily basis is just mind boggling!

Entire books have been written on the topic of product creation alone, but I will give you the key points to look out for in nine steps and save you the read!

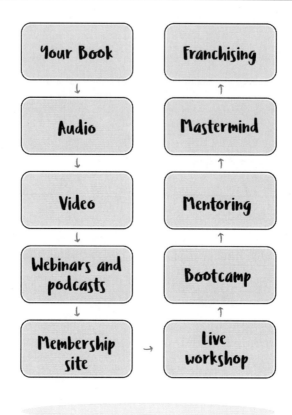

Fig 10.8: Creating an expert's product value ladder

Step 1: Your Book

Find something that you have some level of expertise in. What is it that you know that you can create at least a 100-page book on if pushed? It may be something that you do as part of your job every day. While initially writing a book may seem like a huge undertaking, when it is actually about a topic that you are very comfortable with, it can be a lot less challenging. Now you can be a little clever here, and use some leverage. You can find a professional to do this for you – and for a lot less than the numbers I mentioned in our example earlier in this chapter! Unless you are a writer, they will probably do a better job than you anyway. What you need to do is to define what the main chapters should be about and reach out on Google or upwork.com to find any number of ghost writers who can research and write the bulk of it for you. They will then return the manuscript to you to make the book your own! You can add in your own stories and case studies to make it yours. I was very tempted to do this myself with this book at one stage ;) but once you have an established "public voice" it is more difficult to do. If you are just starting out, I would strongly recommend outsourcing it.

This can mean having your book manuscript all written and ready to go in as little as 4 weeks. Once you get the manuscript back, use this opportunity to add in your personal stories and experiences to make it your own. You can focus on creating a great cover while the bulk of the book is being written for you. I'm sure you have heard the saying before, "never judge a book by its cover", yet it certainly doesn't stop us from doing it in all facets of life! The cover needs to be good, if not great. From a consumer standpoint, the quality of your book will be determined by the cover to a large degree, including the title and the testimonials, etc. on the front and back.

You can create a pre-order page with a free trial at http://resources.rethinksocialmedia.com. You can also download my useful guide on how to have your first book written in just 60 days without any risk at the same location. Before you know it, you'll have a book that you can put up on Amazon, and if you use the right people, you'll have a very good shot of being an Amazon best seller. And then the millions roll in, right? Well maybe in Zimbabwean dollars but not in American dollars! Your book may retail from anything as low as $5 to maybe $15. It is highly unlikely that the book will make you wealthy, but don't worry, this is only step 1! In an ideal world you would create a "pre-order now" page to sell the book in advance and use the proceeds to fund the research and writing phase. You can create a pre-order page with a free trial at www.resources.rethinksocialmedia.com. You can also download my useful guide on how to have your first book written in just 60 days without any risk at the same location.

Step 2: Audio

How can you double or triple the value of your book immediately? One way is to create an audiobook of the exact same book. Once again, there is no need to read this yourself, you can have a professional do it for you, especially if your voice is not publicly known. Costs can vary from very cheap to expensive, depending on your preferences. Perhaps for your first one, to keep the costs down you may read it yourself and use your own recording equipment. This can be so much easier than you think. Using software like Audacity will allow you to record your own voice completely free. You can use the microphone that comes with your smartphone and you're ready to go. Just make sure you are in a quiet place when doing the recording and avoid sounding monotone.

I have specific equipment recommended in www.resources. rethinksocialmedia.com. The reason why audio books are so valuable is that people often prefer to listen to books rather than read them. This has been drilled into us since we were children, when many of us preferred being read to at night than reading ourselves! It is much easier to find time to listen to a book while walking, jogging or driving than to make time to sit down and read. You can also charge more for an audiobook than a book, depending on how long the audio file is. I have paid up to $50 for audiobooks in the past, depending on the length of the book.

The beauty of having the audiobook complete is that you can instantly offer this as an upsell on Amazon or your own site directly after somebody buys your book to increase your income instantly. You now officially have 2 products!

Step 3: Video

At this stage, you can take the material that you have written about and transform it into video form. You can either speak to the camera, which most people would prefer not to do, or create a combination of "how to" videos showing what you are doing on your laptop and using PowerPoint presentations.

The real attraction of these is that you don't need to appear on camera yourself and their perceived value is much higher. The tool I recommend for this would be Camtasia. With video, it doesn't matter how many times you get it wrong, as you can always delete it and start again. It's very good preparation for the next stage of live videos or webinars.

Step 4: Webinars and podcasts

Now with the book, audio and videos under your belt, and surprisingly without too much effort, how do you take it to the next level? The next offering you can create is a series of online seminars known as webinars or web classes to your readers. This can appear a little daunting at first, especially as you have probably never done a webinar before, and what on earth are you going to speak about? Once again, it is easy when you know how. After you have created videos in step 3 and gained a lot of confidence from this experience, this is basically a live version of the same. Let us assume that your book has 16 chapters. What you can consider doing is planning for 8 webinars, one every 2 weeks over a 16-week period.

What do you cover? In each webinar you cover 2 chapters of the book. You don't read out the book, just some key snippets, but you share case studies and some additional examples that can help bring the book to life for the reader and to make it more practical for them. You can also invite readers to get involved and ask you any questions that they may have, and you can answer them throughout the webinar. It is always best to take questions in writing rather than verbally, at least when you start, as you really don't know what kind of lunatic might be on the other side of the screen! Make sure you record each of the sessions so you can create a product that you can offer on an evergreen basis – once you have all the recordings, you have them forever. In the last stages of the webinars you can also make all your followers aware of what the next offering is, which usually entails letting them know what they need to do to get closer to you, the author. With each step in the funnel they are getting closer to you and getting more value, so you price the offer accordingly. If you are ever unsure about how much to charge, a quick acid test I use is this: is the customer who purchases this getting at least 10 times the value of what they are paying?

There are many huge benefits of running a webinar in this way. Firstly, you sell it in advance so if no one buys, you do not waste your time doing it. You can test price points anywhere from $100 to $1,500. You can offer it to your readers and listeners before you run any webinars. If there aren't enough spaces sold to make it worth your while doing them, then you can decide against doing them if you choose. It is a great feeling to be paid in advance before you have even delivered the service and it certainly motivates you to get prepared. Secondly, there is no room hire involved. Using a tool like gotowebinar or webinarjam (both available at http://resources.rethinksocialmedia.com), or many others, you can run the meeting from your own bedroom if you wish. Thirdly, you can have the customers drive the conversation by having them ask questions. The fourth benefit is that you can find ready-made testimonials of your products as people share the amazing insights or feedback that they have had with their experience so far.

The fifth benefit is that you don't have to do them all yourself – you can invite guest speakers to sit in on one of the live webinars. The sixth benefit is that you can also use this as a podcast as you run them every 2 weeks and can launch the podcast separately at a later date as your fifth product offering!

While there are many more benefits, I will leave you with just one more for now: the opportunity you have on a webinar to explain the next stage in your funnel and incentivise your live attendees to get a special offer as a reward for being in attendance live.

Step 5: Membership Site

At this point, you can offer your people a more regular way of keeping in contact with you with additional content and support on a monthly basis. They want regular coaching. This can be set up as a membership site and is a great way of delivering content on a more ongoing basis and not having to worry that you need to create all the content up front. This would be completely unnecessary and possibly a waste of time, as things may have changed as the months pass by. People can then pay you on a monthly basis to receive additional training and support, with you there ready to support them on their journey. It is an excellent product for bringing more consistency to the cash flow in your business.

Deciding how much to charge very much depends on what you are offering. I personally have or have had membership sites ranging from $50 a month to $300 a month and could have a few thousand people in the program at any one time. You need to support it accordingly depending on numbers. For the first time, you may need to hire customer support if you do have quite significant numbers on your membership site.

"How do I create one of those, and how much would it be to set up?" Well first things first, as always let's sell this in advance. Let's get the bookings in before we decide if it's worthwhile creating one.

If I could tell you how to set one up without spending a penny, would you be interested? Ha, I'm sure you would! Well there is a website that I'm sure you have heard of before. You certainly have by reading this far – it's called Facebook! Facebook has a facility called groups and within groups you as the owner of a group, which is free to set up, can make the group public or private. In the private groups you only grant access to the people that you wish to have access to it. You can offer your membership program for a specific cost and then take the payments on something like PayPal or Stripe and then send an email to the customer with their access approved to the Facebook group.

There are benefits and drawbacks to using Facebook groups for this. In terms of the benefits, for starters it is free. It is also very easy to use and to provide the content to your group members. Most people are on Facebook so it isn't a difficult transition for someone to use the system, as they are likely already familiar with it. You avoid having to set up usernames and logins for everyone, as you can control it through Facebook. You also have an automatic built-in forum where people in the group can support each other and even answer each other's questions, while you or your customer service rep can monitor the chat for any inappropriate behaviour. I have a friend in the fitness industry, Pat Divilly, who regularly makes over $40,000 a month running fitness programs through private groups on Facebook.

The other option is to create a fit-for-purpose membership site. This has a lot of advantages over the Facebook platform. Your content is protected by individual usernames and passwords. People can't easily download and share your content with others. You can easily change out older videos and replace them with updated content. You can track where the site is being accessed from, in case the user has shared their login details with others. Of course, the downside is it costs money, so it depends on your budget and your intent. There is some great software out there that does almost everything for you. The software providers can also provide support offerings where someone in their team can set up the platform for you. One huge benefit of the software mentioned earlier that allows you to build funnels, http://resources.rethinksocialmedia.com, is that it has an in-built facility to host your membership site – that is where I currently host mine. In addition, if you are looking for a more advanced software with all the bells and whistles, I can recommend Kajabi.

Step 6: Live workshop

At this point, you may be ready to be brave enough to run your first live one-day event on the book. In this one day, you will make the book come alive with workbooks full of practical steps to show people how to apply the book in day-to-day life. What you charge for this really depends on your status in terms of a following and your own personal confidence of what level of value you can provide on the day. You could bring in guest speakers, but remember the audience are really there to see you. In the past I have charged between $100 and $10,000 for one-day sessions with me, but clearly I didn't start off by charging $10,000 for a one-day workshop! You build your confidence as you grow.

To encourage the people to pay and come see you in person, as it can be a hassle to travel, you can add in many bonuses, such as a signed book and the webinar recordings that you have just completed. Nothing beats meeting your customers in person. You can certainly build a relationship with your social media content and emails, but essentially, they are a replacement for meeting in person. A lot of your customers will jump at the chance to meet with you, while some won't be too pushed either way. That is why your marketing on the webinar and the bonuses you offer them will assist greatly in incentivising and giving them a reason to come and meet you.

Once at the live event, after reviewing the steps of the work book, etc., it is always good to share the success stories of the various buyers of your product, regardless of what niche you are in. It's a great way of building a sense of community and purpose. You might think that this is the pinnacle of products and offerings, but it is not! You can see what happens in the room on the day. People will want more. They love the feel of the tribe and the sense of community, and while some will get upset that you offer them more, most people will expect it, and some will even be upset if you don't at least give them the opportunity to go to another level of training.

Step 7: Bootcamp

What is even better than a one-day workshop? Well you might say, a 2 or 3-day or week-long event. You need to make sure you get your costings accurate on this if you are proceeding to this step. You will most likely be bringing people away for some kind of an intensive bootcamp, where they get the chance to set aside a few days to implement what it is they have been reading and learning about. You will have fewer people on this program than on step 6, but this is the natural stream of the funnel – at each stage you will have fewer who will invest in the next level.

At longer bootcamps like this, it is a good idea to bring other speakers to break up the monotony of listening to you over and over again! You can also have each of the attendees present themselves about their own situation or challenges as they relate to the products or services you are providing.

In terms of price points, it will depend firstly on your fixed costs from the hotel. Is it a 5-star all-inclusive type event? To be honest it probably should be, as this will be what is considered a very high-end program. You could be charging from $10k to $30k, depending on where and for how long, and how much staffing you require.

Step 8: Mentoring

What is the next natural offering that someone might want after an extended time with you? Well, as you move down the funnel, people are continuously getting closer and closer to you. Most likely they will now want to work 1:1 with you and learn directly from you and have access to your personal email and phone, etc. This is the process of mentoring. This is a major undertaking and very time consuming, and as a result it is not cheap for the consumer; in many cases, it can be strictly limited in terms of numbers, as it does use your personal time. You should really think about it seriously before offering it. Start with one person only if you have never mentored before. It is an excellent way to create amazing testimonials, but as I say, the downside is the time commitment. You can always create a waiting list so that in essence you can set it up almost as a very high-end membership site. Mentoring can cost anywhere from $10k to $100k.

An alternative to mentoring at this stage in the process is making the facility available to build a bespoke solution for the client. If you have a team in your business, you can offer that the services will be done for the consumer by your team, a "done for you" offer like we showed in the Bank For Your Book Ltd. example earlier. This could vary from building the customer's internet business, sales funnel, to their social media set up and management, branding, book writing and publishing. It will depend on what you decide to focus on for your business to find out which is most relevant. The price points for these services, depending on how complete the service is, will be anywhere from the $10k to $100k.

Step 9: Mastermind

It would seem that you may be at the end of the line here. Possibly! There is still a strong possibility that a client at this level will also want to be part of a community where they can learn from thought leaders in this field. This can be offered in the form of a Mastermind.

A Mastermind is generally organised by one or more people who are experts in a particular area and they meet up, usually in person every couple of months, to discuss the problems in each other's businesses and collectively come up with solutions for each individual. It is a phenomenally powerful process. Not only do you have your most pertinent business issues solved, you get advice from people who have been there and done that before, who will not be afraid to call it as it is and let you know when you are about to go off the rails. It also has an accountability function, as you must live up to commitments that you made at your previous meetings, regardless of your excuses.

Masterminds are held by various experts in their fields all over the world and the more well-known ones would start at a minimum of $25k per year - an annual recurring charge. I am a member of some myself and consider them an invaluable learning and accountability facility. One other key component of why people attend Masterminds is the calibre of people that they meet at them. One meeting resulting in a partnership may pay for the next 10 years of your Mastermind through only one connection. Setting up something like this is a big undertaking and it is very unlikely that most people will get to this stage of running their own. However, as I will describe in part 3, there is an easier way ☺.

Step 10: Franchising

Really, there is a step 10? How could there be anything more than this? Indeed, there is! Again, it's definitely not for everyone, it will be right up there as one of the highest, if not the highest, offering in your funnel. The next stage is where you can offer your business model as a franchise opportunity for your customers.

Certain customers will be in a position to take this model of yours and to bring it to another part of the world. Depending on exclusivity contracts that determine where the franchise can do business, you can offer them a specific city, state, country, continent, etc. The costs will vary accordingly, but start from as low as $100k to as much as $2 million+ depending on what the franchise is and how large an exclusivity contract you are providing. I have a friend Tom Hua who does this very successfully in China.

Phew! You may have thought step 1, creating a book, would be a challenge, right? It is all very doable, but you do need to focus on step 1 before step 2 and step 2 before 3, etc., or you could give up before you even get started! That is the magic formula for your own products. We looked at the book writing training company example earlier and why as a business owner you should always be looking at how you can add more value to your clients, whether through your or others' products. Now you can see how this can look over a larger scale.

"There MUST be an easier way though, right? We didn't come all this way to be told, 'off you go now and start writing your book' I hope?" Lol! If you are asking that, I can certainly empathise. When I started with my online business, there was just no way I would ever be able to have the confidence to know how to create something to sell for $100 let alone $100,000!

There is some great news though; there is a much easier way, and that is option 3.

Option 3: Other people's products

Let's assume you have read through the first two options and you don't currently have products, or you just couldn't be bothered creating your own. Does that rule you out? Of course not, you are now officially ready to jump into the option that has the most likely probability of success – option 3. This is by far my favourite option, especially nowadays. Selling other people's or businesses' products is such an awesome strategy for so many reasons! Firstly, a product should never define a business. Your business is the database that you build. The people in your database are buying solutions or outcomes from you, not products! They will most likely end up buying products from you that don't even exist just yet! Some poor entrepreneur is busting a gut right now to create this amazing solution that you can decide to sell when it is tested and ready to go. However, selling other people's products It is often misunderstood and poorly explained.

Let me make an assumption: that you have never had an online business, and you are nervous about the prospect of starting one too, as there seems to be SO much to it. Do you know what, you are absolutely right! Yes, you read that correctly. Setting up an internet business, or alternatively bringing you current offline business online, can be a laborious task with lots to learn, and at times it can be difficult to see any progress being made. The reason for this is that many people start an internet business with the intention of immediately creating and selling their own products. This means, among other things, that you will need to learn how to (or pay someone to) do the following:

- Create your own free gift(s)

- Purchase your website domain name

- Purchase and set up your hosting with ftp

- Create at least some of the products from the 10 described in option 2

- Learn how to create all kinds of products on different media

- Design all of the logos and branding for your products

- Build a sales funnel online to allow for people to buy each level of the product

- Employ a sales team to follow up on people who did not purchase

- Potentially start running your own webinars

- Run your own live events, coaching programs, membership sites and mentoring

- Create all of your coaching content and continue to update it as changes happen

- Create sales videos in a professional studio

- Create sales copy, writing like a professional copywriter

- Write a book(s)

- Build website(s)

- Integration with merchant account facilities

- Build up all your social network profiles

- Create and manage all of your social media organic posts

- Interact and respond to all posts and comments

- Run multiple ad campaigns and test profitability of each to each of your opt-in pages

- Build a series of opt-in pages with various free gifts you will need to create

- Assuming someone buys it, deliver the training

- Create a membership site

- Set up a help centre to answer and support any queries

- Keep up-to-date on all the latest changes in your industry so your programmes remain relevant

- Work out all the tax implications of charging people in different countries

- Become a very competent sales person, as you will make most of the sales

- Learn how to communicate with people from both sales and marketing standpoints

- Set up follow-up email marketing campaigns

- Continue to innovate with your products

- Track your competitors continuously to find out what they are changing with their products

- Monitor ongoing price changes in the competitive landscape

- Many more…

How does this sound? Doesn't it make option 2, which seems quite appealing at the beginning, look that little bit less likely? Very few people make it to the top of their game with option 2, at least not to begin with. It makes a lot of sense to have the money come in first with the promotion of other people's products while you embark on creating or promoting your own. This is why I come back to option 3 again and reiterate that it truly rocks!

Look at table 10.1 below, where we show graphically what is involved with option 1, 2 and 3

	Option 1	Option 2	Option 3
Create your own free gifts	✓	✓	✗
Purchase your website domain name	✓	✓	✗
Purchase and set up your hosting with ftp	✓	✓	✗
Create at least some of the products from the 9 options described in option 2	✓	✓	✗
Learn how to create products	✓	✓	✗
Design all of the logos and branding for your products	✓	✓	✗
Build a sales funnel online to allow for people to buy each level of the product	✓	✓	✗
Employ a sales team to follow up on people who did not purchase	✓	✓	✗

Potentially start running your own webinars	✓	✓	✗
Run your own live events, coaching programs, membership sites and mentoring	✓	✓	✗
Create all of your coaching content and continue to update it as changes happen	✓	✓	✗
Create sales videos in a professional studio	✓	✓	✗
Create sales copy, writing like a professional writer	✓	✓	✗
Write a book	✓	✓	✗
Integration with merchant account facilities	✓	✓	✗
Build up all your social network profiles	✓	✓	✓
Build complex website(s)	✓	✓	✗
Create and manage all of your social media organic posts	✓	✓	✓
Interact and respond to all posts and comments	✓	✓	✓
Run multiple ad campaigns and test profitability of each to each of your opt-in pages	✓	✓	✓
Build a series of opt-in pages with various free gifts you will need to create	✓	✓	✓
Assuming someone buys it, deliver the training	✓	✓	✗
Create a membership site	✓	✓	✗
Set up a help centre to answer and support any queries	✓	✓	✗

Keep up-to-date on all the latest changes in your industry so your programmes remain relevant	✓	✓	✗
Work out all the tax implications of charging people in different countries	✓	✓	✗
Become a very competent sales person, as you will make most of the sales	✓	✓	✗
Learn how to communicate with people from both sales and marketing standpoints	✓	✓	✗
Set up follow-up email marketing campaigns	✓	✓	✓
Continue to innovate with your products	✓	✓	✗
Track your competitors continuously to find out what they are changing with their products	✓	✓	✓
Monitor ongoing price changes in the competitive landscape	✓	✓	✗

Table 10.1: Your options for products to sell

I think this table illustrates it best, and if you had made a start at an internet business before and were somewhat unsuccessful, it was probably because of the volume of work you were attempting to do. "Ok, I am convinced, it's option 3 for me BUT I still have the same question, what do I sell? And how does this work? I just don't get it!" Now with the grounding and additional knowledge that you have, it will be much easier for me to explain this to you again. Let me use a widespread example. In chapter 3 I discussed the concept of how affiliate marketing works. The term "affiliate marketing" is often used for this process, but this term also has some negative connotations for people, stemming from some marketers who over the years may have sold products that were not up to scratch. But isn't that the case for any other business? There will always be a few bad eggs.

This is how I like to explain it. Have you ever heard of or shopped at any of the following: Tesco, Sainsburys, Lidl, Morrisons, Aldi, Walmart, Kmart or any of the major supermarket chains? I am sure the answer must be "yes". Have you ever considered their business model? I am sure the answer is most likely "no", or you would already be replicating it!

The shops that I mentioned are multi-billion dollar per year companies in most instances; that's billion with a "b". As a business, what value do they provide? It might seem pretty straightforward, they provide us with the necessities of food and drink and some clothing, etc. at reasonably low cost at a convenient location.

What if I told you that their model is quite simple?

Step 1: Find an empty field near where lots of people live

Step 2: Build a big warehouse with lots of shelves

Step 3: Install some cash registers to accept money

Step 4: Let others' businesses provide all of the products that people want and have them deal with the customer service issues.

Genius, right? Let's build an empty warehouse and let all the individual companies do all the research, product testing, product creation, branding, marketing, customer service and so on. Do you see a resemblance to option 3 above now? This is affiliate marketing at its finest. I strongly suggest you consider becoming a "virtual" Tesco or Walmart, using social media to get to lots of people and then promote other businesses' amazing products. We discussed this in Chapter 3 – positioning yourself in the middle just makes so much sense. And to top it all off, it is so much easier! Why not give people the products they already recognise, are looking for, like, trust and want, where you have the choice to select only the highest quality products available worldwide?

Fig 10.9: The happy matchmaker

That being said, which specific products can you promote right now? You're unlikely to become a Walmart by the morning! The answer is in modelling and leveraging the experts who are already in your niche. Google the top experts in your niche and subscribe to their email lists. Look out for their emails and look at the products they are currently promoting, as these will likely be the top-selling products right now, otherwise they would not be promoting them. You can also model the emails and subject lines they are using with the products so that you are not starting from scratch. Ideally, what you are looking for is to promote a product for somebody who has an entire back-end funnel in place and who pays you a percentage of any upsells that your lead might duly purchase over time. This is fantastic leverage, as you can make sales over and over again of higher value with no additional work on your part.

This is exactly what I provide for my students (and readers)! I invite them to become an affiliate of mine, offering a free 90-minute training or a social media checklist as their free gift and then they make a percentage of any of the sales that their leads may purchase subsequently at any time in the future! So instead of making one sale, you can benefit from the front and back-end funnels later! This could result in thousands of dollars for the affiliate like you from a single lead that you sign up for the free gift ☺. Sounds great, right? If it is something you are interested in, you can sign up to become an affiliate for free and promote some of my funnels through http://resources.rethinksocialmedia.com. You will also find banners for your blogs, to use as advertisements.

Summary

The immediate upsell is an essential part of a highly profitable online business. It allows us to determine which of our leads are buyers instantly, and it also allows us in some cases to liquidate the cost of building our list immediately. It is important to come up with a series of offerings with increasing prices in addition to our core offer, which is known as a value ladder. Once you are clear on the tiers of products, these can now be set up as a front and back-end sales funnel. You have different choices when it comes to which products to sell; either the products of your current business, look at creating your own or alternatively promoting only the very best products of other businesses for a commission.

Traditional Thinking:

With business, it makes sense to create your own products or provide your own services and then offer one core product to your prospects. When they purchase it, your next goal as a business owner is to find more buyers for the same product.

RETHINK:

Business today has changed enormously. Rather than the product being the focus of the business, working out how quickly a new lead can pay for itself through an immediate upsell can often indicate whether your business is worth pursuing. There is no need to create your own product or provide a service yourself in order to have a highly successful business.

Chapter 11: Nurture Your List

"If you are not taking care of your customer, your competitor will."
- Bob Hooey

We are now venturing into the key phase of nurturing the relationship with our leads, prospects, customers and clients. After going through the effort of creating your sales funnels, it is this step that allows you to take advantage of it to its full effect. How you manage your leads will determine how likely they are to progress up your value ladder.

Knowing what to say and who to say it to when it comes to your social media and the complete online experience can be an absolute minefield! It's all too easy to get sucked into the specific technology or tactic being used without taking stock of the bigger picture. In chapter 8, part 3, we discussed the customer journey, moving from awareness to an ongoing relationship over time, using the water font metaphor. Asking someone to marry them on your very first meeting is probably not the greatest strategy if you are looking for that outcome, regardless of whether you are a super stud or not! Communication is a process that evolves with time, and the rules change as common ground, familiarity and trust are established.

As Rollo May puts it, "Communication leads to community, that is, to understanding, intimacy and mutual valuing."

Having previously covered the importance of understanding values and understanding how people view the world in chapter 7, this should have a deeper meaning to you now. In order to better understand this concept, I will subdivide our communication plans according to the part of the "Awareness" to "Relations" journey the audience are at, as we move them from "cold traffic" to "addicts". There is some degree of overlap, but it should start to provide you with a solid groundwork to plan your future engagements.

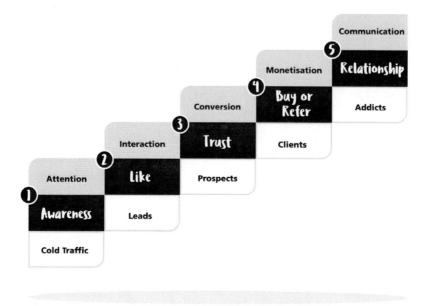

Fig 11.1: Relationship Management journey

Phase 1: Awareness

This is the natural first step in your online journey: Crossing the chasm from being introduced to cold traffic as a complete stranger to somebody that is recognisable and familiar. This is done primarily through paying for advertisements. Traditionally through media platforms, this was performed by running television, radio, magazine and newspaper ads and the awareness process began. However, this ruled out most people and small businesses based on budget reasons alone! The bigger the budget, the greater the reach. Thankfully with social media this has all changed. Nobody is excluded from getting their "Awareness" hat on, even with the smallest of budgets. Here are a number of the main sources that you can get started with:

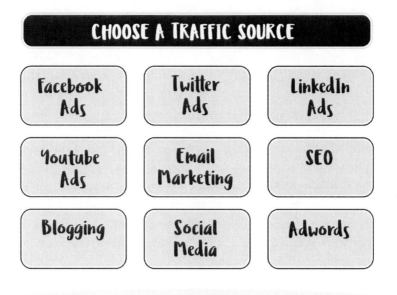

Fig 11.2: Choosing a traffic source

There are multiple means of bringing yourself to the attention of your target market, with the assumption that at first, they do not know who you are. Our goal is to warm these people up sufficiently that they will be interested enough in taking the next step with us, which is the process of requesting the lead magnet. We are NOT looking to make sales, we are looking to build a database.

With this goal in mind, in these advertisements particularly, you must stick to the basics of clearly outlining for the client what the result is that you are promising them. Depending on the source of traffic that you are going to use out of the ones outlined earlier, the method of delivery will vary, but the promise of providing a significant change to their lives is always the same: that is, you will take the consumer from where they are today to some future happier state. Let's take a look at each of these in a little more detail.

The best method I have seen to cleverly implement this in the awareness stage is through something called "eduselling". This is the processing of selling your idea through education. In many instances, people can dismiss products or services immediately for reasons such as cost, when actually that decision was made without them being fully informed. The best way to illustrate eduselling is with an example.

I once had a client who owned a beauty parlour and the most profitable part of her business was her laser hair removal treatments. I asked her if she had as many customers as she wished for specifically for that treatment, and she informed me that she could certainly do with having more customers. I asked her what the primary objections were of her laser hair removal prospects, and she said that there were generally two main issues: Firstly, it was too expensive, and secondly, there was a level of fear around the safety and pain of the exercise.

It was the perfect situation to practice eduselling. Let's assume that we have completely cold traffic coming to a blog post or an advertisement that we have about our laser hair removal business. Rather than offering a discount coupon, which is what most would do, we would not try to sell anything other than the facts. What I asked my client to do was to work out the average amount of money a woman spends in both time and money per year on shavers, blades, creams, waxes, etc. for hair removal and then to work out what that was over 10 years. When these facts were presented as information, it clearly showed that it made financial sense to have laser hair removal! The money objection of it being too expensive was instantly removed. The objection changed to perhaps the treatment was too expensive in one payment, which is a completely different objection and can be managed with payment plans, for example.

The second objection of safety and pain concerns can be handled in the same way. You could start by painting the picture of how unsafe it is to be standing naked on a wet slippery surface, not fully awake, with your children banging at the bathroom door rushing you while you have a razor-sharp blade in your hand! Which is the safer and less painful option? You could of course have fun with this too, and it will act as a pre-frame bridge encouraging people to the next stage, which in this case was to offer a discount coupon for a pay-in-full or a no-interest payment plan offering.

Now let us take a look at each of the traffic methods illustrated above and discuss in some more detail.

Traditional Thinking:

A straight-up discount offering is the best way for a business to make a sale.

RETHINK:

Use the process of eduselling in your communications to educate your leads about why your product or service is a no-brainer.

Paid advertising:

For the sake of simplicity, I will group all of the paid ads together, social or otherwise. Rather than telling you about a one-size-fits-all type ad that doesn't exist, the key here is to gaining awareness of the best ads that are being used within your niche. It is one of the cheapest and most cost-effective ways of learning how to create excellent ads. On Facebook and other networks, you can follow and like the pages of the companies that are already established in your niche to begin with, in order to be targeted by the ads that are working for your competition. This will result in you being privy to the main ads of your competitors, so you can model their advertisements. In fact, you can completely switch your Facebook account to only see ads using the Google Chrome extension BigBigAds. This is when you've officially moved to the dark side – only wanting to see ads on Facebook! For YouTube and Google, you can type in the key search terms that people may want within your target market and then look at the ads you are served within both these sites. The alternative here is that you pay for trained experts to run your ads for you. This is advisable with Google and YouTube advertising, as they are very specialist and well-established. You may want to test Facebook advertising yourself, as it is going to be a key component of your business moving forward, and at least understanding how the ads work will be a very beneficial exercise.

There are six key elements to a paid ad review:

- Irresistible offer

- Engaging copy

- Graphic or video creative

- Trail or scent

- Targeting

- Follow-up retargeting

As you study the ads of your competitors, you should take screenshots of them to study parts 1 to 3 above. The beauty of such advertising is that you can see EXACTLY what ads your competitors are already paying for. You can check out their offers, how they frame them within the copy and what types of videos or images they are using, in order to model the approach yourself.

The "trail or scent", number 4 above, is the sense of repetition or familiarity and continuity between the ad offer and the branding once you click onto the next page from the ad. The closer the ad and the landing page match for language, headlines, imagery and benefits, the more familiar the content seems to the person and the more likely they are to proceed to the next step and become a lead. In order to study how your competitors do this, you can click on their ads and then once more take screenshots and study the landing pages they are using, to give you ideas for modelling what is working best in your industry at this point in time. When it comes to "targeting", or working out who your competitors are targeting for their advertisements, there is an amazing tool called similarweb.com, which allows you to find out exactly what methods your competitors are using for their traffic sources. You can find out where they are placing their ads and find the exact demographics of those that are being targeted by their ads!

Once you click on an ad, it is likely that you are going to be retargeted again by that marketer. Have you ever clicked onto booking.com to look at a hotel and decide not to buy? For the rest of the day that exact same hotel on the exact dates you were looking for seems to follow you around the internet! That is what the process of retargeting is. Just like above, be sure to take screenshots of these ads and track the differences in wording, imagery, etc. on the retargeted ad as opposed to the original ad. You can learn a lot from this one strategy alone.

Traditional Thinking:

Let's pick a budget and start running ads across a variety of platforms, competing with all the experts, hopefully to find out what works by myself.

RETHINK:

Within each of the social networks, be sure to like, follow or subscribe to your competitors so that you are targeted by their ads. This allows you to monitor their ad sets, images, videos, headlines and buttons so that rather than learning the expensive and time-consuming way with your own money, you only leverage the ads that are already being used and tested with other people's money on a regular basis.

Email marketing:

It might appear strange that email marketing is in the list of sources of cold traffic. How can it be cold traffic if you can email people? Surely if we had their email addresses, they would by definition not be cold traffic? Yes, you are correct! In this example you don't have the email addresses BUT somebody else does. A really good strategy to turn completely cold traffic into warm traffic is to partner with somebody who is already established in your niche and ask them to "mail out" for you, recommending you and perhaps offering your gift to their database for free to anyone who chooses to opt in for it. Ideally you would want to know this person and trust their database and the sources of traffic. For someone to do this for you, there will need to be some kind of reciprocal service that you provide in return.

There is an alternative method of doing this, which is paying people to email to their lists directly. This is known as "soloads", where you schedule in the timing for your email to be sent to somebody else's list. This is an area that I have personally had very little success in. The concept of people renting their databases to other marketers does not make sense to me, as it is the most important part of your business to protect.

Traditional Thinking:

Let's buy some soloads to get lots of opt-ins very quickly

RETHINK:

Who do you know in your niche that you can approach and ask them if they could co-promote something with you and have a clear win for them in this arrangement too?

Search engine optimisation (SEO):

With regards to SEO, this is where you pay digital agencies to work their "magic" and hopefully get you listed highly on Google for specific keyword searches. It wouldn't be my recommendation to start with this business, as the costs can be prohibitive for start-ups or small work-from-home businesses.

Traditional Thinking:

You must be ranked on the front page of Google in order to be successful.

RETHINK:

It makes sense to go after the lower hanging fruit first with other traffic sources rather than going down the SEO route, especially when you have a small business.

Blogging:

The concept behind blogging is that you create your own fresh content on a topic in the hope that people are going to be interested in what it is you have to say and come back and read more. It can be a very daunting task for beginners and even established business owners, especially when you are not an expert in your niche, and you may struggle with writing or expressing your thoughts in words. Perhaps you quite simply don't have the time to create new content on a regular basis. My suggestion on this is in order to get you started and to "win over" the cold traffic, share the videos and articles of other experts to begin with (make sure they are freely available to share first) and build your credibility by sharing the knowledge of more established experts. Your blog can be used as a portal or hub for people to find the views of all the experts as opposed to just your own, and as a result your own credibility will increase.

When you have your blog up and running and you're sharing others' content, your next step is to create a post of your own that warms people up to the idea of the specific problem and how it can potentially be solved. These types of posts are known as "pre-frame bridges". They make people much more likely to want to download your lead magnet at the next step. It can be a good strategy to run ads to cold traffic and send them directly to a pre-frame bridge such as a blog post, that then sends them to the lead magnet as warmer traffic and more likely to download the lead magnet, having now being educated more on the subject.

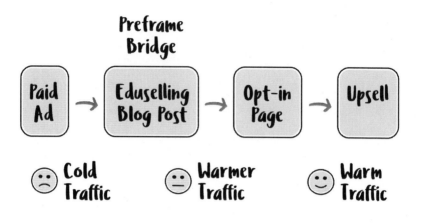

Fig 11.3 Introducing a "pre-frame bridge"

It is also now possible to send people directly from your social media posts or advertisements to an already well-known, highly-established blog's posts, and on this page, have a lead magnet encouraging people to join your list to learn more! For more on this more complex strategy, feel free to download a report at http://resources.rethinksocialmedia.com.

Traditional Thinking: You must spend hours a day creating completely new content of your "own", which is based on completely unique ideas not borrowed from anybody ☺, and share it daily to build up a community of people who will respect you for doing this, and hopefully at some point give you money!

RETHINK: Nobody cares what you have to say on this topic… yet! So give people what they want, which is the opinions of the well-established experts in this niche. Your blog acts as a portal, giving people one convenient location to find all the best information on your topic. You can schedule content once a week to go out automatically. You can then create one great article as a pre-frame bridge for cold traffic to your lead magnet that you can drive your paid traffic to.

Social Media:

As social networks become more and more prevalent in everyday society, the days of being able to just come up with a clever idea and put it up in Instagram or another social network for free, and it suddenly going viral, are all but gone.

There is still a perception that if you do continue to post regularly on social media, somehow your message will eventually be picked up by the right people. Of course, there is always the possibility that given unlimited time and resources, something might eventually work. However, I am here to stack the odds in your favour and show you how to get real measurable profit now, as opposed to following one of my least favourite strategies, the "strategy of hope". With social media marketing, in very simple terms, if you want results fast you must invest in the ad platforms. Let's take that as a given. Please remember we are speaking about small budgets here, as little as a couple of dollars a day. This does not, however, mean that you completely abandon all forms of social media that do not involve ads!

I have listed social media as one of the cold traffic options, as it is still a valid strategy when used in the correct way. You can think of your "free" social media posts as almost a "dry run" for what you may run ads with later. Facebook, Twitter, Instagram, YouTube and more will give you detailed analytics on how that free post is performing without any money behind it. You can find out how many engagements, shares, replies and likes your posts have, and what times are working best. Those preliminary results can give you an indication of which posts are worth "boosting", based on the original small sample size.

"What do I post? Does it need to be unique to me?" These are two very big questions, and they are fundamental to a business' social media strategy. As before, one of the best things you can do is to join the social media platforms of the established experts. They are happy for you to share their content and it really does give you a good feel for what is working for them. This is niche-dependent but it won't take you long to spot trends in what is working for their audiences. In particular, look out for the posts that have received lots of likes and shares already. It is similar to the concept of the blog, but even easier to do within other social networks like Twitter and Facebook.

Content creation:

When it comes to creating your own fresh content, there are ways that you really can be smart about what you do to leverage the time you have as effectively as possible. Our goal remains the same at this point: we want people to become aware of who we are and what solution we have for our audience. The best use of your time in this type of scenario is to create one piece of content, for example a 20-minute video. Be sure to ask people what they think of the content and ask them to share the information – if you don't ask, you won't get! When you are more confident, you can broadcast this video as a livestream across Facebook (Live), Twitter (Periscope), YouTube (Live) for starters, but be sure to make a recording because we have lots of plans for this content!

Rather than just posting the recording out on your YouTube channel and Facebook, etc., our goal will be to repurpose what we have as effectively as possible. The first thing that can be done is to split the video into 10 or more smaller videos, each providing a little nugget or two of information about the result you are delivering. These can be posted on multiple video networks and across Twitter, Facebook, etc., so instead of one video you have at least 11.

You can then have the content transcribed. You can do this yourself or you could use websites such as www.rev.com that will transcribe your video for you at the amazing price of $1 per minute. This will certainly save you a lot of time, effort and headaches. Once you have the transcriptions, you can take some of the text to use directly as tweets or posts. You can also turn some of this text into postcards, which you often see as motivational quotes on your social timelines. There is a nice simple and free way to do this using www.canva.com, which allows you to create banners, images and postcards that you can populate with whatever text you have and then schedule to go out on your various platforms. You could also take the audio file and use it as a podcast at a later stage.

It is amazing what can be produced from one simple video once a week! Best of all, the content is completely unique to you. To begin with, when you haven't built up your confidence, share others until you start to create your own, and then build this up one step at a time. I will refer to when and where to post later in the book in chapter 13.

At this stage of the game, however, remember the purpose of social media is to convince complete strangers who have probably come across you through a shared post that you have a lead magnet that is truly irresistible, and once you get them there, the communication modes change.

Traditional Thinking:

On your social media accounts, post regularly with motivational quotes interspersed with offers and discounts for what you sell. Create lots of unique content to be shared on your social networks.

RETHINK:

The key to the successful use of social media is leverage. Create one decent piece of content per week and repurpose it across all of the social networks where your target market resides.

Phase 2: Like (interaction)

In order to move people through the process from awareness to trust, there is middle ground, which is the "like" phase. Now that you have established the first moves with each of the different tactics above, "liking" occurs through repetition of phase 1. The more often your posts are seen, the more likely they are to bite, so to speak. One key element to remember here in the communications is to add humour. People absolutely love to laugh, and regardless of how serious your business may be, there is always the opportunity to inject some humour. This is the enabler between awareness and like.

Specific retargeting of the people that watched your ads in phase 1 can also be deployed at this point, which means you can reshow your ads, or different versions of the ads, to people that you know have seen you before but haven't necessarily taken the action that you wished, which was to join your database. This is just like the www.booking.com example we mentioned earlier about looking at a hotel and deciding against purchasing, only for that exact hotel on the same dates to follow you around the internet? This is retargeting working at its best, delivering to you what you wanted but with the added incentive of a discount if booked now.

Traditional Thinking:

Move traffic to the sale as quickly as possible.

RETHINK:

You must firstly appeal to your cold traffic audience so that they are willing enough to take a small first step of commitment with a simple like or a follow.

Phase 3: Trust (conversion)

> *"Success comes from taking the initiative and following up...*
> *persisting... eloquently expressing the depth of your love.*
> *What simple action could you take today to produce a*
> *new momentum toward success in your life?"*
> *- Tony Robbins*

In this phase, the person you have been targeting is ready to take things to the next level of the relationship. They are charged sufficiently to engage with you but not enough to be fully "charged" just yet; they are ready to take communication to the next level. If you have marketed correctly and the message has matched the person, the lead magnet was a no-brainer and they have finally taken one of the key action steps that you had planned for. They are now in your database ready for the immediate upsell. Your communication tactic changes now and rapidly picks up pace. You have yet to make money from this arrangement, and the longer you wait to act, the less likely it is to occur. When someone is in the state of having taken action, it is much easier to have them take an additional action and maintain that momentum rather than waiting to come back at a later date. We want to take advantage of this newly-formed relationship and change the relationship as quickly as possible from being a purely informational one to a financial transaction.

What comes in phase 4 is a series of follow-up tactics that you can use as soon as the person has joined your database. It is important to have some kind of welcome message letting the prospect know what to expect next, that this is basically the beginning of something wonderful – the change they have been looking for. It is also a legal requirement, as we will cover in chapter 15.

Traditional Thinking:

Once a person joins your database you must shower them in blessings and free gifts for as long as you can to win them over.

RETHINK:

From the second a new person has joined your list, their level of enthusiasm and interest begins to drop. You must be ready to monetise this arrangement as quickly as possible to qualify your leads.

Phase 4: Buy phase (monetization)

In Chapter 10, we looked at our front-end and back-end sales funnels based on our value ladder of product or service offerings. I did mention back then that these were the "basic" versions. In this "monetization" phase, we can now add more meat to those bones and turn the basic funnel into a much slicker operation.

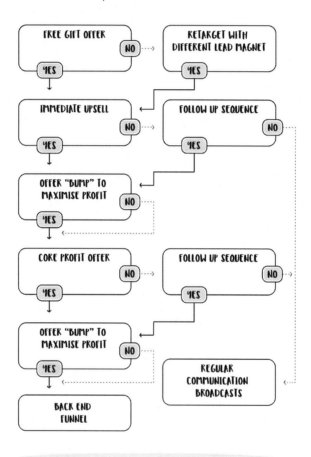

Fig 11.4: Funnels part 2 – ascension through the more in-depth offerings

The key difference to our graphics here is that we are now adding in email sequences that follow up with the lead/prospect/customer and client based on their actions at each step of the funnel. As soon as you get that first "yes" to the lead magnet, you want to immediately make your first offering, as we discussed in chapter 10, with the free plus shipping offering for the book. You want to make a clear distinction between the people who are ready to get serious and the rest. Usually it makes sense next to offer something that is relatively cheap, less than $50, to liquidate the cost of our lead acquisition so that you are in profit right from the start.

Some sales advisers think it's best to immediately promote something more expensive, but it's highly unlikely that you are missing out on too many customers because your offer is too cheap. Regardless, they just need to wait a few more minutes and they can invest a lot more if they wish. There are two options for the individual faced with the offer: to buy or not to buy. Let's deal with the buyers first, as they are our priority.

You can take these people to a much higher-priced and valued product or service, which is your core offering in your back-end sales funnel, either immediately or later through a follow-up series of emails, which I will address in a moment. The price points for these products are a minimum of $500 for this level and anywhere into the thousands of dollars depending on the product, as discussed in chapter 10. Assuming that you offer this core product immediately, clearly there will be a further drop-off rate, as many of your initial buyers are not ready for the next stage just yet. Let's deal with those who choose to purchase first.

There is a real opportunity after that second purchase to further increase your profit margins by adding in some additional offerings that make a lot of sense for the buyer to add to their purchases. Our main goal here is to increase the average transaction value per customer. McDonalds is a prime example of this: they make very little profit until they add in the upsell after their core offering (price points are obviously a lot cheaper than the examples given earlier). The famous question "would you like to supersize your meal?" is more fundamentally asking "shall we make a profit from you or not?"

SPEND $1.91 to get a person in the drive-thru

EARN $0.18 profit on a $2.09 burger sale

PROFIT $1.14 EXTRA on fries and Coke upsell

$1.32 PROFIT
(7.3 times that of the core sale)

Fig 11.5: The famous McDonalds upsell

It could also be some form of a packaged deal, where additional benefits are available. Provided that the buyer decides to go with the upsell, you can continue to extend more offerings; that will clearly eventually run its course as your offerings expire. Or more cleverly, you could use free software like www.wufoo.com to create an application form for a higher level of product offering that may require a sales call and end your transaction (for now at least) at this stage.

The non-buyers will be handled differently. From their first rejection of the offering, the communication process changes. You do not want to bother them immediately by continuing to push something they do not want at this moment. However, there is nothing to say that they may not be ready to come back and purchase on another day. Oftentimes we can forget that people are in the middle of their lives, possibly with children hanging off of them, or rushing from task to task and it just didn't make sense to buy at that moment! Our follow up email sequence is designed to turn these prospects into buyers. The first follow-up series is designed to move the non-buyers of the initial offering to purchase the initial offering.

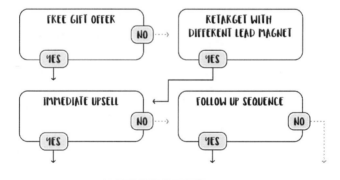

Fig 11.6: Follow-up sequence for initial non-buyers

If they say yes to the initial offering and then no to the core offering, they are added to a follow-up series that extends the core offering to them a few more times, reminding them of the key benefits of the offering and adding some urgency to the action if possible. This is sometimes called the "ascension series", which is a chain of emails designed to take your initial buyers on a journey to investing at the next level. If they say no to the core offering, they will be added to the final stage of this offering, which is the ongoing communication plan.

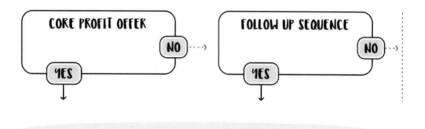

Fig 11.7: Follow-up sequence for core offer non-buyers

With all these "yes" and "no" options, it could quite easily give you a headache just trying to understand it, let alone working out how you could possibly handle all of this from a technology perspective. When I started back in 2009, if you wanted to set up something like this, your only real option was to invest heavily in an autoresponder that had such capabilities. Thankfully, nowadays, the likes of convertkit, which is my personal favourite, allows you to segregate your leads into different lists and different email sequences based on the decisions they made about whether to purchase each offering. Once you understand the logic behind it and have your follow-up sequences ready to use, it is not that difficult to set up. I have provided you with a handy start-up guide on this with everything you need here at http://resources.rethinksocialmedia.com.

You can probably imagine that it makes a lot of sense to make sure these people are segregated into different groups; you don't want to keep reminding someone they should buy a product they have already purchased, as it will lead to annoyance, frustration and, worst case scenario, to people unsubscribing from your database or even requesting refunds.

Traditional Thinking:

Once you offer your list something to buy, continue to repeat the same marketing message to the list, offering it over and over again making some further sales.

RETHINK:

Carefully segregate your database after the initial offering between the buyers who will ascend into the back-end sales funnel and the non-buyers who need more warming up, through a series of emails focusing on the change and new result that this product or service can provide.

Phase 5: Relationship!

As mentioned earlier, the "Relationship" phase is much more than a single word. The relationship with your database is complex and multi-faceted, and it comes with many more "Rs", such as retain, remind, reinvigorate, relevance, refresh, renew, RETHINK, referrals, reward and regular.

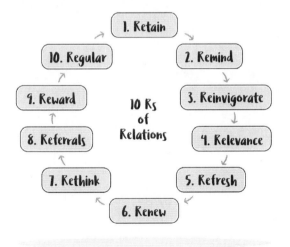

Fig 11.8: The 10 Rs of a relationship

"Wise men speak when they have something to say;
fools because they have to say something."
- Plato

The key here is to always have an intention behind your communication, regardless of the specific tactic. Where possible, always relate your communication method back to the "R" you are intending to achieve. While we set the foundation earlier for the 10 different segments of the relationship, we did not get into the specific tactics that can be deployed to deliver the level of information to keep your audience engaged with you. In the relationship model below, I have listed a number of different methods by which this contact is continued, encouraging our leads to return back to purchase more from us over time.

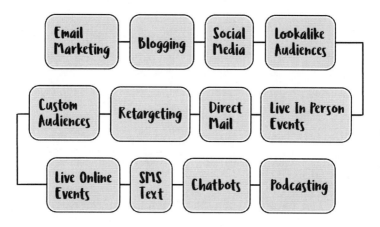

Fig 11.9: Methods for continuing to nourish a relationship

To ascend through the levels from cold traffic to a lead, then a prospect and a customer, to a client and finally to an addict, using a variety of these elements is key. Ideally, we want our clients to become so dependent on our content and knowledge that they become "addicted", to need us and want us as an essential part for their success and become raving fans, mentioning us to all of their colleagues and friends.

Email marketing:

For the segment of your audience that have moved from social media to your database, you will continue to mail them every other day or possibly even daily to keep them posted on the latest and greatest within your niche. Outside of your initial welcome email sequence and any major promotions, I would generally suggest that every second email should be a mix of a content or value email, followed by a promotion email. Schedule these once a week so that this does not become a task that you forget to do. Quite simply, if you are not emailing, you are not making money!

Traditional Thinking:

If you email just once a week, you won't annoy anyone!

RETHINK:

Email regularly, stay relevant and mix up your emails between value and promotions. The more you mail, the more you make! Simples!

Blogging:

As mentioned earlier when discussing blogging, a great strategy when getting started, before you are established as a well-known brand, is to share on your blog the knowledge of already well-established experts in your field. To make the maximum use of these posts and to save you a lot of time, you can place a link in your "content / value" emails back to your blog, where you send people to a specific post or article. There is always a chance of making money from your blog through Google Ads and banners that you may have there.

Traditional Thinking:

You need to write highly informative, completely unique, in-depth articles on your niche on a regular basis to keep your list engaged.

RETHINK:

You can send your list to posts from the well-established experts in your field and position yourself as an expert as you do it. Once you have built your credibility up by acting as a hub, and when there is a demand for your content, that's when you can start to promote it.

Social media:

We discussed in previous chapters the different social networks that you can consider for your marketing channels, depending on who your target market is, and that applies just as much here. In chapter 13, I will give you the template required to plan out your content management and delivery to your followers on social media, but for now, let's discuss the different modes that you can use.

Your goal here, remember, is to maintain the relationship with your social media followers, some of whom are on your list and some not. This will mean that from time to time you will continue to post the same posts you used in phase 1, the awareness phase, to encourage those not on your list to subscribe. The more methods by which you provide your message, the more engagement you should get from your followers. The average social media user now digests their information across five different social networks, and this only continues to increase.

Using forums such as Facebook groups can be excellent for forming a real sense of community and serving the need for a common area to hang out, ask questions and share ideas. It would be wise to keep a couple of things in mind here. Make sure you have express rules as to what the group members can and cannot do, otherwise it can just become a series of sales pitches from some of the members. Have a moderator control the content and the conversations to prevent people with other agendas taking over or attempting to steal your client base. You can break your content into multiple formats of delivery, where people can consume your content by reading, commenting, listening, watching and participating. Always ask for shares to encourage more engagement. As my friend Mari Smith says, "Engagement doesn't pay the bills", but it certainly helps with the next step in our strategy. Let's never forget, however, that we want to move our social media users over to our list as much as is possible. It is fine to have them on both, but your list is the goal.

Traditional Thinking:

Continue to talk about your business and yourself on a regular basis with intermittent promotions.

RETHINK:

Ask questions of your audience, seek engagement, ask what they want and provide it to them regularly and consistently. Remind them why joining your list is an absolute must for them!

Lookalike audiences:

One of the hidden benefits of growing your database is that Facebook, Twitter and LinkedIn, and no doubt more in the near future, allow you to upload that database to their networks, enabling them to crosscheck how many of these people are on their networks so that they can be targeted as a custom audience and, better still, they will allow you to build a "lookalike" audience on their network. This means that Facebook, for example, will perform an assessment on the interests and behaviours of your database and allow you to target similar types of people that are using their network. This is absolutely incredible when you think about it! Where else could you possibly do this in business, where you are building mini clones of your own database to enable you to build your business without ever leaving home?

Traditional Thinking:

Once you have built your email database, you won't share this with anyone at any cost.

RETHINK:

Upload your lists to Facebook, Twitter and LinkedIn to allow you to build similar audiences on those platforms and vastly improve the success of your advertisements.

Custom audiences:

This is another form of retargeting. What if you could target people who already are aware of you, but on an ongoing basis and based specifically on types of topics they are interested in within your niche? Well it is very possible with a feature known as custom audiences. This is powerful on two fronts: they already know who you are, as they have visited your site, and you know what specifically within your niche they are interested in, as you track their behaviour on your site. Let's say, for example, you have a blog about book writing, and you have three different topics that you generally cover within that niche: a. Non-fiction, b. Fiction, and c. Amazon Best Seller Status. Each of these topics has a different focus and they are all attracting people at different stages of their book writing journey.

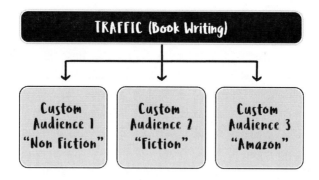

Fig 11.10: Custom audiences within a niche

The ideal scenario here is to collect these people's email addresses based on what their specific interests are. Within Facebook's "custom audience" segment, you provide them with the exact subdomains that you want to track people's behaviour on, and you can then target those people with different ads depending on the subdomain they visited. Similarly, even without having a blog, once you start to get engagement on your social media posts, social networks like Facebook allow you to create custom audiences of the people who watched the video, for example, so that you can reengage with them to encourage further action.

Traditional Thinking:

Your audience will figure out for themselves what they want from the website.

RETHINK:

Help your audience by segmenting them based on their exact wants as opposed to general interest areas.

Retargeting:

Retargeting or, as Google refers to it, "remarketing" is serving an ad to someone based on a prior engagement. This prior engagement can take one or more of many forms. It could be that someone clicks on your ad, your opt-in page, your website or anywhere you have control of for that matter, and you can use retargeting ads to follow up with them to encourage them to take the next step. This point is worthy of a chapter in itself, but for now understanding the general concept is enough. We mentioned the www.booking.com example a couple of times earlier, where they retarget you based on your previous actions. Another example would be if you purchase shoes on www.zappos.com and suddenly the matching clutch bag seems to be following you around the internet!

It works using cookies to stay in front of previous site visitors. A cookie is a file that stores information, and in this case, they will store information about the visit to the website. A piece of code provided by Google or Facebook enables cookies to be used. If one of your visitors has left your site, the cookies let your retargeters, such as Google, know and if there is ad space available on the next site they visit, the retargeter will bid to run the ad and, if successful, the retargeting ad appears. Here are some live examples of retargeting ads following me around as I am writing this for retargeting where to begin with – the resources.rethinksocialmedia.com software referred to earlier is following me around, even on the Spanish internet speed check site of the hotel I am currently in.

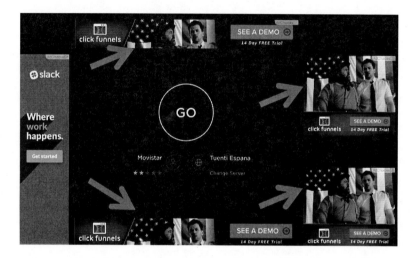

Fig 11.11: Examples of retargeting across other websites

Even as I double check the quotations I am using in the book on entrepreneur.com, sure enough I get targeted by the same advertisements ☺.

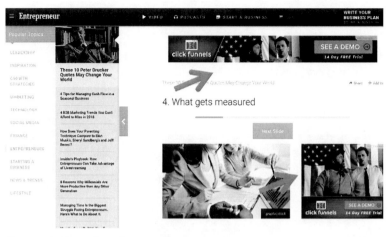

Fig 11.12: Examples of retargeting

Likewise, as I move over to skysports.com to check on the latest sports news, I am targeted both at the top and side of the page with Tai Lopez, another great online marketer's advertisements.

Fig 11.13: Examples of retargeting

And on the side as I scroll down.

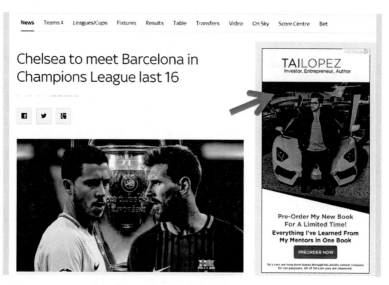

Fig 11.14: Examples of retargeting

Over to Facebook, and more of the same!

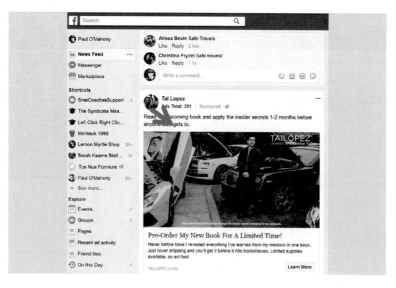

Fig 11.15: Examples of retargeting

Then we get targeted by both at exactly the same time on Facebook!

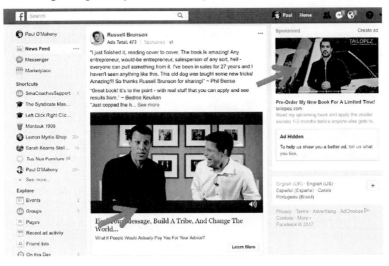

Fig 11.16: Examples of retargeting

And lest we forget our good friends booking.com, they have just shown up on the BBC News site as I checked the latest world news. There is no escape!

Fig 11.17: Examples of retargeting

When you are being targeted by your own ads at the same time, then it is time to smile ☺!

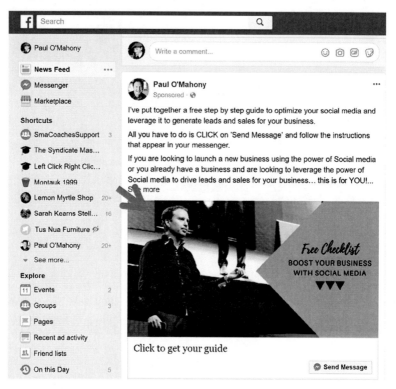

Fig 11.18: Examples of retargeting

It sounds complicated, but it only takes a fraction of a second and suddenly your ad will appear magically alongside the page content, encouraging the viewer to come back. Facebook and Google allow for retargeting, and there are a number of retargeting agencies that you can use, such as AdRoll, SiteScout, Retargeter and Perfect Audience. These are super targeted, super powerful and best of all, they can be a super cheap ad. It works because rather than marketing to a broad group of people, you are being very specific answering an individual's desires. Remember you can find out what sites your competitors are already advertising on with www.similarweb.com.

Traditional Thinking:

"No means No". If your audience says "no" to you on your first attempt, it is a definitive decision.

RETHINK:

"No means not yet, but maybe next time". Your audience has expressed an interest in either your blog post, social media content, your website or your ad, but most people need to see a product or service seven times or more before making a decision. Let's go back again and be persistent. If you don't, someone else will!

Podcasts:

A podcast is probably the most underrated of all of the aforementioned strategies for maintaining relationships. The numbers are just staggering, with almost 100 million listeners in the US alone. Podcasts allow you to deliver content in a completely different way, where the lead/prospect/customer/client/addict can listen to you "on the go". They allow you to really make people feel like they "know" you, as it is very easy to add in some personal touches and fill them in on personal stories of interest. You can bring on guests, and in addition, possibly return the favour and appear on their podcasts as a guest yourself. It is a great way of building excitement about new launches and showcasing your success stories in a non-salesy manner.

The optimum time for your podcast is approximately 30 minutes, but some podcasters like Joe Rogan are known to run on for hours! It's best to record about six of them to begin with so you can launch them at once and then keep them going weekly. My friend Rob Moore managed to make his podcast "The Disruptive Entrepreneur" to the top business podcast in the world, as he says himself, "without being a celebrity!" He has made over $2.5 million of revenue tied directly back to the podcast in just the first two years without running a single advertisement. The industry average rates are $25 to $45 per 1,000 downloads. Other great podcasters include Pat Flynn (Smart Passive Income) and John Lee Dumas (Entrepreneurs on Fire), and look out for my very own "RETHINK Social Media" podcast. If you would like to download "A beginner's guide to making an expert's money with podcasting", feel free to go to http://resources.rethinksocialmedia.com.

Traditional Thinking:

Podcasting requires a lot of technical know-how and expensive equipment, and it's difficult to come up with new content consistently, rarely resulting in real bottom line profits.

RETHINK:

Podcasting is possibly the most underrated method for relationship building with brand new leads, completely cold traffic, or established customers. You can set up all the kit you need for less than $20, if you already have a phone, and get launched within a few hours. It is a highly profitable affair and works very well at introducing people to your back-end and positioning you as an expert.

Chatbots:

A chatbot is a service that is managed by a set of rules or artificial intelligence that allows you to engage with your audience via messenger applications such as Facebook, Slack, Telegram and many more. In simple terms, it works like traditional phone messaging systems of a business that give a decision tree of options based on your requirements ("dial 1 for sales, dial 2 for customer support", etc.) but for a start, it is nowhere near as frustrating – in fact it is quite the opposite; a refreshingly fast and efficient way of getting what you want immediately. One of the reasons it's easier to use is that the users don't have to wait to hear all of the options, only to be faced with then waiting to listen to the next set of options;

instead, you can immediately see what all the options are and click on the appropriate one. You can also include pre-recorded videos to personalise the experience and you can engage live with the person at any time.

This is worthy of some real-life examples as it's difficult to explain this in "theory"! In this example I will show you how you can take completely cold traffic, warm them up and move them into your immediate upsell in less than two minutes. In this example someone clicks on either a Facebook ad that sends them to an instant message or clicks on "Send message" on a Facebook page. Of course, the exact look of these messages will vary across providers and social networks and that will continue, but the concept is the key thing to make note of here.

Fig 11.19 Kicking off the chatbot conversation

In this instance, the first engagement is where the person decides to click on "Send Message" to learn more or receive a free gift. This results in the person being sent a message directly within an instant messenger, such as this one, where Vishal has decided to click on "Send Message".

Fig 11.20: Official confirmation step that person can be engaged with

This personalised message encourages him to continue on with a small commitment which is to click on "Get Started". This commitment is essential as this now allows for you to continue with your marketing. I can give any series of choices that I wish in order to qualify who this person is, including working out what level of experience Vishal may have with online marketing and social media.

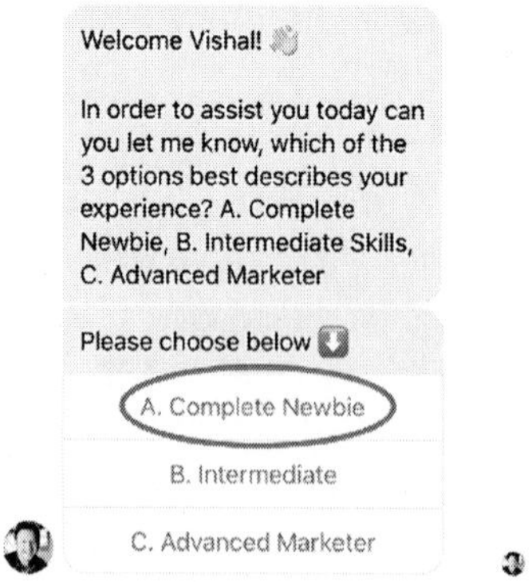

Fig 11.21: Qualifying your lead

I will then have appropriate responses for Vishal, regardless of his level. If he tells me he is a complete newbie, he will then see the following:

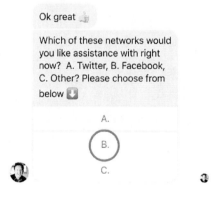

Fig 11.22: Further layering of qualification of your lead

Let's assume the response is A. Vishal wants help right now with a specific social network, and so he will then see the next message he has prompted, but all the answers are pre-prepared in the event of any of the choices Vishal can make.

Fig 11.23: Further layering of qualification of your lead

Let's say that this time it is Facebook that is of interest to them and they choose "B".

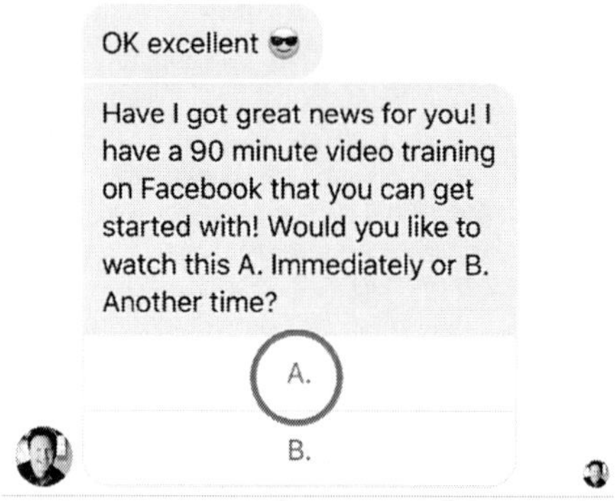

OK excellent 😎

Have I got great news for you! I have a 90 minute video training on Facebook that you can get started with! Would you like to watch this A. Immediately or B. Another time?

A.

B.

Fig 11.24: Moving the lead into the immediate upsell

We have then magically moved Vishal into the pre-registration page for a pre-recorded webinar about Facebook, which is converting at 20%+ for sales of a $40+ product!

Fig 11.25: Registration page for pre-recorded webinar with upsell

As you can see, chatbots can dramatically reduce the speed in moving somebody from the awareness stage to relationship phase. In my opinion, the setup of chatbots through the Facebook Messenger app has the most potential for increasing your level of success in moving cold traffic into buyers than any other right now. There are a number of reasons.

Firstly, as shown in chapter 8, part 4, fig 8.10, since 2015 there have been more users of messenger apps than social networks, and remember we are looking to hang out where people are hanging out! Secondly, the open rate of instant messengers in our experiences is 80-85%+ while email can be 10% or lower. Thirdly, it is instant! You also get to ask all the pertinent questions rather than leaving it up to the person. This makes it easier to move a person through the decision tree to encourage them to download a free gift and purchase a particular product and address any objections within minutes of first engagement. To do the same on email follow up sequences will take days and with every day that passes, the interest level tends to drop. At any point, it is also possible to jump in and take over the chat in real-time. Best practice here is not to pretend it is a real person, you can make it clear it is "Paul's bot" and people seem to love it! If you would like to have one of these bots built for your business, or learn how to create them for yourself, please visit http://resources.rethinksocialmedia.com.

Traditional thinking:

People will never want to engage with automated robots; they want the personal touch.

RETHINK:

With chatbots, you can give people the instant answers they want to bring them to exactly what they are looking for at a fraction of the time and cost of a traditional customer service support team. Once we engage in person, we can work out the exact wants of our audience.

Text messages / SMS:

The traditional text message still has power but can also be misused to a great degree. The first thing to consider with a text message is how personal it is. People tend to get very annoyed when receiving unsolicited text messages, and there are significant fines for businesses that do send them. But they do work well when the relationship is already established and the client has purchased an expensive product from you in the $500+ range, like in this case. The text message can then serve to reinforce the buying decision just made, before the potential "buyer's remorse" or doubt creeps in and reminds them of the next steps. Sometimes emails can go astray, and this is a good back-up plan to have. It can also work very well to remind people about any type of live engagement that you are planning for, whether that is a live webinar or a live in-person event. Text messaging can be fully automated and integrated with your autoresponder or shopping cart with the use of the correct tools, such as Infusionsoft. We use www.fixyourfunnel.com to amazing effect, which integrates all of the text messages with our email follow-up systems.

Traditional Thinking:

Text messaging is expensive and very intrusive.

RETHINK:

When your customers are at the stage in the relationship with you where they have invested heavily or are looking to engage with you in a live format, automated text messaging can serve as an excellent tool.

Direct mail:

The traditional letter or postcard through the postal service still works very well as a means of maintaining relationships with your audience. "Handwritten" or more accurately put, the appearance of personally handwritten, addressed letters, has that air of mystique and shows that you are willing to go that extra mile and put that bit more effort into your relationships. Generally speaking, you would provide clear instructions within that letter, sending people back onto a website where they can complete a purchase or at least express their interest so that they can be retargeted at a later date and moved through the sales funnel and up the value ladder! Direct mailing is expensive relative to many of the other options here, but when done correctly, is a very profitable undertaking.

Traditional thinking:

Direct mail is very expensive and outdated.

RETHINK:

Using direct mailing as part of an overall strategy of relationship management with your list can serve as a highly profitable undertaking especially when combining it with an online element.

Live in-person events:

It is often said that nothing beats the personal touch, and this is definitely true. What better way to reaffirm and grow a relationship with your audience than to invite them to a personal get together with you and similarly-minded people. It creates a sense of community among the attendees and gives the audience the opportunity to meet with you in person, get pictures taken and rub shoulders with their peers. These are an excellent opportunity to give your audience a much bigger product offering, as they are much more likely to commit to a higher investment when they can speak with you in person.

Traditional thinking:

Live events are very expensive and it's very difficult to get people to show up.

RETHINK:

Start to build live communities with sites like www.meetup.com that allow like-minded people to meet up in a coffee shop, bar or town hall, based around a specific area of interest and grow event size starting from there.

Live online events:

If you are not ready for meeting in person just yet, thankfully technology can pave the way for you to still have that personal touch without having to leave home ☺. There is a whole range of options available to you here. Live streaming through YouTube, Periscope or Facebook Live are the easiest to get started with, just press and go! In order to maximise turn-up rate, it would be useful to let your social media followers and email list know in advance. You can then use the live broadcast to inform, educate and give your viewers a chance to engage with you.

Live webinars using one of the many tools available, like gotowebinar. com, zoom.us or everwebinar.com will give you the opportunity to have a more formal catch-up with your audience, which you can charge for or provide for free. If you are interested in learning more about how to run a webinar successfully for profit, you can download a guide here: http://resources.rethinksocialmedia.com. Best of all, you can record one of these live webinars and then allow people to attend it on an ongoing basis, provided you set it up as an "evergreen" webinar. This serves as an excellent free gift and encourages people to take action instantly as your immediate upsell. To see one of these in action, please go here: http://resources.rethinksocialmedia.com.

Traditional thinking:

It is expensive and technically challenging to run live online events.

RETHINK:

There are free trials available on most webinar software platforms, and very extensive trainings on how to run them. The more you practise them with smaller numbers, the better you become for larger audiences.

Summary:

After going to the effort of finding a targeted lead and setting up your sales funnels, nourishing a relationship with this lead, moving them from a lead to a prospect, to a customer, a repeat customer, a client and even an addict is essential for maximising profitability and client happiness! There are 10 separate parts of building this relationship, with the last one, "Regular", being the most important of all. In an ideal world, we would like for our leads/clients to see us in many different media, reminding them of our message and cementing the relationship into a long-term association. The ones that you find easiest are a good place to begin, and always keep in mind that every communication you put out there should have a clear intent behind it – always moving people up the value ladder.

Traditional Thinking:

Let's get our prospect to the finish line as quickly as possible whatever it takes, and once they get there, it's time to find another.

RETHINK:

Winning in business is a long-term play that involves putting people, and specifically relationships with people, first. How well your business fulfils your leads' passions, desires and wants determines how successful your business will be. There is nothing left to guess work here though, your leads will let you know exactly what they want if you work on the relationship. The more time you put into nourishing that relationship, the more profitable the relationship becomes.

Chapter 12: Know Your Numbers

"If you can't read the scoreboard, you don't know the score. If you don't know the score, you can't tell the winners from the losers."
- Warren Buffet

This is it! We are about to cover the final step of the RETHINK model: Part K – Know your numbers. In order to ensure everything that we have put in place up until now fits seamlessly together, we must become fanatic about our numbers. Ultimately our role as a business owner is to work on the business and not in the business, which I am sure you have heard bandied about many times before! If you are to get to this place, knowing not only what your numbers are but ensuring that you are measuring the correct numbers is critical. Admittedly, it may not be the most exciting thing in the world to do, but without it, you will inevitably go out of business. It's quite simply not good enough to just be measuring results; it's about knowing what numbers to measure to ensure we are moving in the right direction as a business.

The RETHINK model has evolved

In chapter 14, we are going to walk through exactly what numbers to look at in our "metrics" segment, but for now we will cover this at a higher level. The metrics that we are looking at here are going to give you the feedback and fuel needed to drive the momentum of your business, propelling it forward.

Up until now, the RETHINK model has been open-ended, without a closed loop as such, as you can see in Fig 12.1 below. However, this is just about to change!

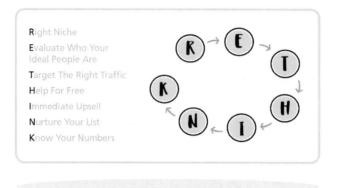

Fig 12.1: Stage 1 – RETHINK Basic Model

We have completed the initial two parts of the RETHINK model, namely the "RE" segment, "Right niche" and "Evaluate who your people are". The RETHINK model now evolves into stage 2, where the business provides feedback, enabling better decisions to drive the profitability. Knowing your numbers and their associated metrics becomes the driver of the new RETHINK propulsion model.

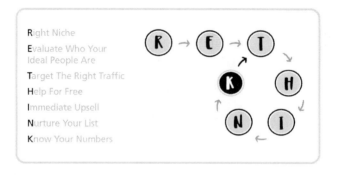

Fig 12.2: Stage 2 – RETHINK "Propulsion" Model

Knowing your numbers is the key to starting the propulsion engine, hence why this section is so important for your new or existing business. However, the numbers alone will not highlight the problem areas or potential opportunities. You need to know that the right numbers are being looked at in the first place!

Once we are looking at the right metrics, they should then be assessed on a regular basis, and only then can the best decisions for the business be made. One excellent way of implementing this is to use the "Thinking Time" idea that Keith Cunningham mentions in his book The Ultimate Blueprint for an Insanely Successful Business. As he puts it, "Thinking time is the singularly most powerful tool in my arsenal. I would gladly forfeit any tool I have before I would abandon Thinking Time".

For our purposes, we will reposition this as "RETHINK Time", specifically for use on the online aspects of your business, as discussed in this book. You can use thinking time for your business as a whole. Once you get your metrics in front of you, there are some key questions that you can ask yourself in order to make better decisions about your business instantly. You will use the time, which can be as little as 2 hours a week, to turn any problems into opportunities, look for potential issues on the horizon and identify what you need to stop and what you need to continue doing.

Date:	Week #:
How do my customers, clients and target market define success specifically?	
What must be monitored, measured and changed to ensure the continuity of our products, success proposition, culture and brand that we may not already be measuring?	
What is the outcome we want?	

What is the REAL reason we have not already achieved this outcome?	
What is the REAL obstacle or problem that is keeping us from achieving this outcome now?	
What does the review of Metrics Essentials #1 show in terms of gaps to be plugged?	
What does the review of Metrics Essentials #1 show in terms of opportunities?	
What does the review of Metrics Essentials #2 show in terms of gaps to be plugged?	
What does the review of Metrics Essentials #2 show in terms of opportunities?	
What does the review of Metrics Essentials #3 show in terms of gaps to be plugged?	
What does the review of Metrics Essentials #3 show in terms of opportunities?	
What does the review of Metrics Essentials #4 show in terms of gaps to be plugged?	
What does the review of Metrics Essentials #4 show in terms of opportunities?	
What does the review of Metrics Essentials #5 show in terms of gaps to be plugged?	

What does the review of Metrics Essentials #5 show in terms of opportunities?	
What does the review of Metrics Essentials #6 show in terms of gaps to be plugged?	
What does the review of Metrics Essentials #6 show in terms of opportunities?	
What does the review of Metrics Essentials #7 show in terms of gaps to be plugged?	
What does the review of Metrics Essentials #7 show in terms of opportunities?	
What are the top 3 things we can do this week to maximise our overall profit?	

Table 12.1: RETHINK time questions

In asking the same questions each week, you will find that your answers will change! You may of course want to add more specific questions as you dig deeper into the metrics, but at the same time you don't want a case of analysis paralysis. It is important to keep going after the biggest bang for your buck, in terms of both reducing expenses and increasing profitability. For example, did you know by cutting your expenses by a mere 12% can increase your profitability by a huge 50%?

Be sure to schedule at least 2 hours into your calendar at the same time each week, even if that meeting is only with one participant to begin with. It will eventually include your team of marketers, who may be running the campaigns for you. This results in the final evolution of the RETHINK model.

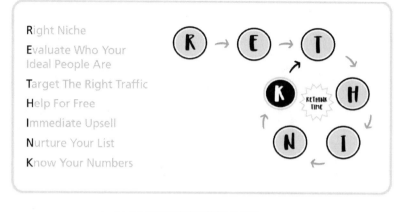

Right Niche

Evaluate Who Your
Ideal People Are

Target The Right Traffic

Help For Free

Immediate Upsell

Nurture Your List

Know Your Numbers

Fig 12.3: Stage 3 – RETHINK "Self-Propulsion" Model

Summary:

Knowing what to measure and making a point of sitting down once a week to review it by yourself or with a team will allow you to introduce a feedback loop into the RETHINK model, resulting in a self-correcting and course-adjusting model that the external environment may require. Use the RETHINK time questions as a guide for what to ask yourself each week.

Traditional Thinking:

The numbers speak for themselves!

RETHINK:

Measuring the right numbers and regular reviews will allow you to continue to reduce expenses and increase profitability of your business. Regular reviews are key to success!

SECTION 5: SYSTEMS & FLOWCHARTS

Chapter 13: Pulling It All Together

"A good system shortens the road to the goal."

- Ralph Waldo Emerson

Now that we have looked in detail at each of the various aspects required within the successful framework, I'd like to simplify it for you and pull together all of the key components into one section. What can seem like a highly complex topic thankfully can be modelled in a convenient way to allow even the least experienced "newbie" to understand and start executing their very own successful online business. Even more conveniently for me, it fits perfectly in line with the concept of the book: "RETHINK".

Step 1 – Right niche:

Before you can do anything with your business, you need to be very clear about the problem you are solving. As I have suggested, getting started with a business area that has a major problem that causes a lot of pain for people who are likely to pay for the solution immediately is key. Otherwise, you can spend a lot of time and energy in business and on social media without turning a profit, like the vast majority of business owners.

RETHINK niche selection:

Niche option	Yes/no
1. Health & Beauty (weight loss, fitness, appearance)	
2. Wealth (make money online, stock market)	
3. Happiness (personal development)	
4. Your own business	
Your final niche choice is:	

Table 13.1: Niche selection options

In order to make a selection from the above, the first question is whether you want to immediately apply what you are learning directly to your current business. If the answer is "yes", then number 4 above is your niche selection.

I suggest that you can learn how to apply the RETHINK model more easily in a niche outside of what you currently do, which allows you to focus exclusively on the marketing to begin with, and you can always come back to your own business later. Assuming that this is the case, then ask yourself the following questions:

"Which of the areas 1-3 above do I have no interest in pursuing as a business at this moment in time?"

"Of the areas that remain, which of these specific areas do I wish to know more about 6 months from now?

Let's say for example that you have no interest in 3. Happiness or 1. Health, but you would be somewhat interested in 2. Wealth. You can ask yourself the second question about which aspect you would like to know more about 6 months from now, such as the stock market or making money online, and then simply select one of those. For the purposes of this exercise, let's assume you chose 2. Make money online. If you are unsure, choose # 2. Make money online (wealth), as this is why you are reading this book in the first place ☺ – to learn how to do this!

Step 2 – Evaluate who your people are:

The importance of thinking about who the ideal lowest-hanging fruit for your business is cannot be overestimated. In order to jump in and get started with this, it is a good idea to think of a specific person that you may already know to help guide you. You will need to make quite a few assumptions to begin with, but an educated guess is much better than leaving blanks. Let's start with the lowest-hanging fruit: the person in the most urgent "pain", who has the money to pay for the solution immediately. Here are some guidelines to assist you.

Category	Best guess
Name:	
Age:	
Sex:	
Country/city of residence:	
Level of education:	
Number of children:	
Ages of children:	
Marital status:	
Years from retirement:	
Employed or self-employed:	

Job title:	
Annual salary:	
Type of car:	
Social networks likely used:	
Hobbies and interests:	
Groups or pages of interest:	
Experts likely to be following:	
Highest values:	
Goals:	
Motto:	
Biggest challenges:	
Main fears and pain points:	
Direct buyer or which part of the buying process:	
Likely objections to sales contact:	
Have I printed out a Google images sample avatar?	

Table 13.2: Avatar data determination

Your job is to create a tone in your marketing that attracts their attention based on matching your message with the biggest challenges and pains that the avatar has at this moment in time, and to keep them interested in receiving more communications from you.

Once you have completed this for your first ideal avatar, you can then move on to do this a number of times, identifying and categorising the different avatars for your niche so that you can target each in turn.

I have a useful pdf file that you can print out and use yourself for your avatar templates, which is available at http://resources.rethinksocialmedia. com. To maximise the benefit from this exercise, print out the avatar documents, complete them and hang them beside you at your place of work, unless you are in Starbucks ☺.

CUSTOMER AVATAR

AVATAR NAME

Age:	**GOALS AND VALUES**	**CHALLENGES & PAIN POINTS**
Gender:	Goals:	Challenges:
Marital Status:		
Age of Children:	Values:	Pain points:
Location:		
Quote:		
	SOURCES OF INFORMATION	**OBJECTIONS & ROLE IN PURCHASE PROCESS**
Occupation:	Books:	Objections to the sale:
Job Title:	Magazines	
Annual Income:	Blogs/Websites:	
	Conferences:	Role in the Purchase Process:
Other:	Gurus:	
	Other:	

Table 13.3: Avatar determination summary

Step 3 – Target the right traffic:

While you were working through identifying the avatar for your business, there were some questions in there that were particularly pointed at giving clues as to where our people might congregate and hang out:

- Social networks likely used:

- Hobbies and interests:

- Groups or pages of interest:

- Experts likely to be following:

With the following template, you can add to the interests and behaviours of your core avatars to give you more and more ideas. A great option to help you reduce the ultimate cost of your ads is to think of other words that people may use for the same interests so that you are competing against fewer advertisers, yet still getting in front of the right people. For example, instead of targeting "make money", perhaps you could look at "work from home".

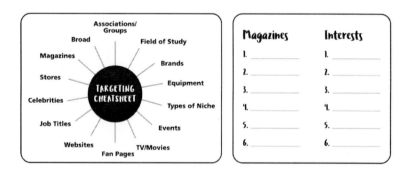

Fig 13.1: Targeting Cheat Sheet

As you work through the details of the avatars, you can then start to look at what particular areas you are going to focus on for your biggest bang for your buck based on those we discussed earlier in chapter 8. We can look to prioritise these traffic-targeting activities, based initially on your own expertise and available budget, and see if you are in a position to get started immediately or need support. Your main goal at this point is to gain AWARENESS and to work out which is the most cost-effective strategy for you.

Strategy	Priority	Resources required	Daily budget required
Facebook ads			
Twitter ads			
Youtube ads			
Linkedin ads			
Email marketing			
SEO			
Blogging			
Google Adwords			
Podcasting			
Social media			

Table 13.4: Ad selection matrix

Obviously if this is all new to you, you may feel a little overwhelmed, but don't despair, you only need to start with one; if you are to choose just one, make it Facebook ads to begin with. Selecting the type of ads to run to find your target market, the images, the videos and the copy could also appear daunting, but it doesn't need to be. That's why I am here to help!

I am a big believer in making things as easy as they can be within your online business. When it comes to the science and art of targeting the right traffic with the right message at this stage, this is particularly relevant. Leverage is critical! It is always a good idea to do some research at this point about what some of your current or potential competitors are currently doing with their advertising. Do some ground work first in figuring out if they are successful with what they are doing. A general guide is to look at how many people are engaging with and commenting on their ads. If there are almost none, you can immediately dismiss them. If the same ads appear again and again on your timeline, those ads are most likely working well for them and you should take note. This is a crude measure, but it is good enough for now!

Look closely at how often you are targeted and across what networks, and click on the ads to learn from the funnels that they are driving their leads into. Take screenshots of their ads, click on them, look at the landing pages and join the funnels yourself, as it will prove a very useful exercise in how to and how not to turn prospects into clients. You can use the template below to do your competitor research.

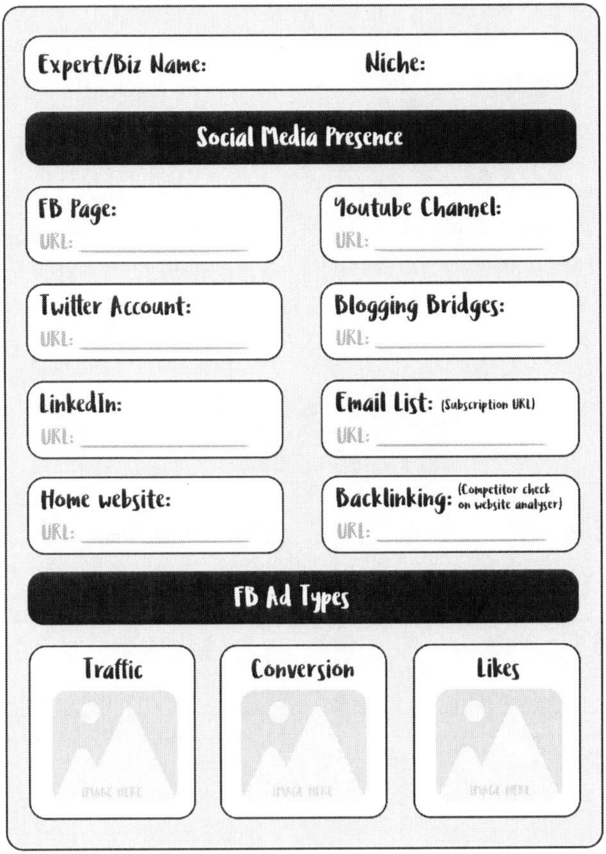

Fig 13.2: Competitor social media research

This template is available to download and use at http://resources. rethinksocialmedia.com. After you have done this exercise and plotted out a map of what your competitors or niche experts are doing, it will give you a much better idea of how you can start to plan yours. A big component of your plan will be determined by the resources that you have. Will it be just you, or will this be handed over to someone in marketing or completely outsourced to a marketing agency? When you are setting out your stall to begin with, it is often best to assume the best-case scenario of how you would like this to work with a fully resourced team and then cut it back according to your resource constraints.

Assuming that you have no social media in place to begin with, we need to plot out a plan for your social media setup, based on what your competition and industry leaders are doing, and opening up your accounts across the board. The following template can provide you with significant assistance here.

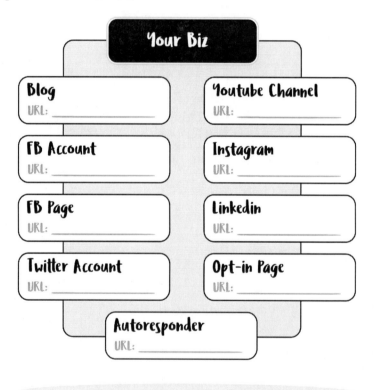

Fig 13.3: Social network matrix

Be sure to have your branding consistent across the platforms so that there is a degree of familiarity for your audience, regardless of where they come across you. You can use www.canva.com for an easy and free-to-use template creator for each of the networks.

You may already have some social media accounts in place and then it becomes more of a case of deciding whether you want to keep those accounts, discard them completely or rename and rebrand them to make use of any relationships you have already built up through those pages. Within the settings of most social networks, you will have the option to select new user names to make it a painless and seamless shift. The Twitter account that ended up becoming my main account at one point was called "fashionguru222" and its profile picture was that of my sister's dog Mary. It proved a lot more popular than any account with my picture and grew a significantly larger follower base than my own account! Later down the line, I switched all Mary's details to mine and suddenly I appeared like a "big deal". I guess the lesson from this is not to take anything too personally on social media; people would indeed prefer to read the jokes on a dog's Twitter account than that of a real human ☺.

The next stage is to work through your specific ad plan, working out the types of ads to use and how you are going to target each group separately. I have included a sample template below that can be used for a Facebook ad, for example. It is a good idea to have one of these for every ad you run, almost like a trading log if you were trading on the stock market. This is where I got the idea from initially and have started to use these to great effect, as have my mentees. Feel free to adapt for other ads that you run across other networks.

Stage 1: Objective	Click on cell for options
OBJECTIVE TYPE	Traffic engagements – likes

Stage 2: advert set	
Advert set name	
Audience location	City 5
Audience interest	Business
Audience age group	45-54
Audience demographic	Both
Audience targeting other	4
Budget per day	Ł5 per day

Stage 3: creative	
Graphic type	Single image
Opt-in page	Yes
Opt-in address	E
Button type	Download
Pixel active	Yes

Stage 4: Results	
# of days:	
Total spent:	
Cost per like:	
CPM:	
Cost per click:	
Cost per purchase:	

Table 13.5: Individual ad performance

You can download access to this template for use for your different types of ads at http://resources.rethinksocialmedia.com. In all the years I have been doing this, I never found a convenient way to keep track of this and make it easy to manage, so I just ended up creating my own and I am happy to share these with you.

Step 4 – Help for free:

This is a two-step process. Firstly, we need to figure out what the free solution, lead magnet or "bait" is and then make it available to download online. In the last section of "Targeting the right traffic", we specifically looked at the types of adverts your competitors are using to attract the right kind of people identified in the Evaluate stage. Once you have set the bait, you need to ensure that it is presented in the correct light to ensure that as many people as possible provide you with their details.

Ok, let's break this down into its two parts, starting with the free solutions that we are providing.

1. Free gifts:

You can start off by listing the biggest challenges that your avatars have within your niche. You will then look for the best ready-made videos on these topics already available online from experts in your field that you can compile on the topic, or alternatively, if you have found a ready-made free gift that you can use, you could choose this option.

Challenges / pain points:	Actions required for free gift creation:	Location of videos
1.	Title:	URL:
	# of steps:	URL:
	Screenshots taken:	URL:
	References complete:	URL:
	Saved as PDF:	URL:
2.	Title:	URL:
	# of steps:	URL:
	Screenshots taken:	URL:
	References complete:	URL:
	Saved as PDF:	URL:
3.	Title:	URL:
	# of steps:	URL:
	Screenshots taken:	URL:
	References complete:	URL:
	Saved as PDF:	URL:
4.	Title:	URL:
	# of steps:	URL:
	Screenshots taken:	URL:
	References complete:	URL:
	Saved as PDF:	URL:

Table 13.6: Pain points of avatar and publicly available solutions

This will not only give you a great grounding for having a clearer picture of what you can create for your free gifts, but it also gives you more ideas for future ones. You can use each of these different lead magnets as different ads at a future stage. Feel free to download the template from http://resources.rethinksocialmedia.com.

2. Opt-in page design:

Presenting your free gift in the right manner is more important than the free gift itself! As we stated before, people just can't help but judge a book by its cover. Creating your opt-in page and using a design that attracts attention and encourages people to take the action required of leaving their data is the next goal.

Rather than attempting to reinvent the wheel and figure this out for yourself starting from the ground up, we will once again use as much leverage as we can here. In the "Target the right traffic" section, we used a template to keep a record of the ads that our competitors were using to give us an idea of the imagery, videos and copy that we can model. The same is true of our opt-in page templates. We should keep a folder of all of the opt-in page templates that are being used by the top people within our niche.

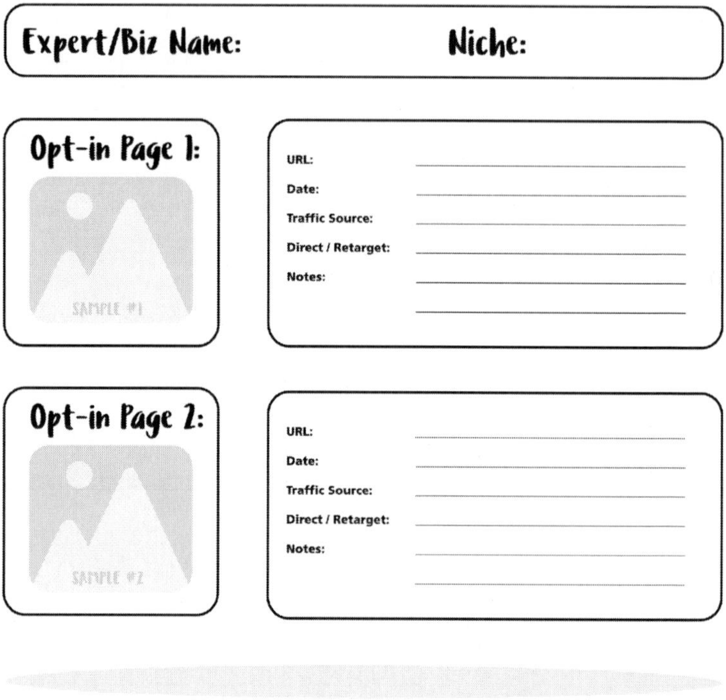

Expert/Biz Name: **Niche:**

Opt-in Page 1:

SAMPLE #1

URL: _____

Date: _____

Traffic Source: _____

Direct / Retarget: _____

Notes: _____

_____

Opt-in Page 2:

SAMPLE #2

URL: _____

Date: _____

Traffic Source: _____

Direct / Retarget: _____

Notes: _____

_____

Fig 13.4: Competitor opt-in page research

Feel free to download the template from resources.rethinksocialmedia. com. Your next step then is to use one of the industry leading software tools to create an opt-in template that takes the best ideas from the various examples you have, and start to test a variety of different examples. I provided more details on the specific software I recommend you can start with for free back in chapter 9.

Step 5 - Immediate upsell:

Now we are ready to start monetising all of the work that we have put in place to find the right people in the right niche at the right time ☺. We want to start off by offering them our initial free plus shipping/postage and packaging or tripwire offering. Rather than doing this in isolation, it is a good idea to plan out what your upsell plan looks like in terms of the products you are going to offer, whether they are yours or somebody else's. Here is a template that will allow you to list the series of products that you can promote; it can be done repeatedly as you add more products to the range. Ideally for each template that you fill out, you keep it specific to one product range that has a natural series of upsells.

Price point	Product title	Affiliate/ promotion link	Average EPC
$10 - $50			
$50 - $500			
$500+			
$2000 +			
$5000 +			

Table 13.7: Products to promote in value ladder

The average EPC is the earnings per click that the product owner provides as an indicator of how much you can expect to make as standard from each click you receive to that sales page. This number often needs to be taken with a grain of salt, as generally it is exaggerated to encourage marketers to promote the products. This concept is explained in more detail in chapter 14.

As mentioned in chapter 10, ideally you want to promote products that have an in-built funnel that allows you to maximise the profit and lifetime customer value from that specific product range. I also mentioned that if you are interested in promoting my products and want to benefit from profiting all the way through the sales funnel, you can sign up to become an affiliate for free and promote some of my funnels through http:// resources.rethinksocialmedia.com.

Once you know what the products are that you are going to promote, you can send your client directly to your affiliate sales page link. If, however, you are creating your own product range, you will need to create your "upsell page" with the same software as the opt-in page creator, which are in http://resources.rethinksocialmedia.com.

It is a good idea to leverage the layout of the upsell and one-time offer pages that you have seen after clicking on the ads of the expert leaders in your niche and joining their lists.

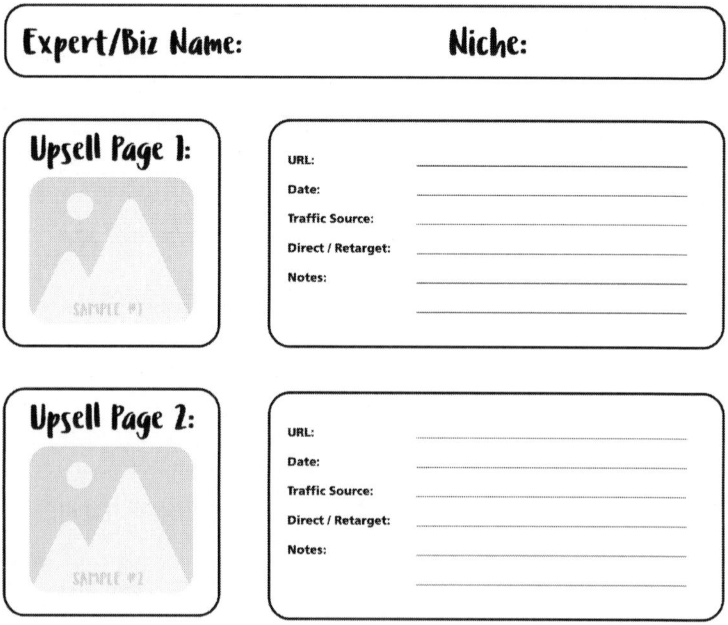

Expert/Biz Name: **Niche:**

Upsell Page 1:

SAMPLE #1

URL: _____
Date: _____
Traffic Source: _____
Direct / Retarget: _____
Notes: _____

Upsell Page 2:

SAMPLE #2

URL: _____
Date: _____
Traffic Source: _____
Direct / Retarget: _____
Notes: _____

Fig. 13.5: Competitor upsell and one-time offer pages research

Step 6 - Nurture your list:

This section is the aspect of social media that people generally focus on as the "social media thing". As you have seen, it is not as simple as making a few posts every now and again and hoping for the best. It is about creating a clear communication strategy planned out across not just the main social networks but the other digital platforms, such as email, webinars and more, that ultimately lead to deeper relationships and a higher transaction value per customer.

Part 1: Leveraging upcoming events

First and foremost, when it comes to planning what to say and when to say it, it can be a complete case of brain freeze! It is a hugely daunting task to plan ahead not just for a week, but for an entire year! That is of course unless you have a clear strategy to overcome this.

I find that opening the calendar for the month is a great place to start, but not just any ordinary calendar! One of the greatest places to draw inspiration from for planning your content delivery is a calendar that includes what is being celebrated on each particular day. For example, as I write, today is "United Nations Day" and "National Tripe Day", while tomorrow is "International Artists Day" and "World Pasta Day". Most days also have their very own celebrated hashtags. I don't know who has the time to invent these "celebrations" but I'm very grateful for the marketing opportunity nonetheless . This makes it very easy not only to plan out a schedule for your content but also to create a clever segue to your content, which you can use for any of the ten "R"s of your relationship management covered in chapter 11.

One of the greatest resources for finding what is celebrated on a particular day is the website www.daysoftheyear.com, and to find the celebrated hashtags of the day please go to http://resources.rethinksocialmedia.com.

An example of one of these hashtag calendars looks like this:

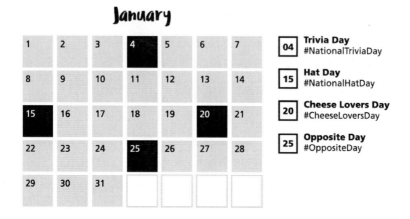

Fig 13.6: Social media events calendar

Once the other "celebration" days get added in, it can start to look quite busy, which is absolutely brilliant for marketers as it gives ample opportunity for ideas for content. Now that I think about it, when I said earlier that I didn't know who had the time to come up with these celebration days, it clearly is marketers!

Part 2: What content will I provide and where?

Once you have the calendar open, you can then decide how many of these celebrated topics you want to take on as part of your content strategy this month. Ideally, you want to be starting with at least one a week. I have included a useful template here to make this much easier for you, which can be downloaded from http://resources.rethinksocialmedia.com.

Monthly Topic:	Relationship Goals:	Types of Content:	Digital Delivery Method:
1.	Retain	Article	Facebook Page
	Remind	Video	Facebook Live
	Reinvigorate	Tweet	Twitter
	Relevance	Short form post	Periscope
	Refresh	Postcard	Youtube
	Renew	Livestream	Youtube Live
	Rethink	Ebook	Instagram
	Referrals	Webinar	Snapchat
	Reward	Survey	Pinterest
	Regular	Podcast	Email
		Product Promotion	Advertisements
		Competitor Share	Blog
		Launch Sequence	Other

Monthly Topic:	Relationship Goals:	Types of Content:	Digital Delivery Method:
2.	Retain	Article	Facebook Page
	Remind	Video	Facebook Live
	Reinvigorate	Tweet	Twitter
	Relevance	Short form post	Periscope
	Refresh	Postcard	Youtube
	Renew	Livestream	Youtube Live
	Rethink	Ebook	Instagram
	Referrals	Webinar	Snapchat
	Reward	Survey	Pinterest
	Regular	Podcast	Email
		Product Promotion	Advertisements
		Competitor Share	Blog
		Launch Sequence	Other

Table 13.8: Content goal and delivery overview

Taking one topic at a time, look at your 10 goals, plan out which of these goals you can achieve and then tick off which particular type of content and digital delivery methods you intend to use. This will give you a very clear indication of what your content strategy looks like on one sheet of paper and declutters the brain in a major way! As I mentioned earlier, one simple video can create enough content for all platforms for a week. It depends very much on how many resources you have to ultimately determine how many topics per week or month you choose to take on. Don't overwhelm yourself here, keep it simple for now!

The beauty of this is that you can easily weave in content related to an upcoming promotion you are doing so that your audience is prepared and anticipating the latest particular solution that is about to become available.

Part 3: When will I publish it?

Once you know what and where you plan to publish, the next step is ensuring that you have a clear plan for delivery. It is back to the calendar time – but a decluttered calendar, exclusively for you to plan out your content for the month, such as the template below.

Enter Month & Year:							
Delivery Type:		Facebook Ad (FA)	Twitter Organic (TO)	Twitter Ads (TA)	Youtube Organic (YO)	Youtube Ads (YA)	
	Google/Bing Ads (GBA)	Live Stream (LS)	Live Webinar (LW)	Blog Post (BP)	Email Send (ES)	Linkedin (LI)	Other (O)
Week 1 Topics	MONDAY	TUESDAY	WEDNESDAY	THURSDAY	FRIDAY	SATURDAY	SUNDAY
1							
2							
3							
4							
5							
Week 2 Topics	MONDAY	TUESDAY	WEDNESDAY	THURSDAY	FRIDAY	SATURDAY	SUNDAY
1							
2							
3							
4							
5							

Table 13.9: Social media monthly publication plan

Once you fill out this template for the month, the benefit is that at a simple glance, either you or your social media manager will know what networks and what content topics will be at a fairly detailed level without knowing the exact posts. Here's an example:

Week 1 Topics	MONDAY	TUESDAY	WEDNESDAY	THURSDAY	FRIDAY	SATURDAY	SUNDAY
1 World Beer Day	■	■					
2 Product Promotion				■	■		
3 Independence Day						■ ■	
4 N/A							
5 N/A							

Table 13.10: Social media monthly publication plan example

The methods of delivery can be changed depending on the latest and greatest digital strategies and you can modify these within the document as appropriate.

You can download the content planning file to use and edit as you wish at http://resources.rethinksocialmedia.com.

Part 4: Execution plan

Finally, it's pedal to the metal time! What exactly are we publishing and when? We are now at a stage with the tools above where we know the dates and the networks on which we plan to share content. The last part of this is to pull together all of the content that is already or will be created in a convenient location and get it organised to be delivered. As I have said more than once, the degree to which you use all of these tools depends very much on the level of resources your business has. You can still use these tools even if you only intend to do one post a week, as they do give you a structure and a plan, and you can always add to it later.

Let's first plan out the days per week and where all of the content is stored and easily accessible before we get to the specific times.

Week 1 Start Date:					
Date	Title	Content Type		Images/Videos	Storage Location	Publishing Channels
			Monday			
			Tuesday			
			Wednesday			
			Thursday			
			Friday			
			Saturday			
			Sunday			

Table 13.11: Social media weekly execution plan

If you really want to take it to the "nth" degree, we can now get into the specific timing of the posts. You would ideally have a staff member or an outsourcer do this for you. Once again, I have included a template below that can assist you with this.

WEEK START DATE:		MONDAY (Date:)	
Time	Social Network	Content	Link
	TWITTER		
08:00			
12:00			
16:00			
20:00			
22:00			
	FACEBOOK		
10:00			
14:00			
18:00			
	BLOGGER		
10:00			
14:00			
18:00			
	LINKEDIN		
10:00			
14:00			
18:00			
	INSTAGRAM		
10:00			
14:00			
18:00			
	LIVESTREAM		
18:00			
	WEBINAR		
18:00			
	EMAILS		
18:00			
	OTHER		
18:00			

Table 13.12: Social media daily delivery plan

Before you start to go into panic mode and think that your life is about to be consumed on a daily basis almost on the hour every hour, we're going to leverage the tools that are available to us. While we do wish for our audience to hear from us on a consistent basis across multiple channels, it is our job to minimise the time that takes from us and set it all up in less than an hour a week.

Fortunately, there now are tools like www.agorapulse.com, www. hootsuite.com, www.sproutsocial.com, www.buffer.com and www. socialoomph.com, which cater for every need, for every business and for every budget. This will allow you to get all of your posts organised and scheduled in one convenient location once a week, allowing you to get on with the rest of your life for the rest of the week ☺.

As a reminder, you can download your content planning file completely for free, for you to use and edit as you wish at resources.rethinksocialmedia.com.

Step 7 – Know your numbers:

This is the process of knowing what to measure as well as how to measure online business performance accurately. As I know from first-hand experience, it is all too easy to fool yourself into a sense of either unfounded optimism or pessimism unless you have a score board to measure your business on.

"Doing the right thing is more important than doing the thing right."
- Peter Drucker

It is critical to ensure that you are measuring the right things and getting accurate results for each. Fortunately, today the metrics are calculated for you by a combination of the ad platforms and software that's used, but it is useful to know where these numbers come from so that you can tackle the root of any issues as they arise.

The numbers themselves are mere symptoms of an underlying problem, they are not the problem themselves! Being able to drill deeper into the numbers and analyse the root cause of the problem is something that we will address in the next chapter with a new concept called "Rethink time". For the sake of completeness in this chapter, I will provide you with the scoreboards to be used here, broken into 7 different layers; these will be fully explained in the next chapter. Depending on your experience, a complete novice will only require Metrics Essentials #1, advancing to Metrics Essentials #7 with time and experience.

Metrics Essentials #1: "Did I make more than I spent last week / month / year?"

Month:		Year:	
Week #:		Date:	
Total Direct Costs:			
Total Indirect Costs:			
Total Income:			
Total Profit / Loss:			

Table 13.13: Overall profit / loss metrics

Metrics Essentials #2: "What is my return on investment?"

Month:		Year:	
Week #:		Date:	
Return On Investment:			
Cost Per Customer Acquisition:			
Immediate Customer Value:			
Long Term Customer Value:			

Table 13.14: High level ROI metrics

Metrics Essentials #3: "What are my ad campaigns returning for me?"

Month:		**Year:**	
Week #:		**Date:**	
Campaign #:		**Network:**	
Return On Investment:			
Cost Per Lead (CPL):			
Cost Per Registration (CPR):			
Cost Per Customer Acquisition (CPA):			
Optin Page Conversion Rate:			
Cost Per Click (CPC):			
Click Through Rate (CTR):			
Relevancy Score:			
Reach:			
Frequency:			
Impressions:			

Table 13.15: Ad performance ROI metrics

Metrics Essentials #4: "How do my ads compare relative to each other?"

Ad Matrix	Lead Magnet A	Lead Magnet B	Lead Magnet C	Lead Magnet D	Lead Magnet E
Avatar A	CPA 1	CPA 2	CPA 3	CPA 4	CPA 5
Avatar B	CPA 6	CPA 7	CPA 8	CPA 9	CPA 10
Avatar c	CPA 11	CPA 12	CPA 13	CPA 14	CPA 15

Table 13.16: Ad matrix overview metrics

Metrics Essentials #5: "How are my emails and promotions performing?"

Date:	Email Subject Line:
Open Rate:	
Click -through Rate:	
Earnings per Click:	
Deliverability Rate:	
Disengagement Rate:	

Table 13.17: Email and product performance metrics

Metrics Essentials #6: "How are my individual funnels performing?"

Ad Set / Campaign #:	Funnel #:	
1. Optin page Version (Ver):	Optin Coversion%:	
2. Immediate upsell offer Ver: e.g. Free + shipping ($7)	Sales Conversion %: Cumulative %:	
3. Additional bump Ver: e.g. add tripwire ($7)	Sales Conversion %: Cumulative %:	n/a
4. Registration for prerecorded webinar Ver: e.g. 90min training	Optin Coversion%: Cumulative %:	
5. What was the show rate? e.g. started to watch webinar	Show Up Rate %: Cumulative %:	
6. How many stayed until the offer was made e.g. 75 mins in	Stick Rate %: Cumulative %:	
7. Upsell during webinar Ver: e.g $47 live 3 hr training offer	Sales Conversion %: Cumulative %:	
8. Additional bump on offer Ver: e.g. $20 for a training recording	Sales Conversion %: Cumulative %:	n/a
9. What was the show rate? e.g. started live training	Show Up Rate %: Cumulative %:	
10. How many stayed until offer was made? E.g 2.5 hours in	Stick Rate %: Cumulative %:	
11. Upsell at live training to core offer Ver: e.g. $2997	Sales Conversion %: Cumulative %:	
12. Application for next level offer Ver: e.g. $9,997	Application Rate %: Cumulative %:	
13. How many purchases post application? Ver:	Sales Conversion %: Cumulative %:	

Table 13.18: Front and back-end funnel conversion metrics

Metrics Essentials #7: "How many income streams are turned on?"

Week Start Date:	Status:	Stream Title:	Monday	Tuesday	Wednesday	Thursday	Friday	Saturday	Sunday	Total
Stream 1										
Stream 2										
Stream 3										
Stream 4										
Stream 5										
Stream 6										
Stream 7										
Stream 8										
Stream 9										
Stream 10										

Table 13.19: Income Stream Panel

Summary:

Social media has a key part to play within all 7 steps of the RETHINK framework. The trick is to work out how it can be leveraged to its full extent in an objective, efficient way that can be tracked and measured as if it were another marketing tactic within an organisation. Fortunately, this is not a pipe dream; this chapter shows that it can be achieved100%. Templates and tables are available for each of the 7 sections to allow you to plan out, execute and monitor for the utmost success and measurable profitability for your business, without wasting thousands of dollars unnecessarily on ad hoc testing and expensive consultants!

Traditional Thinking:

Social media is a "touchy feely" topic where it can be very difficult to tie down the benefits and how it can deliver to the bottom line of your business.

RETHINK:

The ROI of social media is measurable, despite what you may have heard. Successful use of social media relates to how well you plan out its use in advance, followed up by regular monitoring of its results in all areas of the business. Using the templates and tables in this chapter will show you how to do exactly this.

Chapter 14: Metrics

"What gets measured gets improved."
- Peter Drucker

Once you have your infrastructure in place, this entire process becomes so much easier, I'm sure you will be glad to hear! The most difficult part for sure is getting your head around the concepts and then getting the business set up online. However, once in place, it becomes a case of monitoring your numbers closely and learning and iterating as you go, as discussed in chapter 11, "Know your numbers." Our ideal scenario here is that you don't have to work IN your business so much as working ON your business.

It is absolutely key that you "Know your numbers!" Which numbers to look at and how to track them is what this segment is about.

Before I go into this in more detail, please let me add the proviso that this is not intended to be a complete guide for how to monitor the performance of your entire business. I am not going to be discussing balance sheets, profit and loss or cash flow statements. I will solely be focusing on the specific numbers as they relate to your online activities and campaigns. I would strongly recommend you refer to the books Scaling Up by Verne Harnish and Keys to the Vault and The Ultimate Blueprint for an Insanely Successful Business, both by Keith Cunningham, and add them to your library of "go to" books. Your digital and social media marketing is only one component of your overall business. Although everything can be set up and run online, please never lose sight of the fundamentals of monitoring business performance. It would be a good idea to be clear on some of the more fundamental questions like "What is the primary reason I am running this business?" and "What does success look like for my business?"

With that said, a key part of knowing your numbers for your business is to decide what exactly it is that you are looking to achieve for your business as a whole and then look at how your social media and digital marketing feed into this. What are the key performance indicators and measurables of your business? If you are in business already, this will come more naturally to you, but if not, it won't take long to get a handle on the key elements to keep an eye on. Success comes from measuring the correct indicators and making adjustments regularly.

I fully understand that it can be all too easy to ignore the numbers and just keep busy hoping you are focusing on the right things. My advice, though, is that you really empower yourself in this area, and make it your strongest knowledge area of the business; that is, understand your numbers inside out. Reviewing the metrics of your online business can be without doubt a very overwhelming experience, but it does not need to be. The way I will explain this is to go into the varying degrees of depth that are possible but not always necessary, starting with the most essential.

Before we dive in, let's remind ourselves of the importance of the metrics in terms of our self-propelling RETHINK model. It is the key driver, and so finding and reviewing and knowing what to do with the right metrics is of paramount importance.

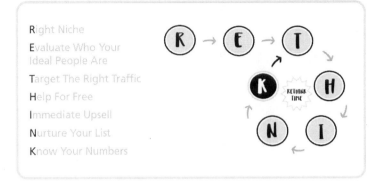

Right Niche

Evaluate Who Your
Ideal People Are

Target The Right Traffic

Help For Free

Immediate Upsell

Nurture Your List

Know Your Numbers

Fig 14.1: RETHINK "Self-Propulsion" Model

Metrics Essentials #1: "Did I make more than I spent last week / month / year?"

This is one of the most powerful questions you can ask yourself and will determine if you are, in very simple terms, running a profitable or loss-making entity over the short term.

Here is a simple little template to allow you to keep a close eye on this.

Month:		Year:	
Week #:		**Date:**	
Total Direct Costs:			
Total Indirect Costs:			
Total Income:			
Total Profit / Loss:			

Table 14.1: Overall profit / loss

Direct costs: The money spent directly on your business, such as on training, mentoring, advertising, software, domains, wifi and hosting. Where you may have annual one-off fees, break the costs out into average weekly costs.

Indirect costs: Money spent on staff, outsourcers or agencies, accountancy fees and any resources being paid to deliver these results. This could also be money due to affiliates or partners to make your sales. This should also include a breakdown on a cost per hour basis of your time.

Total income: Keeping it simple, this is how much money actually came into the business bank account this month as opposed to how much theoretical money you earned.

Metrics Essentials #2: "What is my return on investment?"

Now it's time to get into a lower level understanding of your business without delving too much into the detail.

It is a basic understanding of how much return you are making on your investments within your business. In order to do this, we also want to work out how much you are currently spending to get a customer into your business. Once you have the customer, how much profit on average do you make from them immediately? Finally, what is this customer worth to you over a specific period of time and into the future?

Month:		Year:	
Week #:		Date:	
Return On Investment:			
Cost Per Customer Acquisition:			
Immediate Customer Value:			
Long-term Customer Value:			

Table 14.2: High-level ROI metrics

Return on investment (ROI): There are many different ways of working out the ROI. Coming from my background as a Qualified Financial Advisor (QFA), there are a lot of factors that come into play. For our purposes, we are not looking so much for the strict definitions but getting to the nub of the concept. What is the return we are making on what we are spending? It can be calculated as the

$$\frac{(Gain\ from\ investment\ -\ Cost\ of\ investment)}{Cost\ of\ investment}$$

over a predefined period of time.

This last piece is critical. How long does it take for your business to make money after you spend money on acquiring a lead? For some it could be days, weeks or even months, hence why the conversion funnel or sales funnel with an immediate upsell is so important.

Cost per customer acquisition (CPA or COA): How much it costs you to acquire a buyer. Sometimes this is also called cost per order acquisition. The more you can spend on a buyer and break even or be in profit, the more successful you are going to be. As mentioned earlier, the business legend Dan Kennedy famously says "Ultimately, the business that can spend the most to acquire a customer wins."

Immediate customer value (ICV or IOV): What is my customer worth to me after taking out immediate hard costs? Once you have an immediate upsell in place, you can instantly turn your expense into a self-liquidating offer (SLO) to break even, or better still, into an immediate profit. If this is the case, you scale as much as you can profitably.

Long-term customer value (LTV): How much is the average customer worth to you over a specific longer period of time, i.e. 6 months, 1 year, 2 years, 5 years, 10 years, as they move through your back-end sales funnel and ascend the value ladder? This will of course vary over time as you perfect and improve your average customer transaction value and add more products and services to the mix.

Metrics Essentials #3: "What are my ad campaigns returning for me?"

The next stage is to look at the main cost of your business, which is your ad spend, and to dig in deeper to the analytics and results that are available to you here.

We can break this down into 4 distinct areas.

1. ROI of individual ad campaigns:

This really is when we start to get into the nitty gritty of the business and what is making it tick, or not, be that the case. It depends on many things, such as the market, the sales funnel, the customer journey and the relationship with your database, but we can look at some specific numbers to allow us to make some logical decisions based on facts.

The key performance indicators (KPIs) that you are looking at are the following:

Cost per lead (CPL): How much does it cost you to acquire somebody's contact details from a specific ad campaign? CPL should not be looked at in isolation; be sure to look at the opt-in page itself, which has its own metrics in Metrics Essentials #4. There may also be an ad scent problem if there is a lack of congruency between the ad and the opt-in in terms of language, offering, colouring or imagery. Your targeting could be off too, so ensure that you are targeting the intended avatar. Doubling your opt-in rate means halving your cost per lead.

Cost per registration (CPR): How much does it cost you to have somebody register for a webinar or event from a specific ad campaign?

Cost per acquisition (CPA): We defined this at the previous stage, but it needs to be factored into each individual ad campaign where possible.

2. Conversion rate of opt-in/squeeze/landing page

This is the calculation involved in working out how well your free gift offering is working as a lead magnet. Generally speaking, you want this to be well in excess of 20%, especially when you are paying for the traffic. This is often neglected, but it should be a key point of focus for you, as a simple increase in conversion rates will reduce your costs per lead quite dramatically. Be aware when you are calculating this that you can find the information directly from the software you are using to create your opt-in pages, such as at http://resources.rethinksocialmedia.com.

3. Cost per click, click through rate and relevancy score

Thanks to Molly Pittman, Keith Krance and Ralph Burns and their podcast on Facebook metrics for assisting in distilling down this metric into easy-to-explain numbers ☺. All three need to be looked at, as they all impact on each other.

Cost per click (CPC): How much are you spending on receiving a click? It is very dependent on the niche that you are working in. The cheapest is not necessarily your goal here; a highly targeted click is better than a cheap one in most cases.

Click through rate (CTR): How many people click through onto your landing page? A CTR of >0.5 – 1% or anything above is considered pretty good, although we have campaigns where we have had 50%+ when there is a really good match between the ad itself and the look of the opt-in page.

Relevancy score: How relevant is your ad to the people being targeted? Relevancy score when used in Facebook, is a measure of how much your messaging is targeted at the right type of audience, scored from 1 – 10, with anything from 5 and above being pretty good. A great bit of advice from the team at DigitalMarketer is to think "How can I write a message that people would want to share?" Have your ad speak to your audience in an authentic manner almost as if you met them at a party (but they can hear you, so there is no need to shout).

4. Reach and frequency

Reach: How many unique people have seen your ad?

Frequency: How many times has each person in your audience seen your ad?

Impressions: Reach x Frequency

In the event that you max out on the people that you are reaching out to, you may need to create new content to revive your audience and use the new ad to reengage them. Alternatively, you must find new audiences.

Month:		Year:	
Week #:		Date:	
Campaign #:		Network:	
Return On Investment (ROI):			
Cost Per Lead (CPL):			
Cost Per Registration (CPR):			
Cost Per Customer Acquisition (CPA):			
Optin page conversion rate:			
Cost Per Click (CPC):			
Click Through Rate (CTR):			
Relevancy score:			
Reach:			
Frequency:			
Impressions:			

Table 14.3: Ad performance ROI

Metrics Essentials #4:

While running individual ad campaigns, it can be very useful if you can track more detail about the ad so that you know specifically what particular targeting and ad types delivered these results for you. Here is an advanced version of the template used in chapter 13 (Table 13.4), which allows you to record all the required data from ad objective, to ad set type, to the creatives and results for each individual ad set for whichever particular network you are using, including room for a screenshot of the ad itself.

Stage 1: Objective *Click on Cell for Options*

OBJECTIVE TYPE

Stage 2: Advert Set

ADVERT SET NAME:
Audience location:
Audience interest:
Audience age group:
Audience demographic:
Audience targetting (other):
Budget per day:

Stage 3: Creative

Graphic type:
Optin page:
Optin address:
Button type:
Pixel active:

Stage 4: Results

of days:
Total spent:
Cost per like:
CPM:
Cost per click:
Cost per purchase:

**ENTER SCREEN
SHOT OF AD HERE**

Table 14.4: Individual ad performance

Ideally you fill in stages 1-3 before you open the ad platform, so you have a clear plan in advance of the distraction of the network!

The scoreboard is broken into four parts. The first is being clear on the objective of the ad. Is it to get traffic, likes, clicks or buyers. for example? Stage 2 allows you to keep track of the targeting and the budget being set aside. Stage 3 allows you to record where you are sending the traffic so that you can refer back to this at any stage in the future. Stage 4 monitors the metrics of the specific ad results, which are very useful to have rather than trying to remember the numbers retrospectively! On the right-hand side is where you can place a screenshot of your ad, so that immediately jogs your memory and easily shows you which ads are working best for you on each network. These templates are available for you to access free at http://resources.rethinksocialmedia.com.

Running one ad by itself, however, is not the most efficient way of running a business. Ideally you should be running an individual ad as part of a campaign, where you can measure the "success" or "failure" of the ad relative to others in the campaign. Usually, you can get the best use of this individual scoreboard by setting up a matrix of different lead magnets for different targets or avatars and testing their performance relative to each other. To begin with, you can use three different lead magnets and just two avatars, like below, so that you have 6 ads in a campaign, and you can divide a budget of $12 potentially across the 6 ads, giving you a $2 budget for each.

Ad Matrix	Lead Magnet A	Lead Magnet B	Lead Magnet C
Avatar A	CPA 1	CPA 2	CPA 3
Avatar B	CPA 4	CPA 5	CPA 6

Table 14.5: Ad matrix overview basic

Be sure to use Table 14.4 to track the full data of each individual ad. As you get familiar with the process, you can then scale the number of ads to increase the number of avatars and the number of lead magnets. In the next example we have 5 lead magnets and 3 separate avatars.

Ad Matrix	Lead Magnet A	Lead Magnet B	Lead Magnet C	Lead Magnet D	Lead Magnet E
Avatar A	CPA 1	CPA 2	CPA 3	CPA 4	CPA 5
Avatar B	CPA 4	CPA 5	CPA 6	CPA 9	CPA 10
Avatar c	CPA 11	CPA 12	CPA 13	CPA 14	CPA 15

Table 14.6: Ad matrix overview

You can then measure the results from the 15 ads to find the golden nuggets that you wish to scale. Be sure to scale carefully, adding small amounts to your budget each time until you find the sweet spot. If you have 15 ads running, you would not spend more than a few dollars a day per ad initially, then turn off the ones that were not performing and scale the others. If this seems out of reach right now, don't worry, go back to your first ad and then progress to Table 14.5 above once you gain a little confidence. If you are absolutely rocking it, you can add a couple more avatars to the above to bring the total ads up to 25 in your ad campaign.

Metrics Essentials #5: "How are my emails and promotions performing?"

Next let's move away from ads and look at the performance of your email marketing as we get deeper into the funnel. Your email marketing has the highest potential return on investment of all. Although this data is slightly outdated, in 2015 the Data & Marketing Association in the UK reported that for every £1 being spent on email, £38 was made in return – an enormous 3800% ROI, which was up from 2,493% ROI the previous year!

There are 5 main metrics that I feel are important when it comes to monitoring your email performance. These are:

Date:	Email Subject Line:
Open rate:	
Click -through rate	
Earnings per click:	
Deliverability rate:	
Disengagement rate:	

Table 14.7: Email marketing performance

By far the easiest metric to measure (and an important one for you to keep a close eye on, especially when starting out, as it's within your control) is the open rate, which is calculated as follow:

$$Open\ rate\ =\ \frac{\textit{Unique emails opened}}{\textit{Emails received}}$$

Your autoresponder will calculate this for you, but it is useful to know how the data is generated, especially when you want to improve it! The higher the better. If you are struggling to get open rates over 15%, there are a few things that you can try. Make the headlines more topical about recent news. Make sure that you "charge" the people in the subject line, i.e. create a response; if it is bland or balanced, it does not create much of a "react-ion". Don't forget to study the emails of the leaders in your field and model the subject lines that make you want to open the emails!

The next metric is based on your next goal, to get people to click on the link in order to get them off the email and onto the webpage that will encourage the call to action that involves a promotion of something within the sales funnel.

$$\textbf{\textit{Click through rate} = \underline{\textit{Unique link clicks}}}$$
$$\textbf{\textit{Emails received}}$$

The click through rate calculates how many people end up going to the desired webpage that you wish to send them to. The copy in the email is the key component here. Modelling the leaders in your niche is the best way to leverage your results, especially when you don't have copywriting experience yourself. Watch for trends in whether short or long emails are working in your niche right now.

Once people have clicked on the links, we now want to see how many cross the finish line! How many sales are made? Interestingly, we don't measure this as a quantity of unit sales, as this doesn't account for the price of the product or the quality of the email. Instead, to level the playing field, the measure is earnings per click or EPC. This is the single most important metric of your email marketing campaign and is calculated as follows:

$$\textbf{\textit{Earnings per click (EPC)} = \underline{\textit{Net commissions earned (after refunds)}}}$$
$$\textbf{\textit{Total number of clicks}}$$

If you decide to create your own product, the higher your EPC, the more enticing it is as an offering for affiliate partners to promote for you. When looking to promote products for other businesses, look at the suggested

EPCs of others' products with a healthy degree of scepticism. You may find that they are generally inflated, not taking account of refunds, all clicks, and warm or hot email lists, or even partial email lists.

All of the email metrics discussed so far assume that 100% of emails sent arrived in the inboxes of your leads. This is rarely, if ever, the case, unfortunately. The deliverability rate is a measure of how many emails you sent actually landed in the appropriate inbox.

$$\textit{Deliverability rate} = \frac{\textbf{\textit{Delivered emails}}}{\textbf{\textit{Emails sent}}}$$

This is not a metric that is easy to come by presently, but there are some precautions that can be taken. Always ensure that your spam rating is zero in your autoresponder "spam test" before you send the email. Avoid including attachments in your email. Provide links to download the report instead from somewhere like Dropbox. If you are suspicious that your open rates are way off where you think they should be, as I was at one point, I suggest sending the same email to portions of your database randomly split in two. I found a difference of 23% in open rate recently between two autoresponders to different portions of the same list. Wondering if I had somehow put the most active people into one list, I followed up by completely switching to the new autoresponder as a continuation of the test and sure enough the overall open rate increased on average by 15% per email! That is higher than many businesses' open rates, and that was just the difference... I was flabbergasted! The new autoresponder was convertkit! Sign up for your free trial at resources.rethinksocialmedia.com.

One thing that is part and parcel of email marketing is that every now and again you will upset some of your list. It comes with the territory and cannot be avoided, but with careful management, it can be limited. Disengagement rate is the combination of your complaints and unsubscribes divided by the number of unique opens.

Disengagement rate = <u>Number of complaints + Number of unsubscribes</u>
Unique email opens

While you may make some major whoppers every now and again that most marketers are guilty of, on most occasions, random complaints are not a reflection of the message but more often of the mood that you found your lead in on that particular day. If you do reach out to them personally, you are likely to find that they are super excited that you went to the effort and become an advocate of yours. Ideally, you want to keep your disengagement rate below 0.15%.

Metrics Essentials #6: "How are my individual funnels performing?"

One of the metrics that I feel is essential to track on its own merit is your sales funnel, both front and back-end. Unfortunately, you cannot just Google "funnel metrics" to find bespoke worksheets to track performance, so once more I created my own that we use to monitor the performance of our own funnels.

Given how elaborate an individual funnel may be, the metrics themselves are also quite meaty. Here is a worksheet that you can use for this.

Ad Set / Campaign #:	Funnel #:	
1. Optin page Version (Ver):	Optin Coversion%:	
2. Immediate upsell offer Ver: e.g. Free + shipping ($7)	Sales Conversion %: Cumulative %:	
3. Additional bump Ver: e.g. add tripwire ($7)	Sales Conversion %: Cumulative %:	n/a
4. Registration for prerecorded webinar Ver: e.g. 90min training	Optin Coversion%: Cumulative %:	
5. What was the show rate? e.g. started to watch webinar	Show Up Rate %: Cumulative %:	
6. How many stayed until the offer was made e.g. 75 mins in	Stick Rate %: Cumulative %:	
7. Upsell during webinar Ver: e.g $47 live 3 hr training offer	Sales Conversion %: Cumulative %:	
8. Additional bump on offer Ver: e.g. $20 for a training recording	Sales Conversion %: Cumulative %:	n/a
9. What was the show rate? e.g. started live training	Show Up Rate %: Cumulative %:	
10. How many stayed until offer was made? E.g 2.5 hours in	Stick Rate %: Cumulative %:	
11. Upsell at live training to core offer Ver: e.g. $2997	Sales Conversion %: Cumulative %:	
12. Application for next level offer Ver: e.g. $9,997	Application Rate %: Cumulative %:	
13. How many purchases post application? Ver:	Sales Conversion %: Cumulative %:	

Table 14.8: Front and back-end funnel conversion metrics

As you can see at the top, we start by labelling the particular ad sets or campaigns we are driving to the funnel. Knowing the traffic source is critical in terms of tracking results. We also have a place for identifying the name of this particular funnel. On the left-hand side, we have a funnel leading to a standard opt-in page to a free plus shipping offer. The "Ver" refers to the version of the opt-in page that you are using so you can enter the appropriate number to keep track of which opt-in page you used for this funnel. On the right-hand side, we simply track the opt-in conversion rate over the period of the ad campaign. We then progress through a series of upsells including "bumps"; a bump is where you present the interested person who is just about to purchase something with the option to tick a box that adds in a little bonus or "bump" for an extra few dollars. Usually it might take the form of an audio book, or if it is a live event, access to recordings of it later.

You will also notice the "cumulative %" as we move down the right-hand side. This is how you work out what the overall percentage of people is moving through the funnel at each point as you take account of the drop-off rate at each level, 1 to 13. I have labelled the bumps' "cumulative %" as not applicable. This is because although a customer may not choose to upgrade to the bump, this does not hinder progress through the funnel; the bump is like a bonus rather than a step in itself.

I also added a recorded webinar at step 4 and a live webinar at step 7. This allows you to factor in these types of methods for upselling. When you have a webinar, whether recorded or live, you do need to factor in how many people will show up and then watch them through to completion, as these numbers will also reduce the overall cumulative percentage of people moving through the funnel. I finish the funnel up in this example with an application sales process for a $9,997 offer. This of course does not need to be the end, but it is enough to squeeze into one page for you! When you download this at http://resources.leftclickrightclick.com you can edit it and add more to the funnel, as you wish.

Eventually you are left with an overall cumulative conversion % that factors in each step of the funnel. It can look like a scarily low number overall, BUT when you tackle each step separately, it allows you to plug the gaps very quickly in terms of where the main issues are and of course also see the opportunities that lie within the funnel.

The one thing that I have not added here, purely not to over complicate things (p.s. I can hear you laughing, saying "seriously... lol?"), is the success of your follow-up systems at each step, like one-time offers and follow-up email sequences. You can, if you wish, use the exact same table to track exclusively how your follow-up sequences convert when you are ready for Metrics Essentials #6.

What if, like most people, you have no funnel at all? Do you need any or all of this metric? The good news here is that you can actually still make great use of this tool. Ideally, as I mentioned in chapter 10, you should be promoting another business' funnel that already has high ticket offers in place, rather than an individual product. All you need to work out then is how many sales you make by promoting this funnel for this business, and add in what percentage of buyers you get at each stage. Remember you can sign up to promote by funnels for free at http://resources.leftclickrightclick.com.

Metrics Essentials #7: "How many income streams are turned on?"

At this moment in time, metric #7 is my favourite of them all! It is such a simple tool that I've developed, which has an immediate effect on your business and can instantly bring focus to where your issues lie. As you have probably been made aware of at some point or another in business, it is absolutely essential to have a U.S.P.; that is your Unique Selling Proposition. I would argue that your "I.S.P." is just as important as it can dramatically increase the profits of your business when monitored closely. Your I.S.P. is your Income Streams Panel and it tracks what potential income streams are coming into the business, how many of them are active and what quantity of sales you make with each stream on a daily basis. This turned out to be a complete game changer when I introduced this to my own businesses as it brought focus to the simple question, "What did we do today that allows us to make money tonight?". The more income streams you have active, the more money you should make. We currently have 56 streams of income in one business alone, but when we first used the I.S.P. to identify them, only 7 were active daily. This immediately allowed us to focus on quick wins for the business.

Week Start Date:	Status:	Stream Title:	Monday	Tuesday	Wednesday	Thursday	Friday	Saturday	Sunday	Total
Stream 1										
Stream 2										
Stream 3										
Stream 4										
Stream 5										
Stream 6										
Stream 7										
Stream 8										
Stream 9										
Stream 10										

Fig 14.9: Income Stream Panel

Ok, enough Paul! I'm guessing we have gone much deeper than you expected here, but please let me remind you that you would have to search far and wide from multiple sources to be able to create such a hands-on and usable system of metrics for your online business. The key here is that the metrics match your level of experience and sophistication. If this is all new to you, for now you just use Metrics Essentials #1. With more experience, you will naturally want to know more, and start looking at Essentials #2. This should continue over time until you are using all 6 levels of metrics. These metrics will then form the core of your "rethink time" review that we covered in chapter 12. Don't forget to use the guidelines referred to in the "Rethink Time Guide" to continue to propel your business forward.

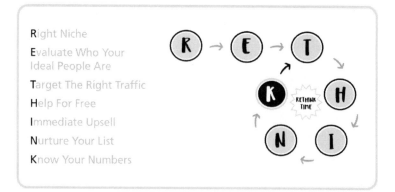

Right Niche

Evaluate Who Your Ideal People Are

Target The Right Traffic

Help For Free

Immediate Upsell

Nurture Your List

Know Your Numbers

Fig 14.2: RETHINK "Self-Propulsion" Model

It is probably abundantly clear at this point that having someone who has done this already to guide you will make your journey so much easier! Please look out for options where I can support you from a coaching perspective in the next chapter.

Summary:

Knowing your numbers gives you, at the very minimum, an awareness of whether you are in a business that has a chance of success! Too often business owners fly blindly using hard work and gut instinct as their drivers and monitoring tools for business success. With traditional business models, where there is a 90% chance of failure, it makes it all the more essential that you are watching the right vital signs from the outset. With the RETHINK framework, you won't leave anything to chance. You have access to varying layers of metrics that will not only enable you to have awareness of the symptoms of some pressing issues, but also give you early signs of where you can hugely profit from upcoming opportunities

Traditional Thinking:

If you keep your head down and work hard, inevitably it will come good in the end!

RETHINK:

If you don't lift your head up and take an overall objective view of your business using metrics designed to focus on the key aspects of your business, you are most likely doomed to fail. Meeting regularly to discuss the metrics allows you to put the RETHINK Model in "self-propulsion" mode for ever-increasing profits.

SECTION 5: CONCLUSION

Chapter 15: Key Watch Outs

"The biggest risk is not taking any risk… In a world that's changing really quickly, the only strategy that is guaranteed to fail is not taking risks."
- Mark Zuckerberg

I hope at this point that you are getting pretty excited about the amazing potential of this business model and are itching to get started! By the way, in the final chapter I will let you know how you can continue your learnings with me immediately.

With any business, there are associated risks. It's part and parcel of business, but with the strategies you are learning in this book, you are consistently stacking the odds in your favour for creating an enduring, highly profitable online business! That said, there are certain things that we should, at a bare minimum, be aware of, to ensure that we steer clear of potential risks. Once we have the awareness, we can start to put contingencies in place to avoid any such scenarios where at all possible. This chapter looks at some of those possibilities and ensures we put plans in place in advance to remedy such potential hiccups. As Warren Buffet says:

"Risk comes from not knowing what you are doing."

So let's make sure we know what we are doing from the very start!

Watch out #1: Increased competition for ad space

When Google Adverts started in 2000, few could have anticipated how successful it would be for businesses all over the world. It became the "go to" place for local businesses, especially in their quest to get in front of the right people at the right time. The interesting thing for me about Google Ads is when I hear people discuss them in general terms, I hear comments that Google Ads are "over saturated" and simply "too expensive" to compete. Being honest, I too subscribed to that theory and never got involved with Google Ads to any serious degree, as I believed the rhetoric. More the fool me! That was until I did a little digging for myself, and uncovered some pretty staggering facts. According to the data provided by Google at the time of Google Adwords' 15-year birthday in 2015, there are only a mere 1 million advertisers regularly advertising with Google! And yes, this includes YouTube! Think about that for a moment, that is 0.014% of the world's population, or 1 in every 7000 people. Is it any wonder that only 0.236% of the world are millionaires? As a result, I started to work with a video ad expert friend of mine Tom Breeze, and I am finally taking advantage of the phenomenal opportunity that Google provides across its platforms to feed my funnels!

You will soon start to hear the same rhetoric about Facebook advertising, with comments like "everyone is using Facebook ads now, you're too late!" Well, Mark Zuckerberg might beg to differ. There are, at the time of writing, only a mere 5 million regular advertisers on Facebook! Yes, you read this correctly. Of the almost 2.5 billion users of the platform, there are only 5 million advertising (0.2%). Picture this for a moment: if you were in a room of 500 Facebook users, statistically speaking you would be the only regular Facebook advertiser in the room! The opportunity is still vast, but of course, like anything when it is this great, it doesn't take too long for others to follow. This is why you must get started immediately, learn what to do and implement it while there is such an amazing opportunity to cash in, regardless of whether you are already in business or not.

Inevitably, as the platforms do become more crowded, the social networks themselves become more innovative. Facebook is a great example of this – advertisers can now place their ads directly within Facebook Messenger to free up more space in the timelines of Facebook users! Remember you just need to focus on what you can control ☺.

Watch out #2: Ad blocker software

There are now multiple software options available for people to use on their desktops and their smartphones to prevent ads from appearing. The Wall Street Journal reports that in 2016, 26% of all online users in the US had ad blockers installed on their PCs. In total, about 11% of all internet users worldwide have installed this technology. The experts on this topic, Pagefair, state that over 309 million users worldwide have them installed on their phones. Adoption varies greatly between countries. In chapter 8, part 2, we looked at the implications of how people within different cultures respond differently when it comes to showing their emotions. I have to say that it came as no surprise to me that in my own country of birth, Ireland, where I declare us Irish as "The most sceptical people on the planet", the ad blocker data certainly backs this up! Ireland leads the way worldwide, with a huge 39% of the population using ad blockers on their PCs. To give you some perspective, in the UK it is 16%. It is estimated that $22 billion in revenue was lost by online advertisers in 2015 as a result of ad blockers.

So what to do we do about it? Panic? Stress? Definitely not. There are plugins available to use on websites that only allow visitors who don't use ad blockers to continue, but I don't feel that this is a solution. In fact, 74% of American AdBlock users say they leave sites with AdBlock walls, which would back up this theory. Sponsored articles tend not to be picked up by ad blockers, and weaving marketing material into posts can work, but only to an extent.

The thing is, you have God on your side here! Both Google and Facebook have huge revenue lines from paid advertising, and they have no intention of stopping them either. You can be absolutely certain that these two "gods" of the internet will continue to innovate to find a multitude of ways to deliver the appropriate ads in a way that is more acceptable to the user, ultimately creating a better user experience for everyone, which is a great end result. My next comment is purely from my own experience from speaking and selling in different countries and cultures, but generally speaking, the people who tend to block adverts on their PCs are resistant to sales in the first place, so they are not likely to be potential buyers in your target market. Ad blocker software is one of those things that is outside of your control, so it is not one to spend much time thinking about; others will come up with the "solutions" ☺.

Watch out #3: Suspension of advert accounts

For the sake of your sanity, one of the first assumptions you should make, even in advance of setting out on your online marketing journey, is that you will at some point have either a social network account or an advert account suspended. That allows you to get over the initial shock and then work your way quickly through the other phases of denial, anger, bargaining, depression, testing and acceptance ☺. Then you are ready to start your online business! Once you accept it, you can plan for it and be ready. The last thing that you wish for is to have a super successful business, with hundreds of thousands of dollars coming in a week like many do, and then suddenly your main traffic source is shut down and the money stops immediately.

You must have contingencies in place. It would be wise to always consider opening a second account with any social network that allows you to do this as part of its terms and conditions. Most will, especially if you are setting one up initially for personal reasons and another for business. Where this can really hurt you, though, is if an advert account becomes suspended. You may have done everything by the book, and it could happen, but you are not the judge and jury, so you may just have to accept it. Fortunately, almost all networks allow you to open more than one ad account, and I strongly suggest that you do this so you have a sense of comfort about the whole thing. The biggest difficulty that people have here is access to multiple debit cards, as you will require different payment cards for each account. Fortunately, you can use the likes of www.N26.com, which will open a new bank account for you in less than 8 minutes and issue up to 5 debit cards for free! Now there is a tip and a half ☺.

As a general rule, as soon as you are running ads and issues with a personal representative from a company like Facebook, email them your ad for review prior to going live just to ensure that everything is by the book. In the event that there are issues, you have the proof of communication that you received the ok from a representative of that organisation to run that advertisement in advance just in case!

Watch out #4: The ever-changing environment of social networks

"There is nothing more constant than change."
- Heraclitus

Heraclitus must have been on Facebook when he first wrote this ☺. Even the most basic user of social networks will notice that every few months the network has changed its interface. It feels awkward for a few days and before we know it, we are dreading the next inevitable change. By their very nature, if they are to stay relevant, social networks must innovate and change to constantly match the ever-evolving needs of their users. This creates sheer PANIC in most businesses when it comes to their social media! As soon as they feel they understand it, a change happens and inevitably there is a major over-reaction and demands for the previous version to be returned.

Where people see problems with this, I see MASSIVE opportunities. Why? Quite simply because it means that most businesses are always playing catch-up on social media, using tactics that worked 12 to 24 months previously. This means that those clever people who keep their finger on the pulse will always be the first to adapt and get the first mover's advantage on all the latest changes and strategies. The key thing to remember here is that social networks want to make the experience for businesses on social media more profitable. They know that the more money businesses make with the networks, the more they will spend with the networks. What you can do is to join a coaching program that does the research for you, so that you only need to use the most recent of tactics that are working today.

More to follow on this. This means that you will always be the quickest to learn and the first to profit from the inevitable changes.

Watch out #5: The "demise" of email marketing

Ever since I started with my online business, I have been listening to the eulogy for email marketing ☺. It's rare that a month passes without an email arriving in my inbox (ironically) about how email marketing no longer works! As mentioned earlier, studies have shown that there is up to a 3800% ROI for businesses on the money they invest in email marketing, and it continues to rise.

I totally agree with the fact that we all receive more emails nowadays. On average, we receive 125 business emails per day. If you think about it though, do we receive more emails because they are not working for businesses or because they are working? The Radicati Group's study on the topic showed that there is an expected increase in email users worldwide from 2.6 billion in 2015 to 2.9 billion in 2019, over a third of the world's population. This growth is despite the increased user adoption of social networks and instant messaging.

Although it has been around since 1965 and started to get popular around 1993 with Outlook and AOL, email has certainly stood the test of time. I am a realist, however, and there is no doubt that its success may decrease over time, like any marketing strategy in its own right; just look at radio, TV and newspapers! It is highly unlikely that it will disappear anytime soon though; the more likely scenario is that we start to adopt to other versions of the same concept.

What can we do to make sure we are prepared regardless of what happens? Firstly, in chapter 14, where I wrote about email deliverability rates, I mentioned a number of things that you can do with the emails you send to increase the likelihood of them being received. Secondly, we adapt! Instant messages through the likes of Facebook are getting open rates of over 80% on average, which is amazing news! As a result, what we do is we use both email and social networks' messaging systems! We invite people to join our email lists through our lead magnets and continue our communications in the traditional manner, BUT we also cater to those who prefer not to move out of the social network environments and we communicate with them right there within the messaging environments of the various social networks. The beauty of this is that we are getting our message to the same person in multiple ways, each time reinforcing the building of trust in our relationship.

Watch out #6: General Data Protection Regulation (GDPR)

From May 25th 2018, a new regulation will impact database owners (like marketers) all over the world who collect people's data or have databases of the personal information of anyone within the EU. In simple terms, this would cover pretty much all online marketers worldwide! It seems scary at first, but like most things, once we get into the detail, it can definitely be managed without hitting the emergency button. A huge thank you to the team at http://resources.rethinksocialmedia.com, who have assisted me in ensuring that everything mentioned here stands up against any legal checks.

This section is not by any means meant to be a complete guide to navigating the GDPR and ePrivacy Regulation, but instead, more of a starting point; I will refer you to resources that will provide you with more in-depth follow-up information. The GDPR applies whenever you process personal data (for instance, email addresses) – whether it is data about employees, customers, suppliers or anyone else. Then there is also the new ePrivacy Regulation that is specific to electronic marketing and applies as soon as you start to market to people through electronic means (for example, by email, by SMS, through a downloadable app or on social media).

That means when you are carrying out electronic marketing, you are going to have to deal with both sets of regulations: GDPR and the ePrivacy Regulation. To put that into context, for online businesses, imagine a customer comes to your opt-in page or website. From the moment that user finds your website or lands on your landing page, you're most likely already collecting personal information about them. Whether you know it or not, you may well already be automatically collecting their IP address (personal data) and will have to comply with GDPR.

What if that person then fills in a form on your site? Again, as soon as they fill in that form, giving their name or email address, they're providing you with, and you are processing, personal data. As soon as you have that personal data you need to comply with GDPR. It is only when deciding what to do with that data that the ePrivacy Regulation starts to come into play. So, if you decide to send a response to that person, or you want to send that person marketing information by email or text, or you want to direct that person to your website, at that point you need to comply with both GDPR and the ePrivacy Regulation, which means that there's more law that you need to consider.

Firstly, the recipient's consent must be "freely given". In other words, it can't be required of the person to give that consent in order to continue to download a free gift. In essence, you can't require that person to give you their consent to marketing as a condition of them receiving your goods or services. Secondly, it must be "un-ambiguous" – in other words, it must be very clear to the person who is signing up what they are signing up to, and each purpose should be set out clearly. The person who gives their consent must know, at the time they give their consent, exactly what it is they are signing up to, and what your purpose is in asking for their details. Thirdly, it must be a "clear, affirmative action", in other words, it will no longer be acceptable to have a pre-ticked box that says "we assume that you are happy to accept your details but unclick if you are not". Fourthly, it will be important for you that you can prove how and when you received that consent.

So in short, you're going to have to tell the person what you're going to use their data for (under GDPR). You're therefore going to have to provide a "privacy notice", and you're also going to need consent wording when you capture the data that asks the customer to agree to that use. I have provided you with a "privacy policy" and a template for your "consent cording" – wording that you can use where you capture personal data at http://resources.leftclickrightclick.com.

Best practice would be for the short consent wording to appear immediately next to the area where the customer provides you with personal data, so right next to the sign up form on your landing page and your website (if you have one), and for there to be a tick box next to it. Your privacy policy (or rather a link to it) should appear everywhere on your website and opt-in page but also in a link from every single email that you send out. If you already have an extensive database and are unsure what to do, or where you stand, please go to resources.leftclickrightclick.com., which explains what you need to do in order to be compliant. Whilst it may sound as if some of these steps might scare customers away, the reality is that, armed with the right knowledge, you're likely to have an even more responsive list than ever before and, as a result, a much more robust business.

Watch out #7: Surrounding yourself with the wrong people

The final watch out is a more general one, but it's a crucial one! It is being very careful about who you surround yourself with and who you get your advice from when it comes to learning how to create and grow your highly profitable online business. This is relevant at all times of your business, and it's one of the key "hidden factors" that can hold you back on achieving your goals.

There are two aspects to this. The first is on a day-to-day basis: be very mindful of who you speak to about your online business. It is all too easy, especially at the start of your journey, to have your confidence knocked by somebody who knows very little, if anything, in this space. If, for example, you know people who use terms like "If it's too good to be true, then it probably is" or "If it was that easy, everybody would be doing it!" they are most likely not going to help you on your journey of setting higher standards in meeting your newly-stretched financial goals. Another classic is "Surely everyone knows the internet is a scam!" There was a time where I would have started defending the internet, but now I know to just agree and change the topic. In my experience, there is no point in attempting to change someone else's mind about any subject. I find it a much better us of my time to focus on what I can control, and that is focusing on learning and growing my own business, and finding others who are willing to do the same. Your confidence will be gained by surrounding yourself with people on the same journey who are looking for solutions rather than problems. Remember, only 0.0216% of the world's population are millionaires, so if you are taking advice from the other 99.98%, it is very unlikely that your financial situation will change.

The second aspect is WHO you learn from. I have met hundreds of people who tell me they are going to "try it for themselves first" and then later pay for coaching. I can tell you that not even one of those people who said this to me have ever been successful by themselves. "Self learning" in this space is a non-runner! I have yet to meet a single person from the tens of thousands I speak to each year that has told me they have figured it out for themselves by watching videos on YouTube. Success leaves clues, and if you want to be successful with your online business, make sure you get a coach on board. Look at every expert you know in any arena, whether business or sports – all of those on the top of their game have coaches.

So who should you learn from? Clearly, I am biased on this topic! You can learn "social media marketing" from thousands of "experts" every day of the week, but my advice is look for the evidence of their successes. There is a huge difference between learning how to open up social networks and fix up your profile and actually building a profitable business that is built to grow and to last. I can assure you that in my experience, over 90% of the experts I have met not only don't have front-end or back-end sales funnels, most of them don't even fully understand the concept, so be very careful. As a result of this, I want to make this choice easy for you. I would like to offer my coaching services to you at no risk. I have opened a coaching program specifically aimed at the readers of my book, where I will guide you on your journey to the creation and continued growth of your online business. You can start by visiting nextsteps.rethinksocialmedia.com.

Summary:

With any business, it would be foolish to focus exclusively on your day-to-day tasks without keeping an eye on the external environment. It is here where you may find both potential threats and opportunities in equal numbers. The 7 key watch outs we have identified are: 1. Increased competition for ad space, 2. Ad blocker software, 3. Suspension of advert accounts, 4. The ever-changing environment of social networks, 5. The "demise" of email marketing, 6. General Data Protection Regulation (GDPR), and 7. Surrounding yourself with the wrong people.

Traditional Thinking:

In the event of some "failures" or "warning signals" in the online marketing space, it may be time to completely reconsider what you are doing there and possibly abandon it, especially as email marketing is dead!

RETHINK:

It is important to keep an eye on what potential issues are around the corner for your business. Having regular weekly rethink time meetings can certainly bring your focus on upcoming challenges, threats and opportunities. Get advice from the people in the know rather than listening to hearsay and rumours.

Chapter 16: Final Wrap

"If someone offers you an amazing opportunity and you're not sure you can do it, say yes – then learn how to do it later."
- Richard Branson

Without any shadow of a doubt, you must be feeling like you were just hit by a bus right now, especially if you tackled this book over a short period of time! I have taken almost 10 years of experience in the online marketing space and compressed it into a single book, which can certainly result in that effect ☺. I could have left out at least half of the material here, but I decided against it. I could have finished it earlier without getting into the detail of the metrics, which no doubt may have lost some of you, but only for the time being.

This, however, is a journey! This will not be built overnight, but it certainly can be created successfully – and highly profitably – over a few weeks or even months. I want you to think of this as your complete handbook for your social media and online business that you come back to and refer to over and over again and hopefully recommend to others (but make sure through your affiliate links ☺). The more advanced you become, the more you will get from it and the more ideas you will pick up.

There is a whole series of digital and physical resources available to you, which have been mentioned at various points in the book. I have also referred you to training videos in the areas where I feel there is a likelihood that changes will occur over time after this book was first published. You can continue to come back to this handbook and the videos will continue to be completely up-to-date, which was my initial goal: to make this a book that stands the test of time.

I am a very visual person and I feel that possibly one of the easiest things that you can do immediately as a little gift to yourself is to order a RETHINK model roadmap, which is an A3 poster that you can hang on your wall that shows the entire model and where each template sits in its own rightful place: resources.leftclickrightclick.com. Before long, with that baby in front of you, the overall jigsaw will start to make a lot of sense – and a lot of profit!

> *"Social media is not a fad, nor a silver bullet."*
> *- Paul O'Mahony*

Social media has been around for thousands of years and most likely will endure for thousands more, although the format will change. However, it is not the "be all and end all" in itself for a business' success. It is a very important step, but only one cog in a much larger wheel; very few people realise this, which is why we need to RETHINK social media. When treated as a tool in the right way, it can turn you or a brand into a sensation almost overnight, gaining you immediate "credibility" and much appreciated attention for your business ☺.

To recap one final time, here are the 7 steps again:

1. **R**ight niche – Choose a niche area which is already proven to work rather than reinventing the wheel.

2. **E**valuate who your ideal prospects are – Understand the interests, the mindset and perspectives of the people who have these problems and assess where they hang out online.

3. **T**arget the right traffic – Target these people online with different traffic strategies such as advertising, testing different networks as you go.

4. **H**elp them for free – Offer a free and incentivised solution to the problem in exchange for their contact details.

5. **I**mmediate upsell – Learn how to offer a product or service immediately after contact details have been exchanged.

6. **N**urture your list – Go through the process of building a long term profitable relationship with the people you are assisting through email and other means.

7. **K**now your numbers – Understand the key indicators that will drive increased profit from your online business, allowing you to adjust as you progress.

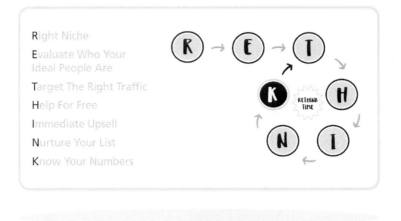

Fig 16.1: RETHINK "Self-Propulsion" Model

Our RETHINK model shows how you can take this 7-step model and apply it to your brand new or existing business, to make it a highly profitable business with the smallest possible levels of risk, scaling appropriately as you proceed.

The primary reason I ended up being relatively successful with my businesses to date was because I sought out expert help very early in my journey. I had played around but didn't make a single cent until I got a coach on board! If you know that this is something that you would love to do, I would love to have you work with me on an ongoing basis, so I can drip-feed the required trainings to you over a period of time in the comfort of your own home, giving you time to implement as you go. And you can get started completely risk free on me. - Find out more about it at www.rethinksocialmedia.com/nextsteps.

Please refer to this book over and over again as you progress through your journey, as each segment will mean more to you as you implement it. And ENJOY the journey! As I say, to fast-track your success, feel free to reach out to me to get you onto your next step of our journey together.

You will start with a free training call with me, and after that… well, you know the drill! One of the things you can do from now to advance your learning enormously as I assist you is to start to learn not only through the eyes of a student, but through the eyes of a skilled marketer. Please understand that you, me, and almost everybody you know are already in sales funnels and the more we are aware of it, and appreciate the learnings from them, the sooner we can rethink how to use them in our own business and profit for life! This will allow us to switch from being the target to doing the targeting ourselves.

We mentioned earlier in the book that 90%+ of businesses fail in the first 10 years because they are sticking to an outdated model. Times and technology have changed beyond recognition, especially in this last generation alone. Smartphones, iPads and laptops are not second nature to our children, they are first nature! This is why I have created a company called Funancial Freedom, specifically for the education of children. The mission is to teach children all over the world how to become financially free before they ever leave school, by learning the skills of money management and internet business creation.

Any child on the program in the developed world will in turn sponsor a less fortunate child in the developing world, sharing with them the same skills that they are learning and together changing this world for the better, one generation at a time. A portion of your investment for this book has already helped in making this dream of mine a reality. You can find out more about it here at funancialfreedom.com. This is something I could never have anticipated only a few years ago, before I opened that very first Twitter account.

Rethinking social media has allowed me to quite simply RETHINK my finances, my life, my aspirations and my potential global impact on our next generation. It may well be the right time for you to RETHINK the opportunities that sit in front of you today and realise that you can have a life that you once only dreamt was possible for you and your family. Please have a RETHINK… And use the power of social media to do something extraordinary on this planet!

Join me at http://nextsteps.rethinksocialmedia.com